More Praise for *The Co*

"*The Compromise Trap* will confirm the experience of all who work in systems. It is insightful and well written and aims us in the right direction."

—Peter Block, author of *Stewardship* and *The Answer to How Is Yes*

"Human nature has a strong compassionate, cooperative base that needs to be rediscovered. Elizabeth Doty's systemic and realistic approach provides guidance on how we can make the world a better place for everyone, not just for ourselves."

—Napier Collyns, cofounder, Global Business Network

"*The Compromise Trap* is thoughtful, pragmatic, and provocative and a pleasure to read."

—Joseph L. Badaracco Jr., John Shad Professor of Business Ethics, Harvard Business School

"Elizabeth Doty has brought greater depth of understanding to one of the major dilemmas of organizational life: what causes people to do what they believe is not right? I hope this book encourages everyone to avoid the compromise trap and provides leaders with insight that will help them create healthy organizations where people and the business thrive."

—Nancy Southern, Chair, Organizational Systems Program, Saybrook Graduate School

"*The Compromise Trap* clearly and directly addresses an essential principle for navigating toward a more sustainable economy—acting from the center. Without acting from what is true for each of us, our collective actions may not realize our intentions, which is a great risk indeed."

—Stacey Smith, Managing Director, Advisory Services, BSR

"An engaging and easy-to-understand analysis of the traps we weave at work and, frankly, in our daily lives. This book is relevant to anyone looking to 'redefine the game.' With the ethics breakdowns in business over the past decade, it is a must-read for every business school student and businessperson up to and including the C-suite and the board."

—Steven F. McCann, retired Executive Vice President and Chief Financial Officer, Longs Drugs Stores

"*The Compromise Trap* reveals the pandemic of incremental soul-selling in the workplace, as people compromise bit by bit until one day they wake up in disbelief at the full cost. Read this book and liberate yourself and your colleagues from the indentured spiritual servitude that sometimes seems required to earn a living. A how-to on the emancipation of the soul at work."

—John Renesch, businessman-turned-futurist, senior executive adviser, and author of *Getting to the Better Future*

"I agree with Doty: you cannot outsource your integrity to your leader. *The Compromise Trap* is an important book, not only for our corporate lives, but also for our health and wholeness as a society."

—Roger Saillant, former senior executive, Ford Motor Company

"Elizabeth Doty has touched on one of the often-secret dilemmas of organizational life: how to stay true to your deeper 'knowing' as you navigate the delicate terrain of organizational politics, ethical forks in the road, personal well-being, and competing loyalties. Her pioneering illumination of practical steps we can take, both individually and collectively, to embrace the higher possibilities inherent in even the most difficult situations is a great contribution to organizational leaders and members everywhere. Brava!"

—Juanita Brown and David Isaacs, cofounders, The World Café, and coauthors of *The World Café: Shaping Our Futures Through Conversations That Matter*

"Stephen Covey once told me, 'Integrity is the value you place on your relationship with yourself.' *The Compromise Trap* addresses how to deal with the small temptations that chip away at that value and shows us how to protect the integrity and purpose in our lives. *The Compromise Trap* is absorbing and entertaining, but, most important, it's a book for our times."

—Mike Harvey, Change Facilitator, Dow Chemical Company

"Doty explores the tangles of thought, feeling, loyalty, and pain that we all carry in our hearts. How do I rationalize my values with those of my organization? What do I do when they are in conflict? Can I fully participate in the moves of the organization while still honoring my deepest values? This book offers us a way to think about that trap and six valuable tools for setting our own path, shedding light on a powerful hidden force that slows much of our individual and shared success."

—Herb Wimmer, retired Facility Manager, Chevron Corporation

The Compromise Trap

The Compromise Trap

How to Thrive at Work Without Selling Your Soul

Elizabeth Doty

BK

Berrett–Koehler Publishers, Inc.
San Francisco
a BK Business book

Berrett-Koehler Publishers, Inc.
235 Montgomery Street, Suite 650, San Francisco, CA 94104-2916
Tel: (415) 288-0260 Fax: (415) 362-2512 www.bkconnection.com

Ordering Information

Quantity sales. Special discounts are available on quantity purchases by corporations, associations, and others. For details, contact the "Special Sales Department" at the Berrett-Koehler address above.

Individual sales. Berrett-Koehler publications are available through most bookstores. They can also be ordered directly from Berrett-Koehler:
Tel: (800) 929-2929; Fax: (802) 864-7626; www.bkconnection.com.

Orders for college textbook/course adoption use. Please contact Berrett-Koehler:
Tel: (800) 929-2929; Fax: (802) 864-7626.

Orders by U.S. trade bookstores and wholesalers. Please contact Ingram Publisher Services, Tel: (800) 509-4887; Fax: (800) 838-1149; E-mail: customer.service@ingrampublisherservices.com; or visit www.ingrampublisherservices.com/Ordering for details about electronic ordering.

Printed in the United States of America

Berrett-Koehler books are printed on long-lasting acid-free paper. When it is available, we choose paper that has been manufactured by environmentally responsible processes. These may include using trees grown in sustainable forests, incorporating recycled paper, minimizing chlorine in bleaching, or recycling the energy produced at the paper mill.

Library of Congress Cataloging-in-Publication Data

Doty, Elizabeth.
The compromise trap : how to thrive at work without selling your soul / by Elizabeth Doty.
p. cm.
Includes bibliographical references and index.
ISBN 978-1-57675-576-1 (pbk. : alk. paper)
1. Business ethics. 2. Success in business. I. Title.
HF5387.D68 2009
174--dc22

2009034362

14 13 12 11 10 09 10 9 8 7 6 5 4 3 2 1

Interior design and composition by Gary Palmatier, Ideas to Images.
Elizabeth von Radics, copyeditor; Mike Mollett, proofreader; Medea Minnich, indexer.

To my grandparents, Wayne and Roma Rieker,
whose professional quest went by the name of "total quality";
and to my family and all my partners in parallel inquiries
for the loving encouragement necessary for the birth of a book.

Contents

Foreword

By Art Kleiner

One of the great modern parables for working adults is the children's story *The Silver Chair* by C. S. Lewis. In that book, which is part of the Chronicles of Narnia series, two children named Jill Pole and Eustace Scrubb are drawn to a magical kingdom by Aslan, a godlike lion who oversees that world. The lion takes Jill to a mountaintop and tells her that she and her friend will have to make their way through a series of dangerous adventures in the valleys below to rescue a lost prince. They will safely fulfill their quest, he says, if they follow four signs: they must greet an old friend when they first see him, they must journey north to an old city, they must follow instructions written there in stone, and they will know the lost prince when he says to do something in the name of Aslan. He makes her repeat the signs over and over until she is certain she has memorized them; then he sends her to rejoin Eustace below.

Sure enough, in the ensuing adventures the children (and their traveling guide Puddleglum) flub one sign after another. They don't recognize the old friend, and he sails away without helping them; they get distracted from the road to the old city and wind up there only by accident; and the written instructions, when found, are overlooked and virtually unreadable. Finally, they meet someone, a most unlikely and intimidating individual, who invokes the name of Aslan, and they do the right thing in the end—but only after several minutes of dithering and hedging. In three very clever lines of dialogue, Lewis shows us what real-life ethical debates sound like:

> "It's the sign," said Puddleglum.
>
> "It was the words of the sign," said Scrubb more cautiously.
>
> "Oh, what are we to do?" said Jill.[1]

This might almost be the dialogue from the members of a management team, facing the fine print of a contract that has gone awry, a deal that has some unexpected conditions, or an obligation that they had hoped never to have to fulfill. It turns out that sticking to the rules and the ethics of a mountaintop ideal is a lot harder—it's even much harder to recognize them, let alone to follow them—when you're down in the workaday world.

That's why business ethics is such a thorny issue and why (I suspect) business schools continue to try to teach it and fail. Even if they get the signs and the signals right in the lecture hall and on the midterm, people are bound to lose their mountaintop perspective once they're caught up with the constraints, compromises, and connections of everyday business (and everyday life). Indeed, the more confidence people have that they know the signs, the more likely they are to have lost touch with them.

Hence the value of this book: the questions it raises about organizational ethics and its underlying message about the practice of healthy compromise. There are many equivalents to Lewis's signs in real-life business (and government and anywhere people congregate to get things done). These signs are ambiguous and easy to misconstrue, but they have immense significance for anyone seeking to balance the goals of making a difference and making a living. And that balance—the need to work for an organization *and* for your own sense of purpose and your own values without losing your loyalty to either—is the core subject of the very original and incisive book that's in your hands.

Elizabeth Doty is a longstanding manager, consultant, and educator in the field of organizational learning. We first talked about the ideas embedded in this book in the early 2000s, when I was working on a project of my own about organizational power and privilege. It soon became apparent that she was onto a distinctive insight that is frequently overlooked. The relationship between an employee and an organization is critically important to both, and when it is compromised both the individual and the institution suffer—and so does the world around them. Moreover, most of these compromises are unnecessary. It is possible to work for a large organization, to give much of yourself over to it, and to develop your own character and values in the process if, as Doty puts it, you learn to "redefine the game."

I should add that I'm personally grateful to Elizabeth for writing this book. Last year I published the second edition of a book called *The Age of Heretics* (San Francisco: Jossey-Bass, 2008). It's a history of countercultural management thinking, and it's built around the idea that "heretics" are the source of great business ideas. These "heretics" are people, throughout business history, who see a truth that contradicts the conventional wisdom of the organization they work for and who remain loyal to both the organization and the difficult truth. In my own history, I didn't quite explain how to navigate that dilemma. But *The Compromise Trap* does exactly that.

Doty began her research by asking people to tell about the times they felt compromised—when they felt pressure to go against something they believed at their core. Betraying one's inner beliefs, it turns out, has serious consequences at both a personal and a professional level. You'll see many examples in this book of people who had to cope with those consequences. And other examples will undoubtedly occur to you of compromises that have come home to roost.

There are plenty of examples from business history (like the cigarette executives who suppressed reports about the addictiveness and the health hazards of smoking in the 1950s—and then spent decades watching customers and colleagues die of cancer). And from current-day headlines (such as all the financiers and auditors who recognized the risks of unfettered lending but found no way to communicate those risks in time to make a difference, not even with one another). And there are plenty of less prominent examples from everyday working life. The head of human resources for a major company I studied was intentionally placed by the CEO as a corporate "hatchet man," deliberately punishing people who offended the CEO by shortcutting their careers. Then, after the CEO retired, the "hatchet man" was left behind with a new executive team—full of people he had betrayed.

But just because we see its consequences doesn't mean that the compromise trap is easy to avoid. People do not fall down a slippery slope of bad behavior overnight. It happens gradually, by degrees. Nor is the slope avoidable because any business practice involves trading with someone, and just about every trading partner is compromised in some way. Indeed, the more closed your mind is to "evil," the more susceptible you are to falling because the true danger is not temptation but ignorance.

Those who navigate business ethics well, and who manage to do the right thing, are the ones who understand compromise and are experienced with its pitfalls. They know which acts will be impossible to return from and how to distinguish them from the acts that will, in the end, be worth some ambiguity. And they know, most of all, how to transcend the dilemmas of business life: how to be bigger, wiser, and longer-thinking than the problems facing them and the short-term incentives that make it all too easy to slide.

Finally, you will find a great deal of guidance in *The Compromise Trap* for transcending the trap, for consciously choosing how you engage, and for participating in (and helping build) enlightened organizations (that are also more successful than their counterparts). And the guidance arrives not a moment too soon. As I write this, in May 2009, the Western economy is trying to climb out of a recession that looks like it could go on for years. Many people, including myself and those I know, have been personally affected—with lost jobs, ravaged finances, and short-circuited dreams. Conceivably, much worse will happen to many more people. And there is a prevalent awareness that much of this meltdown could have been avoided with a modicum of restraint and ethical capability on the part of a relatively small number of people. (Well, perhaps a few thousand people in the financial services industries and the regulators who oversaw them.)

The outrage over this is widespread and slow building. It will not go away. And it is understandable. But it is also, in a significant way, misplaced because it doesn't recognize how to prevent similar crises from occurring in the future. Yes, rules and punishments will be needed, and regulations should be clearer (and more transparent and better enforced); but these will not be sufficient. Nor can we prevent such problems in the future by encouraging "values" and good intentions. These, in themselves, will not prevail.

The answer is to build ingrained practices that build people's conscious focus. You design organizations in ways that, day by day, procedure by procedure, meeting by meeting, and deal by deal, make it easy for people to do the right thing.

This kind of capability doesn't come quickly. It is built up gradually through ongoing discipline—not just on the part of individuals but embedded in the fabric of corporate practice as well. It is no coincidence that most companies known for their ethics—Toyota, Procter & Gamble, and Springfield Remanufacturing Company come to mind—are also known for diligent, day-to-day production practices that lead people, continuously, to think about improving their performance. (By the way, these three companies come to *my* mind; Doty wisely avoids the temptation of singling out any particular organizations as virtuous. As you'll discover that's not the point of the book; it is aimed at getting to the heart of a dilemma that is present in all companies.)

In short, good business practice and ethical behavior come from the same types of activities, and they all have to do with high aspiration, continuous improvement through observation of the world as it is, and relentless discipline. Great companies are those that make it easy for their leaders and employees to be good. Great individuals, within companies, are those who learn how to "redefine the game" and engage at a higher level (as Doty describes it) and help their bosses and companies excel.

The Compromise Trap helps show how both of these dynamics can be nurtured through the way you think about your own purpose and ethics. This book won't solve the problems of corporate malfeasance on its own. No book could because the solution is forged in the heat of day-to-day decision-making. But Doty has given us an essential part of the solution, a vehicle for expanding our own awareness of virtue, and a way to start building up our own capacity as leaders and employees.

Navigating the compromise trap is much easier if you're capable—and if your company is capable as well. Building that capability will take time. The changes may not be perceptible at first, but in the end, if you can make the shift, it might be the single most powerful thing you can do to improve your company's future—and your own. This book can be both a helpful guide and an inspiration.

Introduction: Seeing with Peripheral Vision

This book is for people who are striving to live with integrity and purpose at work but are increasingly troubled by the compromises, double-binds, and contradictions of organizational life—and for those who want to avoid such messes in the first place. It is for professionals at all levels, at all stages in their careers, who bring energy and commitment to their work but have a growing uneasiness with ways they are not being fully true to themselves—whether breaking promises, stretching the truth, or something more severe. And it is for those who are not sure.

In this book we explore the problem of unhealthy pressure to compromise at work—the feeling that you may have to "drink the Kool-Aid," "play the game" in negative ways, or "sell your soul" to survive or reach your goals, compromising your personal values, commitments, or professional standards in the process. Drawing on in-depth interviews with more than fifty businesspeople in a variety of industries—as well as on my own experiences in the trenches with a global corporation; nineteen years of consulting experience diagnosing breakdowns and dysfunctions in large, complex organizations; and a number of studies in social psychology—I hope to show how, over time, unhealthy compromise actually becomes a self-depleting trap, hurting you, your organization, and your organization's ability to fulfill its commitments and obligations to the larger world. My goal is to invite you instead to redefine the game—to engage at a higher level, deliberately reconceiving what your work is about, knowing that it is not just a game but real life.

Compromise is a tricky subject. Compromising on anything never feels completely right or satisfying. And it is always challenging to look at a problem when you are not sure there is any other option. I hope that the ideas presented here will solidify more options in your mind so that you will feel more confident reflecting on which compromises involve making the best of a bad situation and which go too far.

In a way this book is about seeing with your peripheral vision; that is, recognizing what you partly know but that has not yet fully come into focus. The periphery of awareness is often where you learn the most, as old habits make what is right in front of you too familiar for insight. By widening your gaze to include what is just outside your normal focus, you can sometimes see what you have been missing—and increase the possibility of actually learning from your experience.

My own first glance into peripheral vision happened back in 1993. Two years out of business school, I was working for a group of brilliant and passionate reengineering consultants as the "numbers person" responsible for calculating the client's financial payoff for project proposals to streamline processes, provide better technology tools, or train frontline client staff. When I first started, I was absolutely convinced of the massive potential for improvement and reflected those assumptions in my analyses. It was only after seeing the realities of large-scale organizational change on several projects that I began to realize how unrealistic my projections were. Thus after my third major engagement, I felt a profound uneasiness as I sat with one of our senior leaders, making a pitch to a prospective client: "We think you can get a 35 percent reduction in cycle time and a 20 percent reduction in unit costs by the end of the year." I knew as soon as the words came out of my mouth that they were false. What had at one point been a passionate conviction was now a lie.

I call this a case of peripheral vision because the facts of the situation had not changed, but inside I saw things differently. Something tipped the moment I actually spoke the words, and I suddenly knew what I really thought. This experience and others like it forced me to confront the ways I sometimes tune out data that contradict my preferred beliefs. At first, facing these discrepancies caused me much private angst.

Unhealthy compromise so often comes with the option to avoid realizing that fact—to tune it out, rationalize it away, or change our standards. We don't *have* to see. Though Enron's motto was *Ask why,* one ex-trader said, "If I had questions, I didn't ask them...because I didn't want to know the answer."[1]

Sometimes it seems easier to shut out the data that raise too many unsolvable complications, but there are some very good reasons for tuning in to peripheral awareness.

First, seeing more of reality makes us saner. Things make more sense. We don't have to spend all that psychic energy tap dancing around the minefields of awareness, trying not to think what we're about to think. This means we can actually make a change. For example, it was not long after facing my own compromise in my work situation that I made the commitment to pursue a different type of consulting that more openly acknowledges the challenges of large-scale change—the brand of consulting I practice today, almost two decades later.

This brings us to the second reason for tapping what is at the edge of our awareness. Peripheral vision reveals gold along with lead. It gives us glimpses of who we really want to be, what we really want to do in the world, the passions and the talents we may have put on hold, and the missions big enough to truly engage our creative energies.

I learned this during my second glance into peripheral vision in 1998, when I was talking with two friends after watching a documentary about the Vietnam War. The movie zeroed in on the soldiers' spouses and how they decided whether they really wanted to know what their partners were involved in during the war. Sparked by that question of whether to see, my friends and I asked ourselves, *What is going on today that, if we were to fully look at it, might call us to take some action?* It was a fishing line into peripheral vision. What surfaced were the dormant missions that lay waiting for us to pay attention—missions that each of us is still actively working toward today, ten years later.

For me that conversation helped clarify the core inquiry that has energized my most interesting work since: *how do people reconcile the contrast between what they care about as people with the societal challenges that the organizations they work for may sometimes contribute to creating, intentionally or not?*

That question led me to embark on a series of interviews with fifty-two businesspeople in a variety of industries over the past four years, and their stories form the core of this book.

It is also why I find the topic of unhealthy compromise at work so important. It is a challenge with consequences at multiple levels. First, our lives are so intertwined with our identities at work, it is hard to imagine a satisfying life without work in which we can take pride. Second, when organizations create too much unhealthy pressure to compromise, they speed faster along the route to dysfunction and limited results, cutting off intelligence about how ineffective policies are undermining larger strategies to retain customers, engage employees, and deliver for shareholders. And, finally, lots of individual compromises, however reluctant, can add up to organizations that gradually erode their own integrity—tuning out the ways they cause harm or reneging on commitments and obligations to customers, employees, shareholders, the larger society, and the natural world.

So, I hope that as you explore this book you will not only take away deeper confidence and an increased ability to live up to your personal and professional commitments in the face of unhealthy pressure at work but also feel inspired to participate more actively in helping your organization act with integrity, fulfilling its commitments and potential for positive action in the world.

What to Expect

Our journey involves three primary topic areas:

- Understanding how unhealthy compromise can become a trap
- Learning what it means to redefine the game and engage at a higher level
- Taking practical steps for strengthening your ability to engage at that higher level in a wider range of circumstances, including unhealthy pressure from your organization

My hope is that having a greater understanding of the challenge, knowing how to access your sources of strength, and seeing multiple constructive options for action will give you the confidence to step up to the challenge of bringing your personal and professional commitments more fully into your day-to-day work.

We will talk about ethics, but we will go beyond traditional discussions of ethics in three ways. First, rather than examine the right thing to do in a situation, we will focus on how to strengthen your ability to live up to the values you already hold. Second, we will go beyond basic ethics and integrity to the other personal and professional commitments and values that affect your sense of being true to yourself, including what sort of person you want to be, your commitments to your family, your professional standards, what you consider worthwhile work, and your health and self-respect. Third, it is useful to understand how other factors such as groups, authority figures, and situational forces affect our choices, so I will bring in references to these factors from the fields of psychological ethics and social psychology where they are helpful.

In some sense what we explore in this book is integrity in its broadest sense. Not just consistency between your words and actions but the wholeness and the vitality that come with seeing the world as it is, sustaining your relationships, and fulfilling a worthwhile purpose.[2]

Chapters 1, 2, and 3—"The Compromise Trap," "A Devil's Bargain by Degrees," and "Ten Misconceptions about Compromise at Work"—explore what unhealthy compromise means, how it becomes a trap, and why we fall into that trap.

Chapter 4, "How Do I Redefine the Game?" tackles the challenge of how to engage at a higher level even when your organization or leader does not encourage it. Drawing on a variety of models from systems thinking to the pro-democracy movements in central Europe, I hope to convince you that far more is negotiable than you think, making it possible to act on your principles and values even in the face of unhealthy pressure.

Still, you will need more than a "just say no" strategy if you are going to pull it off without hurting yourself, so chapters 5 to 10 cover the personal foundations that make up your internal reinforcement system and enable you to redefine the game: "Reconnect to Your Strengths," "See the Larger Field," "Define a

> **Integrity** Being true, whole, undivided, and sound, which includes consistency between words and actions, being open to seeing the world as it is, sustaining relationships, and fulfilling a worthwhile purpose. Put most simply, integrity involves seeing, caring, and action.

Worthy Enough Win," "Find Your Real Team," "Make Positive Plays," and "Keep Your Own Score." These are the practical how-to chapters, outlining how to see past the blinders that hide choice points and options, demonstrating the importance of a "professional quest" for keeping you focused, and describing five positive plays you can make in the face of unhealthy pressure (fighting back is only one of them).

In the last two chapters, we connect the dots. In chapter 11, "Thriving at Work," I ask you to step back and reconsider your assumptions about what it takes to thrive. You'll see that though it seems riskier, redefining the game at a higher level actually has all the core ingredients for greater well-being for yourself and as a positive model to those around you. Finally, in chapter 12, "It's Bigger Than a Game," we see that responding to unhealthy pressure is not just an individual challenge but part of a necessary evolution toward organizations that act with integrity as a whole.

What I offer here is from the perspective of one who has been on the inside of large organizations (during my eleven years in hospitality management), who has struggled to integrate my values and my work without marginalizing myself, and who is now part of the support system for others who are doing the same. The stories you read here have all happened as reported, though I have omitted names and sometimes disguised industries to avoid embarrassing those involved.

How to Use This Book

To get the most out of the book, I encourage you to let it serve as a catalyst to uncovering the lessons in your own experience, a prompt to tap your own peripheral vision. My primary thesis is that when you broaden your perspective, you naturally see the costs of unhealthy compromise, the priorities that provide true security and satisfaction, and the hidden options for action that may not be apparent when you feel cornered into compromise. The whole story is about making better choices because you see more clearly. So, the examples and the ideas here should serve as prompts for telling your own story in a way that makes new sense and offers new guidance.

At the close of each chapter, I offer a few questions for reflection to spark your thinking and help you apply the concepts to your own situation. In chapters 5 through 10, you will find practical "Decision Point Tools" to help you address a specific problem or pressure. And, finally, I have included a section at the back of the book called "Individual and Small-group Activities," which includes six additional in-depth activities designed to take you from the compromise trap to the excitement of redefining the game, in whatever situation you find yourself, over a period of several weeks or months.

If you are stuck in a stressful situation, I hope this book will give you the reinforcement you need to recognize that investing in your personal strength and ability to be a positive force is not a luxury for another day but a way to create more flexibility, freedom, and respect in even the toughest settings. It will be important for you to read the early sections about how simply going along with pressure can backfire and become a trap so that you are clear about why it's worth investing in your personal foundations and adopting a "professional quest."

On the other hand, if you have already redefined how you engage or have embarked on a professional quest, you may want to jump to the later chapters on personal foundations to add options and reinforcement for the path you have already undertaken.

This is a broad territory to explore. To keep it focused, I have tried to include just the critical ideas you need to push back the barriers to redefining the game and engaging at a higher level. I hope you will view each chapter as a stepping stone on the path to ongoing personal development, which will expand your range even further should you choose to pursue it.

One last note before we dive in: for clarity's sake, I speak to "you" as the reader when I have a suggestion to make or a proposition to offer. One downside of this convention is that it implies a teacher/student relationship that just doesn't fit here, especially given the thorniness of the topic. I realize that I have much to learn myself and could just as easily speak to what "we" need to do—you and I both. What I offer is based on my best understanding to date, given prolonged study, application in my own professional life, discussions with countless individuals, and ongoing conversations with several thought leaders in the field. As a reminder that these ideas are meant for both men and women, I have opted to vary gender pronouns throughout the text, rather than adopt the more awkward convention of adding "he or she" at every turn.

The payoffs for embarking on this journey are the increased vitality, energy, confidence, security, and excitement that come with redefining the game based on your own independent decision to do so. In the process, you change yourself from a cog in a machine to a "hidden degree of freedom in the system's unexpressed creativity,"[3] contributing in unexpected ways to the evolution of the larger institutions where you work.

Thank you for choosing to pick up *The Compromise Trap.* I look forward to working together to strengthen your ability to redefine the game and engage at the level at which you truly want to engage.

1

The Compromise Trap

"You have to interview me again," said a voicemail from Jim, a sales manager I had interviewed eighteen months earlier when I was beginning my research for this book. "My story has changed."

Jim was the first of the fifty-two businesspeople I have interviewed over the past four years. These conversations were all part of a quest I embarked on in 2005 to understand how businesspeople see their personal values connecting to their work.

I met Jim at a conference on sustainable product design, where his company's innovative carpeting and flooring products were featured (among other things, they made carpet squares that were recyclable). We agreed to meet at a local pub several weeks later for an interview. He arrived almost an hour late, just as I began to wonder if I was insane to venture into such idealistic territory. But then he rushed in, breathless and eager to explain that he was late because he had had the chance to tell his company's "sustainability story" to a new customer.

"Initially, these interior designers can't believe they can do something good without hurting their business," he said. "The idea that they can get cutting-edge flooring designs without all the chemicals that leach into the landfill from broadloom carpeting is electrifying to them. I think it is a relief because they want to do the right thing while meeting their business objectives." Jim had been slow to get on board with the new product line himself, initially thinking it was just marketing spin. Then he did some research and found out how remarkable his company's products really were. "Previously, I didn't understand the issue or what we were doing about it. Shame on me. Now I preach this story every day. I'm on a mission."

When I asked, as my interview protocol required, whether he ever felt any tension between his personal values and his work, he replied, "It really matters whom you work for. When you work for an employer where your values are aligned, you do not confront those sorts of dilemmas." He was a subscriber to what I later dubbed the "playing for the good guys" strategy for finding alignment at work.

Now, eighteen months later, his voicemail said his story had changed.

We met at the same noisy pub. As we moved through the crowded room and I swept old peanut shells off the table to make room for my recorder, I could tell that Jim felt a sense of urgency, a need to clean up his story.

"I feel as if I was duped. Just like the movie *Who Killed the Electric Car?* my company got the pilot teams all excited but didn't make a full commitment to the sustainability strategy. Now I have tarnished my reputation, selling what they told me to sell, convincing myself they were serious."

His doubts had begun with a memo. Shortly after he and his family moved cross-country so he could take over as sales director for the new sustainable product lines he had told me about, he received a brief interoffice memo stating that he was required to sell the *entire* line of products—including the old broadloom carpeting that was the worst offender for landfill.

This caused a minor crisis for Jim. "How could I tell the sustainability story in good conscience if I was pushing broadloom right alongside it? Did they really believe the sustainability strategy they were promoting? Or were we just 'greenwashing'?" But his leaders assured him that they were actively pursuing ways to reuse the nonsustainable product lines and that the company was firmly committed to more-sustainable products.

So, Jim compromised. He continued telling the "sustainability story" to his customers, assuring them that the company shared his passion for diverting the harmful products going to the landfill and that if they bought broadloom carpeting, there would be some way to reuse it in the near future. But a year went by with little progress on solving the broadloom landfill problem, and gradually the initiative faded from corporate communications. Jim tried to find out the status, asking whether the constraints involved resources, executive support, or technology. "But every time I asked, I got silence," he said quietly. He looked down for a moment, and the din of the pub intruded on our conversation. I wondered if the recorder would catch his words at this low volume. "To tell you the truth," he concluded, "I am getting more and more disappointed with how things work."

Healthy and Unhealthy Compromise

Compromise is a fact of organizational life. You couldn't get anything done if you did not have some willingness to adapt to the competing priorities and interests that are part of accomplishing any meaningful goal with other people.

Most of the time, compromise is healthy. It is the spirit of compromise that allows people to cooperate to achieve shared goals, allocate scarce resources, smooth over personality differences, leverage diverse points of view, change with the changing world, and learn anything new.

Yet, as Jim found, compromise can be unhealthy too.* When you compromise on something you believe in, it just feels wrong. There is often a strong visceral reaction, like feeling sick to your stomach or having something "stick in your craw." Perhaps that's why having "qualms" means having both doubts and a nauseated feeling. Going ahead with these unhealthy compromises takes a bite out of your passion and vitality, leaving you with nagging doubts and uneasiness, regrets and disillusionment, or even dread and deep remorse if severe enough. Jim's compromise on selling broadloom carpeting left him feeling foolish and guilty, deeply uncomfortable about the false promises he had made to his customers.

On an organizational level, compromising too far can erode quality, lose customers, demoralize employees, damage shareholder value, destroy trust with outside stakeholder groups, and even jeopardize the firm legally and cause great harm to the larger world. A recent news story showed how the agencies responsible for rating mortgage-backed securities made incremental compromise after compromise in their standards until they were touting very questionable mortgages as top quality. During a congressional hearing on the crisis, one representative cried in frustration, "You are the gatekeepers; you are *the guys!* That's why you're there! Now we face a situation where we've got a house of cards that has fallen."[1] In this case, compromise contributed materially to the global financial meltdown with which we are all contending.

How does this happen? Greed is too simplistic an answer, especially in an economic system that is supposed to run on

---

*As I am using the term, *unhealthy compromise* can refer to any of three typical conflict strategies—compromise, accommodate, or avoid—as described in the Thomas-Kilmann Conflict MODE Instrument (*www.kilmann.com/conflict.html*).

self-interest. We all need to better understand the dynamics of unhealthy compromise, the true costs, and what you can do instead without committing career suicide.

But why would you make a compromise that didn't sit well?

To start with, you don't compromise if you can have your cake and eat it, too. Compromise is a way of adapting to the pressure created by competing interests, others' demands and expectations, or circumstances themselves.

The type of pressure you face is part of what leads you to unhealthy compromise.

Healthy and Unhealthy Pressure

Healthy pressure drives you toward healthy compromise. Audacious goals, intelligent strategies, and challenging targets create rewards for pursuing higher priorities and values and/or penalties for pursuing lower ones. They give you a reason to stop squabbling over little stuff and get on with what really needs to be done.

Healthy pressure Expectations, demands, or circumstances that create rewards for pursuing *higher* values, wants, and priorities and penalties for pursuing *lower* ones. *Examples:* a drive to win new customers by earning their trust, a directive to make cost reductions needed to save the business, or a cultural norm that enforces accountability.

Healthy compromise Adapting to pressures or constraints by sacrificing *lower* values, wants, or priorities for *higher* ones. *Examples:* contributing toward shared goals, sharing costs, deferring projects due to scarce resources, adapting to others' personalities, or giving up old ways to learn new ones.

Think of the last great boss you had. Chances are he inspired you by engaging you in a really big challenge. When something is truly important, the natural response is to rise to the occasion, and this involves healthy compromise: putting aside your personal preferences, sharing resources, perhaps putting in longer hours, maybe even relocating with your family as Jim did.

At its core, healthy compromise means adapting to pressures or constraints by sacrificing lower values, wants, or priorities for higher ones. In other words, it's giving up something less important to get something more important, just as in negotiations you might make a concession to reach a mutually acceptable settlement.

But as we have seen, pressure at work can be unhealthy as well. It is harder to know how to respond when this happens.

Unhealthy pressure drives you toward making unhealthy compromises. The price of doing the right thing goes up. You still have a choice, but with unhealthy pressure you face penalties for pursuing higher values and priorities and/or rewards for pursuing

Unhealthy pressure Expectations, demands, or circumstances that create rewards for pursuing *lower* values, wants, or priorities and penalties for pursuing *higher* ones. *Examples:* expectations that salespeople will lie to customers, a directive to cut costs for appearance's sake, or a cultural norm that enforces posturing.

Unhealthy compromise Adapting to pressures or constraints by sacrificing *higher* values, wants, or priorities for *lower* ones. *Examples:* agreeing with the boss although you see significant flaws, manipulating numbers to win awards, destroying family relationships to gain a promotion, or overworking until you deplete your health.

lower ones. In other words, it becomes increasingly expensive—in terms of energy, political capital, or personal security—to do what you think you should do.

For example, in good economic times when there are plenty of jobs, when your company has an ethics hotline and a culture of high integrity, with senior leadership that walks the talk, it is very difficult but not mortally terrifying to report an unethical boss. But the same situation becomes much more difficult when the circumstances are less supportive—if you don't know how senior leaders will respond and whether you will keep your job or be able to get another one quickly enough. These are the classic dilemmas faced by would-be "whistleblowers."

Consider Thomas Tamm, the federal employee who reported a government program he believed carried out unconstitutional warrantless wiretapping on U.S. citizens. As he made the call to report the wiretapping, he realized that some might interpret his actions as treason, a capital crime that could earn him the death penalty. Would he be tried and executed for going public with a civil-rights violation? That's a pretty high price for doing what he considered the right thing.[2]

Contrary to popular wisdom, unhealthy pressure at work is not uncommon. Many people I spoke with in my research described situations that pressed them to violate a professional standard, a promise, an important personal value, a personal commitment, or their basic ethics.

For example, an intensive care nurse started having panic attacks after her patient load tripled with managed care. "I was terrified that someone would die on my shift," she told me, shivering at the thought. A bank loan officer felt cornered into choosing between making unsound loans and losing the respect of her board of directors, who thought her "overly cautious." Salespeople

Types of Compromise

- Honesty
- Laws or regulations
- Your professional standards
- Your promises or commitments
- Your desire to do good work
- Your relationships
- Your values or principles
- Your objectivity
- Your health
- Your character
- Your purpose or mission

for a network equipment company confessed their worries to a sales trainer, believing they were supposed to mislead customers by assuring them that every single one of their components was the best in its class, which was not true.

Unhealthy pressure can come from an unethical boss, an organizational culture, a company policy, or even a line of products, as it did for Jim. You may face unhealthy pressure in the midst of an organization you otherwise believe in. The pressure can even come from internal personal issues, as when financial need or an exaggerated drive for the trappings of success leads people to step over the line into cheating, backstabbing, fudging the numbers, or outright fraud or illegal actions. (Of course, you can also have healthy internal pressure such as the desire to do well by doing good.) There is no stark dividing line between healthy and unhealthy pressure; they lie on a continuum of the rewards and the penalties they generate.

Just as the natural response to healthy pressure is healthy compromise, the default response to unhealthy pressure, much as we wish it were otherwise, is unhealthy compromise—giving up something of higher value, like being honest with a customer, for something of lower value, like winning an award. This might mean making a decision that undermines a larger goal, betrays a core value, breaks an important commitment or obligation, or jeopardizes your health or future productivity. For example, playing to the boss's ego by supporting a shortsighted strategy feels to many people like an unhealthy compromise. Of course, what counts as higher priorities or values varies by person, but everyone has some that are higher and some that are lower, and there is a surprising amount of overlap among us.

The essence of unhealthy compromise is the feeling that you are breaking a commitment to yourself or someone else, failing to protect or live up to a responsibility. This is the sort of compromise that fits the less common dictionary definitions, where *compromise* means (1) exposing something to danger or suspicion, as when a military mission is compromised, or (2) impairing the health of something, as when an organism is so depleted it can no longer fight off infection. For example, Jim felt he had tarnished his reputation because he had a commitment to serve his customers' best interests by advising them accurately about his company's products and in retrospect he had been misleading them about the broadloom product line.

The irony is that most people make these concessions reluctantly.

But what do you do when the pressure is on? Do you dare speak up when you know the boss hates being challenged? What do you do when, like in Jim's case, a company policy or unwritten expectation requires you to do stupid things that cost the company customers, destroy employee morale, or waste the shareholders' money?

This is where many people get muddy.

How Shall I Engage?

When the price of doing the right thing goes up, many people feel they have no choice but to conform, especially when their careers or their families' well-being are at stake. It is particularly challenging when the unhealthy pressure comes from the organization or when others think it is okay to go along. For example, a senior human resources (HR) specialist in a growing technology firm noticed that important decisions were increasingly made with very little thought. She found it harder and harder to ask her colleagues to stop and think before making a decision about whom to hire or where to assign them. "You become the bad guy if you slow things down. I have to use my political capital very carefully."

Anytime you face pressure like this, the first question is: *How are you going to engage?* Are you going to play along with the game, shrinking yourself to fit a bad situation? Or are you going to play big, redefining the game so that you can engage at a higher level? (See figure 1-1.)

Figure 1-1 How Shall I Engage?

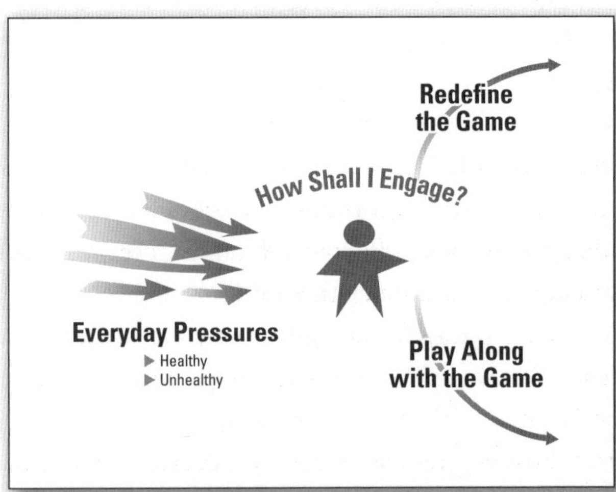

Playing along with the game often feels like playing small, "sinking to their level" as some people say. By contrast, when you choose to redefine the game in a positive way, it feels like "being big," rising above, and bringing the game itself to another level.

For example, Jim in our opening story could now take a narrow perspective, focusing on how to ensure that no one blamed him for unfulfilled promises to customers while turning a blind eye to the company's shifting priorities; or he could choose to take a broader perspective, focusing on making accurate commitments and, ideally, ones that fulfilled the sustainability story.

According to the conventional wisdom about organizational life, you need to "play the game" to get along and get ahead. Yet it is often precisely this playing along that disturbs people most—whether that means giving lip service to a poor idea, feeling forced to enact a dog-eat-dog mentality, or focusing too much attention on power plays and status rather than the real work and the real value.

Given the intense pressure to play along, it is easy to miss the fact that you do have a choice about whether you accept the terms of the game as defined by others or handed down by history—that is, you have a choice about how to engage.

How you engage refers to the orientation or stance you bring to any situation. You can think of this as the "game" you are playing, in the sense that how you engage determines what you consider a win, whom you include in your thinking, how long a time horizon you project, what questions you ask, what you pay attention to, what options you will consider (and those you won't), and how you keep score, among other things.[3]

As a strategy for being true to your values and higher aims, redefining the game means defining a pursuit or an enterprise to be *for* something rather than against someone. That is what that great boss you recalled earlier was probably doing, in which case,

Playing along with the game Letting others define the terms of engagement and your options, generally focusing on self-protection or winning as the primary concern. Tends to solve for a narrow set of interests and a short-term time horizon.

Redefining the game Consciously choosing to engage at a higher level, orienting toward whatever matters most, considering a bigger win, over a longer time horizon, involving more interests and higher values as well as practical outcomes. Generally tries to act as a positive force to help the right thing happen, for oneself and others.

your entire team was probably redefining the conventions of your organization or industry. It is what a breakthrough innovation does and what a true leader accomplishes: setting the terms of engagement at a whole new level.

When you redefine the game, you are engaging at a higher level. You are orienting toward what matters most, considering a bigger win, over a longer time horizon, involving more interests and higher values. Ironically, this means your "game" is about bringing in more of reality and acting as a positive force to help the right thing happen rather than just trying to overcome a threat. It is a far more creative and flexible strategy as a result.

Theoretically, it *is* possible to convince yourself you have to play along in a negative way even when the pressure is healthy. Those who cross lines for personal gain often feel "this is just how business works," though they are choosing a very cynical view. I am sure you know someone who feels they have "no choice" but to lie, cheat, steal, or mislead for their personal gain. They are making unhealthy compromises with themselves—betraying their own principles, the company's values, others' trust, or even the law—to advance their self-interest. They are solving for themselves, in the short term, and typically count only external measures of success such as money, power, or prestige.

This is what most ethics training is focused on preventing. If that person justifies his actions by feeling he has no choice but to go along with the game, why don't you do it, too?

Because you made a choice to engage at a higher level than that. At some point you decided to step up to the challenge of actually creating value, of truly winning new customers, of inspiring employees, and of finding more-innovative or more-efficient ways to operate, rather than simply meet your goals or company targets by cheating. That is why you choose the admired company or work for a visionary boss. *But can you step up in that way when the pressure turns unhealthy? Can you afford to swim against the current? How do you do it?* These are the questions at the heart of this book.*

Without workable answers to these questions, you are likely to feel that your only choice is to play along with the game if the pressure becomes unhealthy. And, based on my research, that is going to lead you into a trap.

The Compromise Trap

The choice to play along with the game in the face of unhealthy pressure is often automatic, a gut-level response to a threat or risk.

---

*For simplicity's sake, I will speak from here on as if *redefining the game* and *engaging at a higher level* are synonymous; the reader should recognize that technically it is possible to redefine the game at a *lower* level, though this is simply a shortcut into the compromise trap. Conversely, playing along with the game generally means compromising on higher values, so I will refer to *playing along with the game* and *engaging at a lower level* as roughly synonymous. Again, technically you could play along with the game and pursue higher values in a passive way, which has its own risks.

For example, I distinctly recall sliding discreetly backward in my chair during a meeting where a senior executive was upbraiding a team—just to stay out of his line of sight. It was a gut reaction out of fear that came from worrying only about myself—and not one I am proud of.

Once you've taken that narrow perspective, it looks as though your most viable option is to make the unhealthy compromise required by the pressure you face. Most people feel that the costs of fighting back or quitting are just too expensive, but they fail to estimate the full costs of unhealthy compromise. This path is both self-depleting and self-reinforcing over time, which is why I call it "the compromise trap." (See figure 1-2.)

Like all traps, the compromise trap offers enticing bait: the promise that you can win or protect yourself if you will just compromise on a few minor scruples. And like all good traps, the catch in this offer is hidden. The catch is this: you play along with the game because you don't feel big enough to take on the unhealthy

Figure 1-2 Playing Along with the Game

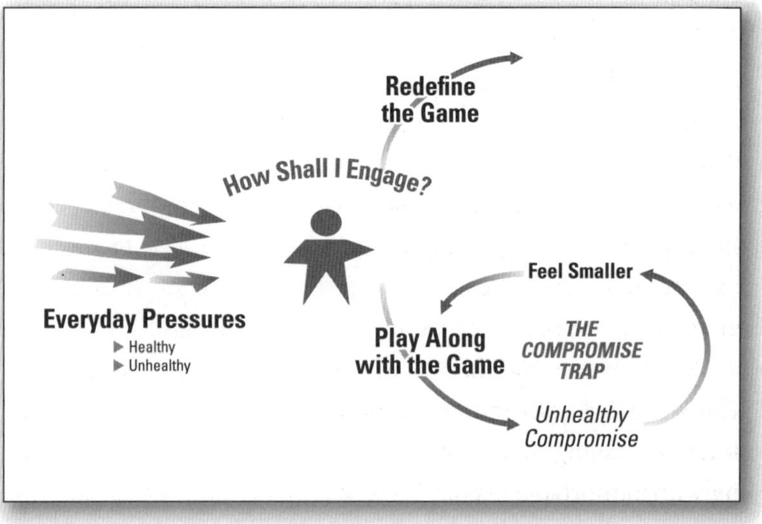

> **The compromise trap** The gradual erosion of vitality, passion, and confidence that occurs when you deal with unhealthy pressure by playing along with the game and compromising in unhealthy ways.

pressure, but each unhealthy compromise leaves you feeling even smaller and less capable.

Every time you cross a line or betray a commitment, you take a bite out of your self-respect, your confidence, and your passion for what you are doing. It is mentally, emotionally, and physically depleting to go along with actions with which you disagree.

For example, when Julie, the chief financial officer/chief operating officer (CFO/COO) of a Fortune 500 company, turned a blind eye to some questionable employment practices it "tore her apart." Eventually, she started getting sick and couldn't keep up with her responsibilities. Externally, unhealthy compromise undermines your influence, setting precedents with those around you and teaching them to expect you to comply, or costing you allies as you show that you may betray their trust when the chips are down. Finally, as you lose faith in your courage, creativity, and judgment, you become more dependent on external indicators of success, so you are more driven and willing to do "whatever it takes" next time, tuning out the warning signs that might reveal the trap. This is the meaning of the word *demoralize:* to cause to lose confidence, spirit, courage, or discipline; to confuse or disorient; to lower morale; to cause to lose moral bearings.

For example, Karen, a marketing communications director who struggled with the posturing her role sometimes involved, described feeling more and more driven even as she felt increasingly uncomfortable inside: "I was riding high on the surface but full of dread underneath. I learned to tune out reality, to rationalize to myself."

The end result is that you become a bit like the monkey with his hand stuck in a hand-trap: he can get his empty hand into and out of the trap, but while clutching the food his hand is too big to fit back through the opening, so he's starving because he won't let go of food he cannot eat. To the outside world and your peer group, you may seem quite successful. You may not even be able to see the harm you are doing or the true costs to yourself until you leave the situation. "Life began for me when I left Wal-Mart," said an ex-manager who agreed to be interviewed for the documentary *Wal-Mart: The High Cost of Low Price.* "When you're in the culture, or the cult, you don't see any other way."[4] As mentioned earlier, this process can envelope entire companies. For example, you might say the rating agencies Moody's and Standard & Poor's fell into the compromise trap during the mortgage-lending boom. Caught in a market-share war, each was convinced it had to do whatever it took to win business from the other. Because their business models involved earning fees from the very companies whose securities they rated, they had a built-in incentive to erode their standards. In a recent PBS special, Standard & Poor's executive Frank Raiter describes the subtle pressure to compromise that infected his agency during the mortgage-backed security boom. "I was amazed at what they [the division charged with rating collateralized debt obligations] were doing. I saw an erosion of standards in the face of pressure to close a deal."

Another executive, Richard Gugliada, explained that they had no choice. "[We had] no way of obtaining the information we would normally use, so we needed to come up with a shortcut way of doing it. Otherwise the deal would be unratable; it couldn't be done." In other words, he felt there was no choice but to act in a way that ultimately led to devastating negative side effects, causing incredible damage to the company, the industry, and, some would argue, the stability of the entire global credit-rating system.[5]

The point is when you let others define the choices for you, it is easy to miss the larger stakes and what you truly have to lose.

Redefining the Game

When you are caught in the compromise trap, it feels as though you are selling pieces of your soul but with very few other viable alternatives. Yet a large subset of the people I interviewed actually saw other alternatives and acted on them.

Roughly eighteen of fifty-two people described redefining the game in a positive way in the face of unhealthy pressure, acting courageously to "help the right thing happen" for themselves and others. In the process, they exercised a level of leadership far above their official roles.

For example, Roberta was a young sales director who had gotten on her boss's "bad side" and found that no one in her office would speak to her, preventing her from doing her job. As her performance ratings slipped, she spent months in worry and self-doubt, yet she stayed because she desperately needed the job. Then one day, thanks to some encouragement from a couple of courageous co-workers, she decided to take a risk. Recalling her strong performance in prior jobs and reminding herself that her goal was to help the company succeed, she walked into her boss's office and said, "Boss, you cannot treat me this way any longer. This is not okay—it is insulting to me, and it is disabling my ability to create the results I promised you. So, I recommend either I quit today or you start treating me like a member of the team." She fully expected to be let go, but that's not what happened. He acknowledged the problem, changed his behavior, and she went on to become one of his top salespeople!

As Roberta's story shows, redefining the game for the better is not about ignoring hard realities but deciding to be a positive force in the face of them. You bank on your own potential and capability while including other people's interests in your thinking, considering a longer time horizon, and defining a win in terms of higher values and goals. This is what gives you the courage to engage at a higher level rather than shrink to fit the game you are being pressured to play.

Jim shows us how this can be done even when exiting a situation.

Shortly after our talk in the pub, Jim decided he needed to act on the broadloom issue. First he talked to his family about his concerns and plans. He then went to check out the competition—but with a completely novel approach. "Even though I was just interviewing for a frontline sales management job, I insisted on speaking with the CEO [chief executive officer] and other senior leaders. 'Are you guys serious? Do you really mean this stuff, or are you full of crap?' I asked them. I guess I was pretty direct, but I knew I could not sell the product if they were just playing a game. They understood my questions, so they took me through the manufacturing process and showed how the same philosophy was in use there. After several meetings and more tangible examples, I became convinced that it was a real mission and a mindset, not just a marketing pitch. Though they still had things to work on, I could live with it, given that it was a real commitment."

Meanwhile Jim talked with the leaders at his current employer because he wanted to stay on if they were truly committed to sustainability. He told them he really believed in their mission but he wasn't sure they were serious and he couldn't stay if they weren't. They were polite but didn't address his concerns, which gave him his answer. Eventually, he moved over to the competitor. He is now thriving as a passionate advocate, speaking at conferences and training his team on all the advantages of the sustainable products. "It is a pleasure to work with these guys," he told me in a follow-up call. I have a personal suspicion that his graceful way of exiting may have influenced one or more people at his former employer, though we'll never know for sure.

The people I met who were engaging at that higher level consistently demonstrated this sort of positive approach to negotiating conflicts and dilemmas. They often startled me with the way they thought about things. For example, an HR director described moving *closer* to difficulty rather than away from it. In describing the greater range of options available when you realize you can redefine the game, one marketing manager said, "It's almost as if you cross over into a parallel universe; there's so much more you can do." And once they had adopted this path, it became self-reinforcing, just as the compromise trap did: each positive play left them feeling bigger and more capable, more able to engage at that higher level the next time. (See figure 1-3.)

Figure 1-3 Redefining the Game

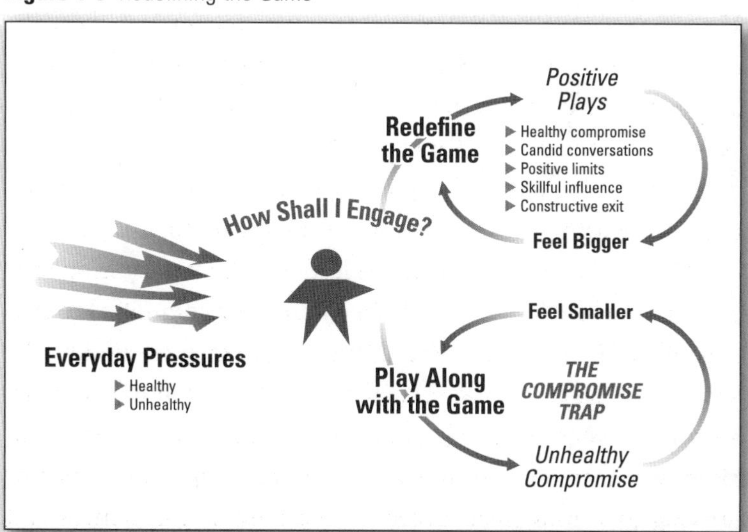

So, what enabled these eighteen people to risk redefining the game in the first place, daring to set their own terms on how they would engage? Were they independently wealthy, with all the freedom many of us dream that will bring?

In a way, yes.

Personal Foundations

What the people who dared to redefine the game and engage at a higher level had in common was an internal reinforcement system that increased their sense of security, confidence, independence, well-being, creativity, and courage.

Engaging at a higher level under *healthy* pressure earns you all sorts of recognition and rewards for rising to the occasion. But with *unhealthy* pressure, when the system creates penalties for doing the right thing, you need additional support to not be drawn off course by the dysfunctional incentives.

So, the first step in strengthening your ability to redefine the game for the better is to switch to your own personal foundations for support. (See figure 1-4.)

In studying patterns in the stories of those who successfully redefined the game under pressure, I identified six personal foundations that make a difference. We explore each of these in depth in the second half of this book, so you can adapt them for your own uses, regardless of the pressure you face.

The Six Personal Foundations

1. **Reconnect to your strengths** This allows you to access confidence and creativity and provides self-awareness to guide your choices.

Figure 1-4 Tapping Your Personal Foundations

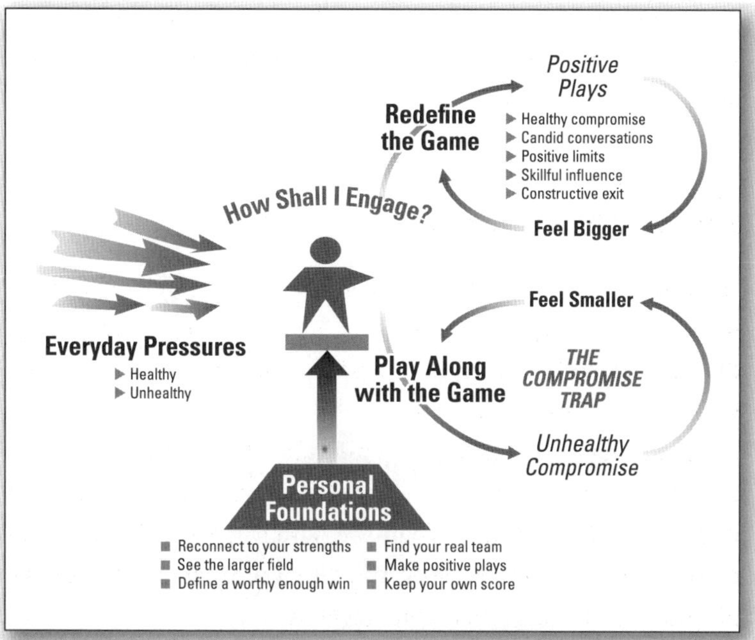

2. **See the larger field** A broad perspective reveals hidden choice points, costs, and opportunities, so you can be proactive and creative.

3. **Define a worthy enough win** This gives you a reason for courage and helps you weigh hard choices.

4. **Find your real team** This provides access to added resources, validation, and support and ensures that your priorities are aligned with your family's.

5. **Make positive plays** This gives you a range of options that enable you to be true to yourself while minimizing retaliation; they include healthy compromise, candid

conversations, positive limits, skillful influence, and constructive exit.

6. **Keep your own score** This frees you from comparing with others while providing reassurance of your impact and helping you learn.

With these six personal foundations supporting you, you will have access to a much broader range of options for courageous, constructive action. You will no longer be dependent on your organization for whether you can engage at the level at which you really want to engage.

Thriving at Work without Selling Your Soul

As poet David Whyte once said, "Taking any step that is courageous, however small, is a way of bringing any gifts we have to the surface."[6] Learning to redefine the game in the face of unhealthy pressure means you can not only survive but thrive and contribute in a broader range of circumstances. When you are creatively engaged in pursuing what you are passionate about, even if it is difficult, you feel more alive. Acknowledging the unhealthy pressure leaves you feeling a little more sane, with more access to your creativity and resourcefulness. And when you step up to a higher level of engagement and purpose, you remind others that they have the freedom to do the same—sometimes even those who are pressuring you. A single role model has a dramatic impact on others' awareness of their choices.

It all begins with a decision.

"I decided I was no longer going to cave out of fear," said a marketing manager after several episodes that undermined her self-respect. "I might have to make hard decisions, but I wasn't going to cave."

Suppose you too made the decision not to cave in to unhealthy pressure—or to expand your range beyond your current comfort zone. What support would you need to follow that through?

As you consider that question, in the next chapter, "A Devil's Bargain by Degrees," we explore the stories of those who discovered firsthand that the compromise trap is a losing proposition. If nothing else, this should convince you that playing along with the game is not as safe as it may seem.

But first, here is a recap of this chapter's key concepts, followed by a few reflection questions to connect what we've discussed here with your own experience. You may also want to skim "Individual and Small-group Activities" at the back of the book to see the sorts of practical activities we will use throughout our journey.

KEY CONCEPTS

- **Healthy pressure** Expectations, demands, or circumstances that create rewards for pursuing *higher* values, wants, and priorities and penalties for pursuing *lower* ones.
- **Healthy compromise** Adapting to pressures or constraints by sacrificing *lower* values, wants, or priorities for *higher* ones.
- **Unhealthy pressure** Expectations, demands, or circumstances that create rewards for pursuing *lower* values, wants, or priorities and penalties for pursuing *higher* ones.
- **Unhealthy compromise** Adapting to pressures or constraints by sacrificing *higher* values, wants, or priorities for *lower* ones.
- **Playing along with the game** Letting others define the terms of engagement and your options, generally focusing on self-protection or winning as the primary concern. Tends to solve for a narrow set of interests and a short-term time horizon.

- **Redefining the game** Consciously choosing to engage at a higher level, orienting toward whatever matters most, considering a bigger win, over a longer time horizon, involving more interests and higher values as well as practical outcomes. Generally tries to act as a positive force to help the right thing happen, for oneself and others.
- **The compromise trap** The gradual erosion of vitality, passion, and confidence that occurs when you deal with unhealthy pressure by playing along with the game and compromising in unhealthy ways.
- **Review figure 1-4,** Tapping Your Personal Foundations, which graphically summarizes all the concepts covered in this chapter.

REFLECTION QUESTIONS

- Find a copy of your résumé and read back through your work history. What thoughts, feelings, or images come up as you recall each role and organization? What sort of healthy pressures do you recall? Where and when did you feel unhealthy pressure? How did you respond to it? Notice how thinking about these affects you mentally, emotionally, and physically.
- What pressures in your current circumstances might lead you to make an unhealthy compromise? Why? How would you like to redefine the game if you could?
- Recall a time when you chose to redefine the game in the face of particularly challenging unhealthy pressure. How did you feel just before you took action? What enabled you to take that path? How did you show up differently from normal? What happened as a result?

2

A Devil's Bargain by Degrees

"I can't tell you exactly the moment I changed," Amrita told me as we sat in the spacious den of her colonial mid-Atlantic home. She had retired a month earlier from a position as senior vice president of a global petrochemical company. "I worked in a very competitive culture, and I felt I needed to fit in. First, I gave up the *bindi* and sari of my Indian heritage.* Gradually, I gave up myself. I tried to act less feminine. As I moved up, I became more and more competitive. Then one day, as I was getting ready for work, I looked in the mirror and I did not recognize my own face—I mean literally. I saw the lines, the tight jaw, and the cold eyes, and I put my hands up in shock. *Who have I become?* I asked myself. It was a terrifying moment."

An Appreciative Inquiry into the "Dark Side" of Work

As I mentioned in the Introduction, this book is largely the result of a research project begun in 2005. Inspired by my own

*A bindi is a small colored ornamental dot worn in the middle of a woman's forehead, especially in Hindu and sometimes Sikh cultures.

challenges and by my observations of troubling patterns in client organizations, I embarked on a quest to understand how businesspeople see their personal values connecting to their work.

The fifty-two individuals I interviewed were mostly current and former midlevel leaders in public and private corporations. I interviewed recent college graduates, professionals at the peak of their careers, and recent retirees. Anyone who was willing to spend a few hours talking was a potential participant, from business school classmates and former co-workers to family, friends, clients, and tired travelers waiting in airport lounges. Each interview lasted two to three hours and covered the person's work history, where he or she felt pressure to compromise, how he or she adapted (or not), and his or her highest values and concerns as a parent, spouse, citizen, or grandparent.

In addition to these fifty-two formal interviews, I have held informal conversations with at least sixty-seven more individuals on the topic of compromise at work. Although this sort of study does not allow statistical generalizations, it provides a rare window into people's experiences and thought processes about work, especially with its firsthand accounts of pressure to compromise. Of course, to get this level of candor I had to promise not to reveal individual or company names. (See "Online Resources" at the back of the book for a link to more information about the interviews.)

As you will see, the project was conceived less as an exposé than as an appreciative look into the dark side of work, a solution-oriented investigation into the barriers to living up to values you already hold. There was nothing anyone described that I could not imagine doing myself in similar circumstances, even though some of their decisions had indeed contributed to harm. Perhaps the most valuable takeaway is the realization that anyone can get off course from his or her own values and that there are indeed workable strategies for staying true.

Most surprising in my conversations was how much unhealthy pressure people felt to compromise and how much those compromises cost them over time. Amrita's story was not an isolated case. More than 130 hours of recorded interviews, plus notes from the many additional informal conversations on the topic, suggest several overarching themes:

- There is often intense pressure to conform at work.
- Unhealthy pressure to compromise is routine and can happen even in the best companies.
- A devil's bargain is often made by degrees.

As you review these themes and the quotes that accompany them, I encourage you to mentally compare and contrast them with your own experiences.

General Pressure to Conform

The first notable pattern in my conversations was widespread and intense pressure to conform to organizational norms of any type. Participants described "having to drink the Kool-Aid" (a reference to a tragic mass suicide that is now commonly used to refer to making a full commitment to a team, company, or strategy); "being assimilated" (a reference to a *Star Trek* episode involving a hivelike alien that takes over individuals' wills); and being "sucked in," where there is "no halfway."

"You have to conform or you will be ejected," said one marketing manager. The intense threat of social ostracism or retaliation left many people uneasy about their ability to be true to an independent set of values. And apparently, the perceived risk increases with rank.

"There's more ownership [of your psyche] as you go up," said Joe, an HR vice president at a Fortune 100 public healthcare company. According to some people I spoke with, just this general cultural pressure to conform led to various unhealthy compromises, including acting hyper-competitively, becoming a workaholic, gossiping, drinking too much, or faking certain political beliefs to fit in. For example, one HR director confessed, "I see now how easy it is for me to make 'devil decisions' when I am around people who make me feel important."[1]

It was not always obvious to people when this pressure to conform was healthy or unhealthy.

Most people tend to assume that unhealthy pressure at work arises from unethical demands; but as specific incidents from the interviews showed, unhealthy pressure can come from distasteful cultural norms or from organizational double binds as well. Organizational double binds are policies, directives, or situations that put you in conflict with your values but which you cannot discuss for fear of being labeled a "resister." (*Double bind* is a psychological term that refers to a mixed message or contradiction that is undiscussable and whose undiscussability is undiscussable.)[2]

For example, an information technology (IT) team in a Fortune 50 computer and office equipment company was pressed (against their better judgment) to promise higher service levels to their internal customers. Three months later they were floundering, as the result of a predictable reorganization that drastically cut the capacity of the internal supplier they depended on, making delivering on their promises impossible. Their leader, however, hesitated to speak up for fear of looking like a whiner. As Jim found when he could no longer sell broadloom carpeting, or when I realized I could no longer make such ambitious projections for reengineering projects, unhealthy pressure like this may be gradual and reach a critical threshold only over time.

This is crucial to understanding the compromise trap because it means you may develop a habit of conforming and then be unable to recognize unhealthy pressure if and when it shows up, especially if it is just a piece of your overall experience of an otherwise healthy company. Books on professional ethics refer to this risk when they discuss the potential for groupthink or the ways professional roles can impair ethical awareness.[3]

Routine Pressure to Compromise

The second most notable finding from my interviews is that unhealthy pressure to compromise is relatively routine and can happen even in the best companies and even in the midst of otherwise worthwhile work. A significant number of the companies my participants worked for had received awards for being "most admired" or "great places to work" or otherwise recognized as values-based businesses. Yet fifty-one of the fifty-two people I interviewed experienced some form of memorable and uncomfortable unhealthy pressure to compromise, and many of them experienced some degree of unhealthy pressure while working for those companies. This is consistent with the findings of a recent survey, which found that companies with a strong ethical culture *are* better to work for but are extremely rare (9 percent), and even then 24 percent of respondents from those companies still observed at least one incidence of ethical misconduct within the prior twelve months.[4]

As a very rough overview, here are the specific areas in which people I interviewed felt pressure to compromise. (See figure 2-1.)

Being honest and following the law As you can see at the far right of the chart, only a small portion of those I spoke with faced pressure to lie, cheat, or break the law or collude in doing so. Similar to the bank officer I mentioned earlier who was pressed to make loans based on false information, others were pressured to lie to or

Figure 2-1 Where Participants Felt Pressure to Compromise

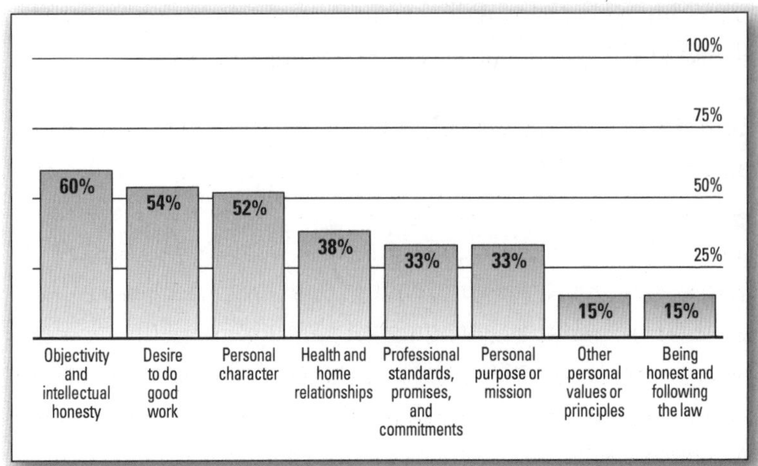

mislead their customers, hire employees based on sexual attractiveness, use broad layoffs to get rid of certain individuals to avoid discrimination charges, sign off on inaccurate financial reports, or alter official documents. These clear-cut cases were actually relatively rare, mentioned by only 15 percent of those I interviewed.

Objectivity and intellectual honesty At the other end of the spectrum, the most common pressure by far was to alter professional judgment based on a business interest or office politics. Thirty-one of fifty-two people described being unable to say what they really thought professionally due to the need to play politics. According to one CFO, "You have to demonstrate *total* commitment to an initiative. Throw the *frosting* on it. 'It's *fantastic.* What can I do to help?'" Others stated categorically, "You cannot disagree or you're out." Some younger leaders were coached to "be more confident" though they did not really know the facts of a situation. Others referred to tendencies in their field with interesting phrases, such as "pencil-whipping" or "fudging" the numbers.

"It was never outright lying, but you try to position [a project] in the best possible light, and sometimes you eliminate information that might be questionable," said one finance executive.

Desire to do good work; professional standards, promises, and commitments Organizations routinely press their members to "buy in" to new strategies or processes, often in promising new directions, sometimes about missions people truly care about. Yet if other policies and incentives seem to contradict the new direction, or the strategy seems irrational or ineffective, you can wonder if leadership is really serious. This puts you in the awkward position of making commitments to others based on something that rings false.

For example, Bruce, a midcareer publishing executive, found himself laying off the people who had most bought in to a company directive and made it profitable. "My bosses challenged me to turn around the Florida operation," he later recalled, "to get it up to corporate standards because they didn't want to have to shut it down. It turned into a fantastic assignment. I worked with dedicated people who were intensely proud to be part of the company. After eighteen months we had met the company's most ambitious targets. Then, actually because of our strong performance, the corporate folks decided to dramatically increase their growth projections. That meant they had to shut down the Florida operation anyway because only the corporate operating facility was set up for such high volume. I understood the decision, but telling the team was one of the hardest things I ever did. It was translated into Spanish as I spoke (half the team was Spanish-speaking), and for a good 90 seconds they were all smiling at me as the translation happened. They thought they were going to get a bonus, not be laid off."

Like Bruce, others described working hard to create dramatic improvements only to have a new leader casually drop the programs and have results deteriorate. One longtime company leader was torn because, so far as he could ascertain, winning a promotion meant he would have to sacrifice the company's true best interests and maneuver to get short-term results.

All these dilemmas show that the second most common pressure, the desire to do good work, is closely related to the fifth most common pressure—maintaining professional standards, promises, and commitments. Participants were particularly troubled when their work was misrepresented to customers, shortsighted layoffs were used to achieve executive bonuses, poor processes prevented delivering to customers on time, or executives arbitrarily undermined commitments to valued professional connections, "making me a liar" as one marketing communications director put it. For example, an editor in an ad agency had nagging doubts about some of her responsibilities. "I'm doing fact checking on medical-related advertising, and I don't have a medical or scientific background. That worries me."

What is most interesting about these four categories of pressure to compromise—honesty, objectivity, doing good work, and maintaining professional standards, promises, and commitments—is that holding the line helps the company itself, at least in the long run. Clearly, organizations have an interest in minimizing this type of compromise.

The next four areas are more specifically individual, though they have an indirect impact on the organization's results.

Personal character; health and home relationships As Amrita found when she looked in the mirror, adapting to organizational pressure can have a profound effect on you personally. Twenty-seven of the fifty-two people I spoke with described pressure to give up the qualities they considered part of being a good person: "wearing a mask" or "walling off parts of themselves" and distorting themselves to be more arrogant, competitive, or ruthless in a culture that was "kill or be killed." Even my most ambitious business school classmates wished for a chance to relax more or to be able to emulate an admired relative though they worked in the "shark tank" every day. They struggled to carve out time for health and balance or to honor commitments to family and close relationships. People described "sacrificing their health," having "no time for exercise," "owing the company everything," even though "I never see my wife" and there's "no time for developing the community relationships that really nurture me."

Bill, the CFO of a global retail bank, said, "I didn't think I should really start dating before my career was on track. Now I'm forty-three, and not too many women of the age to start a family want to date a guy that much older. I guess I may have lost my chance to have children." Companies were sometimes quite explicit about expecting leaders to sacrifice their family relationships. A director of training and development recounted, "The new woman CEO told us, 'Children are a compromise to your career.' What does that say about what it takes to be a woman leader around here?"

Dave, a thirty-four-year-old technology entrepreneur, demonstrated the sort of "whatever it takes" attitude that that CEO would have admired. "It took us five years of driving hard—days, nights, weekends—doing deals, promising the moon, then pushing to meet impossible deadlines without enough staff. But when we sold the company last year, we made it big," he said, rising from his seat where we sat talking. Playfully, he stretched out both arms overhead in a kind of salute, and added, "I felt like Caesar returning to Rome after conquering the Gauls. That was my triumph." I could see how he inspired his team.

After such a success, it can be shocking to find out what "whatever it takes" truly means. We may find ourselves unable to sustain our tough attitudes. For example, when Dave cashed in, he left behind a partner who hadn't benefited on the same scale. "You follow the lure of the money," he said, "but the M&A [mergers and acquisitions] people don't tell you about the downside. Your partners are going to feel betrayed. I succeeded, but it ended one of my closest friendships. Now I have to ask myself, 'Am I a good guy?'"

Personal purpose or mission; other personal values or principles Twenty-five people mentioned struggling because their work seemed irrelevant, purposeless, or otherwise violated their values. "You put on your game face—but for what?" said a software-marketing manager. "I went to work for the energy-trading division of an oil company—me, the power-to-the-people activist!" recounted Mitch, an organizational effectiveness executive. "I rationalized to myself that at least it wasn't Exxon and the *Valdez.* But where I was working was basically this company's version of Enron, and I was helping them be more aggressive traders."

These values may seem like luxuries to you compared with survival and feeding a family, but one of the most devastating realizations for professionals is finding contradictions or harm at the very core of their business.

For example, the division vice president of a soft drink manufacturer once traveled to a South American megacity with his team to better develop their sales strategy. They were toying with the idea of offering drinks in smaller sizes to be more affordable. Then one day he and his team visited one of the barrios in their target market. Looking around him, seeing signs of the most abject poverty, the leader was suddenly overwhelmed by the incongruence between his sales tactics and the reality of the neighborhood around him. At one point he stopped cold and hunched over, hands on his knees, unable to breathe. The reality of the situation fell on him with a sudden weight: *These people don't need soft drinks!* he realized. "They need a lot of things, but soft drinks is not one of them. What we were promoting was not only irrelevant but harmful." Nothing he did for his company was the same after that moment.

Clearly, knowing whether your work adds value or does harm is important to getting up in the morning. In fact, it can be debilitating to find out things don't quite work the way you think they do.

For example, Greg was a corporate officer for a financial services firm—until the senior officers (including his boss) were indicted and sent to prison for embezzlement. Greg was no naïf; he'd spent years in investment banking. He had come to this last firm specifically because he thought it was an unusually ethical place where he could escape those pressures. That only made the shock of the alleged wrongdoings more painful. Three years later, when I met him one evening over dinner, he had not gone back to work. He articulated the bewilderment he still felt: "I believed in these people. I respected them; I even loved them in some way. Was I an idiot to be part of this? I can't reconcile it in my mind." He felt adrift, distrustful, and unsure of his own instincts. "I guess I'm suffering from the wounds of commitment. It was like a relationship that had gone awry," he confessed.

This quick review reflects the most common values and concerns of those with whom I spoke. You may care about some of these and not others, or you may have a separate list entirely. The point is whatever you really do value in your heart of hearts, compromising that is going to take a bite out of you—unless it is for something even more important.

Making a Gradual Deal with the Devil

Given the general pressure to conform and the fact that unhealthy pressure and compromise can come in subtle forms, it is not surprising that the third overarching theme is how difficult it is to know if you are crossing a line you will regret. Many people I spoke with worried about making a devil's bargain or selling a piece of their soul and not knowing it.

It is interesting how frequently the concept of a "Faustian bargain" comes up in business conversations. You wouldn't expect such an old story to capture such modern professional dilemmas, but apparently it does. According to the original legend from the late 1500s, Faust was a disenchanted scholar who made a pact with the devil, Mephistopheles, selling his soul in exchange for supernatural powers and the secrets of the universe. The irony is that although he makes the deal to be free, it actually enslaves him, alienating him from himself and destroying his closest relationships, so he cannot enjoy his powers and ends up more and more dependent on entertainment and distractions as he "storms through his life."[5]

I've come to believe that Faust's story captures the feelings that go along with unhealthy compromise: the vague sense that you may be sacrificing something too valuable to lose but you can't pinpoint exactly what is off base. What makes it all the harder is that, unlike Faust, most people do not confront the choice in a single instant.

More often, according to those I spoke with, a devil's bargain is made by degrees. "You wonder if maybe you've made a deal with the devil—but you can't really tell," said a process excellence director.

Partly this is because most people, when they first start out, are focused on proving themselves, not questioning their organizations. "No one in my family had been a professional. I knew I wanted to be around smart people. I had something to prove," said Gary, the CFO of a nationwide manufacturer about his early career as an accountant.

Yet years later this same CFO discovered that proving himself had some pretty high costs. "I was working for a very high-performing manufacturing company, a growth *machine.* All the company cared about were the numbers, *whatever* trade-offs were required. They would beat the hell out of you, but I overlooked it all. I told myself what mattered was money, recognition, and promotions. I thought it was okay to be the "bad guy" if it was for the company. I was not a nice person to be around. Later I was shocked to find out how little my peers trusted me, how they saw the bosses using me. And I made some serious trade-offs in my marriage. I was going for the American dream; I wanted money and recognition and was working ninety- to one-hundred-hour weeks to get them. But were those my wife's goals? I had never asked. And no, they weren't."

Many of those with more career experience described having gotten caught up in an unhealthy compromise without fully realizing it, making subtle adjustments to their values and their behavior that added up to a significant problem in retrospect.

"Over time my values mutated. I compromised," said Mitch, an organizational effectiveness executive. "I moved from social service into business. I got a great job in Europe with more responsibility and great bosses—but I became a drunk. The sense of service and contribution faded. I ended up working for a military contractor, which I disagreed with but rationalized away. Over time my soul receded. There was a spiritual gap."

One investment banker saw this same mutation happening to those around him. "I got my MBA degree and went back to the business and did well for a while. Then I started looking around, projecting myself out twenty years. Would I be like those at the top? They were extremely unhappy. They were aggressive as hell. They were divorced. They had trouble with relationships. They disliked each other. And they were very rich. That wasn't a package that was worth paying that price for in my mind."

These stories illustrate the painful experience of playing along with the game and the unhealthy compromise it entails. But how exactly does this become a trap?

How Playing Along Becomes a Trap

The nature of any trap is that you capture yourself through your own actions. The trap just helps you along by luring you to focus too narrowly on an immediate gain or threat (the bait) so that you ignore the larger potential for loss (the catch). This is true whether we are talking about a monkey hand-trap, a confidence game, a military maneuver, or a tantalizing credit card offer.

Playing along with the game becomes a trap because it typically leads to unhealthy compromise. And basically, every time you make an unhealthy compromise to reach your goals, it is like paying for them with a credit card. You can extend yourself a little in the short run if you have the discipline to repay as you go, but if you rely on this with any regularity, you are setting yourself up for regret.

Whenever you trade off your higher values in favor of lower ones, you create an obligation, a debt to be paid before you can feel completely free. This could be a literal debt, such as when you overextend yourself financially to maintain an image you cannot afford, or figuratively, as when you betray an important commitment to please the boss or avoid a confrontation. In either case, your success becomes encumbered by a liability on your inner balance sheet. This is the "bite" that unhealthy compromise takes out of you that makes you wince when you think about it.

But of course, as with any credit card, what really trap you are the finance charges, late fees, and penalties, so the debt multiplies as interest compounds over time. Because this is typically obscured amid the pressure to play along with the game, you don't see the ultimate costs of crossing your own lines.

In most conversations about ethics, people talk about considering the cost to your reputation if your compromise were discovered. But my interviews and other research suggest that these hidden costs go further. In fact, near as I can tell, there are actually seven "hidden charges" that compound the costs of unhealthy compromise, making it harder and harder to pay down your debt and achieve the freedom or well-being you seek.

The Costs of Compromise

The total "costs of compromise" include the financial, social, or psychological sense of debt or obligation created by an unhealthy compromise plus seven additional hidden costs that continue to compound over time.

1. The "internal stress" cost "It just makes you crazy!" said a former lawyer, describing the internal effects of unhealthy compromise. Research on cognitive dissonance (the conflict or anxiety caused by holding two ideas, beliefs, attitudes, or opinions that are psychologically inconsistent) shows it is mentally, emotionally, and physically draining to live with contradictions between your actions and your beliefs.[6] Dealing with this stress can drag down your day-to-day functioning, as you have less access to your creativity, courage, confidence, and resourcefulness. As a marketing communications professional put it, "My therapist said she could put me on medication, except that this wasn't a Prozac problem—this was an integrity problem."

2. The "tuning out" cost Because the stress of inner conflict is so uncomfortable, human beings are wired to tune it out through various forms of rationalization and self-justification. To cope you may put your values on hold, compartmentalize them between work and home, deny the situation, or engage in heroics to fix things. As you tune out the contradictions, you become increasingly acclimatized to the compromise and less able to see the full costs or new alternatives. "I had to tune out the larger questions about the industry," said Rick, a retired midlevel executive of a Fortune 50 petrochemical company. "Otherwise I couldn't be a 'player.'" This comes with its own penalties, as you start to think you really do have no choice but to go along next time.

3. The "escalating commitment" cost Human beings are also very susceptible to irrationally escalating their commitment to a goal, particularly when their ego is involved.[7] When this happens you narrow your perspective, tuning out other factors and "doubling down" to reach the outcome you think will satisfy your interests. Unfortunately, what you are tuning out are data that tell you that the costs may be too high and the goal may not be what you really want. Several people described driving even harder as they started to have questions about their work, becoming even more committed to achieving the rewards that would let them be done with it. "You think of wealth as freedom; then you are not subject to someone else's whims—you can go your own way," said a high-tech executive.

4. The "external validation" cost Once you tune out your internal compass and guidance, you are naturally more oriented toward external signals to guide you. In the famous Milgram experiments, where ordinary people followed orders even when it seemed to cause harm to others, Stanley Milgram observed an "agentic shift" that as people crossed more and more lines, they gave more and more of their judgment and decision-making authority over to the scientists directing them.[8] In a similar vein, as you lend more credence to others' power to punish or reward you, you become more oriented toward external validation to know you are doing well. "It's a bit masochistic, the way we think we need *the company* to say it, to tell us we're competent," said one vice president.

5. The "bullying" cost In the field of conflict management, the number one rule for dealing with power imbalances is to watch for precedents; that is, how your acquiescence on one issue can set a precedent and invite the other party to apply power on another issue. When you succumb to unhealthy pressure by playing along, you are effectively teaching those with a competitive approach that you will respond to threats. If you are dealing with a bully, this may escalate until you ultimately confront her. Roberta's story about being disabled by her boss until she confronted him shows how this can happen.

6. The "reputation" cost Conversely, unhealthy compromise damages your reputation, as allies and those who depend on you discover that you may betray their trust under pressure. In the extreme this can result in the classic *Wall Street Journal* ethics failure: seeing your actions portrayed on the front page of the newspaper in a way that costs you your reputation and self-respect. This also happens on a more incremental scale, as Jim, the carpeting sales manager, worried about tarnishing his reputation with customers. This has both personal effects and business ones because without others' trust it is very difficult to get anything done.

7. The "business backfire" cost Finally, research shows that shortsighted business fixes, many of which involve compromise rather than facing the root cause of an issue, tend to backfire and cost more.[9] For example, one high-tech equipment company pushed its salespeople so hard to meet their numbers that at the end of each quarter many of them shipped products that customers had not ordered. (This is illegal.) The sales were recorded as revenue in that quarter and adjusted off the next quarter when the customers returned the unordered product. Over time they had to ship a greater number of products at the end of each quarter to look like revenue was growing steadily. This did nothing to address the core drivers of their business and damaged relationships with many customers who recognized the fraud.

These seven hidden costs add up to a set of potentially huge and unknown liabilities you create with each unhealthy compromise—almost as bad as taking on an adjustable-rate mortgage with a payment you cannot afford for a home that is overvalued. If you fail to recognize that you are in a trap, you may misread the signals that say you are in trouble and think you need to drive even harder, more and more convinced that you need to play along with the game and achieve the goals that will supposedly set you free, meanwhile increasing your burden, just as consumers end up in destructive cycles of ever-increasing credit card debt.

The end result is that you can feel like Jacob Marley in *A Christmas Carol,* weighed down by chains of his own making. Though you started out seeking freedom and respect, you end up having lost your autonomy, with so few options that you are effectively at the mercy of other people's decisions. "I lost the will to say no," said one executive indicted for misconduct. Even if you achieve your externally visible goals, you may be so depleted on the inside that your net well-being is negative. A quote from a CEO in a recent article makes just this point: "If this is success, how come I feel like a boiled chicken? A lot of my friends envy me…the title, status, power, money. But the truth is that the seemingly endless treadmill I'm on is soul-destroying and provides me with little real personal satisfaction. If only they knew!"[10]

How Do You Know If You're in the Compromise Trap?

As I have mentioned, the jaws of the compromise trap close slowly, so it is hard to recognize when you make the choice that sets the process in motion.

For example, Julie, the CFO/COO we met earlier, did not realize until late in her career how playing along with the game was depleting her. When she was thirty-two, a recently divorced single mother of two with no college degree, she had decided she was going to prove to herself, her kids, and the world that she could be a winner. Years later she realized that the price of that goal was simply too high:

> I drove myself like a machine. I became superwoman. I learned to play the part, how to think, how to dress, how to speak, how to act like you don't have kids, how to boost the boss's ego. It worked. Gradually, I moved up in accounting until I was promoted to senior director of a Fortune 50 consumer products company. I learned all about playing with numbers—like using layoffs to meet financial targets. You get a bonus, and the truth gets buried. The money became the most important thing; where you live, what car you drive—they become like credentials. It ate at me, but I stuffed it, though I sometimes erupted at home, where my kids got the brunt of it. I turned a blind eye as the company used job elimination to get rid of people they didn't like, to avoid discrimination charges. I participated in it. Doing that sort of thing goes against everything

> you believe in; it tears you apart. But living in a fear-based culture, it feels like there is no choice but kill or be killed.
>
> Then one day, while I was working as the CFO/COO of a Fortune 500 company, my son and daughter sat me down to talk. "Truthfully, Mom, we don't like you very much as a person. Maybe this is how you have to be for your work, but don't tell us you're doing it for us because we don't want it."
>
> I was devastated. Because I *had* been doing it for them. I thought I *had* to do it, that this was the way life was supposed to look, with all the cars and expensive vacations and homes. Looking back, moving from $125,000–$250,000 to $300,000–$350,000 per year was just a number. But the price? I lost myself in the process and did irreparable harm to my relationship with my daughter.

Julie's story is a good example of the typical stages in the compromise trap. Let's consider these in terms of our credit card metaphor.

Typical Stages of the Compromise Trap

1. Signing up Pulled by dreams of winning, freedom, and success and pushed by fears of failure and poverty, Julie entered the work world ready to adapt. Like a consumer with a preapproval notice, she signed up to play the game and do whatever it took when she got the chance, and she would have engaged at either a higher or lower level depending on the situation. She was probably not able to tell healthy from unhealthy pressure at this point. *Key indicators:* unquestioning cooperation and adaptability.

2. Getting hooked As Julie got a taste of the rewards, money became the important thing. During this stage there is a sort of "high" surrounding promotions, recognition, and even intellectual stimulation that encourages you to narrow your focus and drive harder to succeed. Like the consumer enjoying a new standard of living, you may tell yourself you cannot think about unhealthy pressure or compromise until you are firmly established, just as Julie stuffed her concerns about playing with numbers. *Key indicators:* compulsive focus on narrow goals; nagging background doubts about unhealthy pressures and compromises.

3. Getting stuck in the cycle As Julie gained experience and responsibility, the unhealthy pressures became clearer and the compromises more conscious. As you see more and know more, you recognize unhealthy pressure but see few options other than continuing to play along with the game, especially given your actual financial obligations and your discomfort with facing any damage you have done. In terms of our credit metaphor, this stage involves making just the minimum monthly payments and trying not to think about how the balance is increasing with time. You may even find yourself buying more, compromising *more,* just to deal with the stress. If you do not hit a limit, you may find at some point you go from compromising to *being compromised,* which is an extreme of self-alienation. Even then, though, the process is not irreversible if you are willing to go through the hard work of facing what you have avoided. The key indicators of this stage vary based on your strategy for dealing with the unhealthy pressure. The following strategies are variations on playing along with the game.

- **Playing to win** resolves unhealthy pressure by putting values on hold until you get to the top; this may show up as driving harder so you can get out sooner. *Key indicators:* health issues; emptiness and isolation.
- **Playing to live** resolves the pressure by compartmentalizing work life and home life; you invest only what is required so

that you can survive at work and try to get real enjoyment elsewhere. Can include emotional disengagement, where you avoid disappointment by adopting a cynical attitude or denying your real dreams and goals. *Key indicators:* motivation issues; nagging doubts; protective cynicism.

- **Playing for the good guys** means you seek out companies or leaders who share your values so that there is no unhealthy pressure. What starts out as a way to engage at a higher level becomes a damaging compromise, though, if you discover unhealthy pressure and continue to play along, tuning out uncomfortable facts rather than face the organization's contradictions. *Key indicators:* frantic heroic efforts to fix the organization so you can believe in it again.

4. Hitting the limit For Julie the confrontation with her kids was a wake-up call that forced her to face the real costs of "whatever it takes." This step often involves a personal crisis, a health problem, or even a work setback that reinforces your limits—just as when a creditor reduces your limit or cancels your card. Paradoxically, this process can raise the deeper questions that help you see what you truly want and how you really want to engage. For example, one executive asked, "A part of me is crying out for an answer: when is it okay to be happy?" By facing and gradually accepting hard realities you have avoided, you eventually gain access to more of your vitality and capacity. For some, hitting the limit can lead to a strategy of rebelling—avoiding the trap by fighting back defensively or falling into cynical resistance. This is a close cousin to redefining the game, though it tends to be more reactive and antagonistic, and it has high costs and consequences that make it unattractive to most people. *Key indicators:* questioning; stepping back; or, with the rebelling strategy: defensiveness and all-or-nothing thinking; reactive opposition.

5. Freeing yourself Once you recognize the full costs of unhealthy compromise, you may literally or figuratively cut up your credit cards. No longer convinced that unhealthy compromise is your best choice, a new level of perspective, creativity, and resourcefulness kicks in. You may reevaluate your goals and whether all those "purchases" give you what you really want. You may change your work situation, or, like Roberta who challenged her boss, you may dare to redefine what the game is about right where you are. You start to include more of what is really at stake, which the lure of the trap tends to obscure. You reconsider the rules, reevaluating your aims and your options, knowing that you won't get where you want to go by complying. Ironically, this recalibration brings you closer to self-understanding and self-acceptance, which is akin to the freedom you originally sought. *Key indicators:* increasing courage, vitality, creativity, resourcefulness, perspective, humor, and self-acceptance. This is typically when you will discover or return to a sense of a professional quest to guide your decisions—but one now based on the internal reinforcement of your personal foundations.

- **Redefining the game** accepts unhealthy pressure as a common occurrence and yet consciously chooses to engage at a higher level, orienting toward whatever matters most, considering a bigger win, over a longer time horizon, involving more interests and higher values as well as practical outcomes. Generally tries to act as a positive force to help the right thing happen, for oneself and others. *Key indicators:* strong pragmatism coupled with an ability to question assumptions and a willingness to be a positive force.

How to Free Yourself

For Julie the process of freeing herself began with a period of soul-searching following the conversation with her kids. It was then that she realized she already had far more freedom than she thought:

> I thought about why I cared so much about what other people thought. I realized it came out of a personal deficit, the search for a sense of self-worth through what I could buy. Now, I am more okay with being different and asking questions that cause people to think.
>
> I needed to forgive myself for what I did. Communicating with my family was the first step. Second was to take a company through bankruptcy. But this time I did it the right way, talking to people, sharing the burden. The third step was to thank my kids for being my mirror. They are my purpose, the root of my love.
>
> I have learned that profit and human ends are not either/or. Competition can be healthy, and companies are pretty good at bringing people together for a common good, but being professional means being a good person too. I am not bitter; these are gifts. Now I am okay with the person in the mirror. I feel myself rising to my natural authority now, clearer about what I am here to do.

Like Julie, many people found after some reflection that feeling small and dependent on external validation, rather than actual financial need, was the root cause of their willingness to compromise.

"The problem was in me," said Mitch, the organizational effectiveness executive we met earlier. "There was a hole in me. I was unsure of myself, so I kept looking for where I fit, where I could be accepted." Karen, a marketing communications director, gave a similar account: "I think on some level, I thought that if I was good enough, I would be loved. Well, I got the goodies, the rewards, but

I found them meaningless, and they came with empty relationships—and there was no love after all."

"We keep thinking the system will give us freedom as a reward, but it doesn't come from there," said a former high-tech engineer. "After you get over feeling sorry for yourself when it doesn't turn out the way you want, you begin to develop a new confidence in what you offer, how you learn, what you know how to do—something no one can take away from you."

Like Amrita, whom we met at the start of the chapter, we all have the potential to wake up one day and not recognize our face in the mirror. Given the general pressure to conform and the amount of unhealthy pressure you are likely to face at work, it is perfectly natural to think that your best option is to play along with the game, to take care of your own. Yet as we have seen with Julie, Gary, Mitch, Karen, and others, if this involves unhealthy compromise, as it so often does, it can amount to making a devil's bargain by degrees, as you build up obligations and regrets that leave your net well-being in the negative.

When you are playing from a sense of internal deficit, you narrow your perspective so you don't see all the options and, like Julie, you don't question your assumptions. You amplify the prizes and the threats but miss your true priorities, the interests behind your goals, and the full costs of what you have to lose. It's natural for imagination to conjure up the worst.

This is not to say that the risks and the threats are not real but that resolving unhealthy pressure through unhealthy compromise is a losing proposition. It is only hard to see because it is so gradual and because the ways people cope with the discomfort of unhealthy compromise, by tuning it out and focusing more narrowly on their goals, is exactly what makes it hard to draw the connection between your choice and its consequences.

This means you can free yourself the minute you begin to reconsider your assumptions. For example, as Julie looked back on her experience, she saw that what got her into the compromise trap was surprisingly simple: "You know, all this heartache came out of two unquestioned assumptions: you can't set boundaries at work, and this is what my kids want."

I wonder what unquestioned assumptions might be narrowing *your* options.

The first step in avoiding or getting out of the compromise trap is to take off the blinders and look with fresh eyes at your real goals and what your experience really teaches you about pressure, survival, and winning. On a practical level, this is what it means to redefine the game.

In the next chapter, we explore the most common misconceptions about compromise so that you can see and reconsider some of the limits that may be constraining you.

KEY CONCEPTS

- **The devil's bargain by degrees** There is widespread and intense pressure to conform to organizational norms of any type, and unhealthy pressure to compromise is relatively routine, occurring even in the best companies. Thus it is surprisingly difficult to recognize when you are crossing a line you will ultimately regret, as one does with a devil's bargain.
- **The total "costs of compromise"** This includes the financial, social, or psychological sense of debt or obligation created by an unhealthy compromise plus the seven additional "hidden costs" that continue to compound over time: the "internal stress" cost, the "tuning out" cost, the "escalating commitment" cost, the "external validation" cost, the "bullying" cost, the "reputation" cost, and the "business backfire" cost.

- **Typical stages of the compromise trap** The five stages of the compromise trap are: signing up; getting hooked; getting stuck in the cycle (and its variations: playing to win, playing to live, and playing for the good guys); hitting the limit; and freeing yourself.

REFLECTION QUESTIONS

- Have you ever shared Julie's two core assumptions? How realistic do they seem to you now? What other assumptions or beliefs might have contributed to your decisions about how to engage at work?
- Revisit figure 2-1, Where Participants Felt Pressure to Compromise. Which three areas are most important to your definition of being true to yourself? Why?
- Write down your top three sources of stress at work. Reflect for a moment on each stressor: What is the root cause of the stress? Does it involve compromising on any personal or professional commitments? What are the symptoms for you of making that compromise? Now revisit the typical stages of the compromise trap. Do you recognize any of the key indicators in your current situation? Which stage, if any, might best describe you now?

3

Ten Misconceptions about Compromise at Work

In 1979, Jose Gomez was a rising star, one of the youngest certified public accounts (CPAs) ever to make partner at Grant Thornton accountants; he was well respected and active in community affairs. But just after making partner, two officers from one of his auditing clients, ESM Government Securities, let him in on an accounting ruse that was hiding millions of dollars in losses. Warning him repeatedly how embarrassing it could be that he had signed off on two previous annual audits without discovering the issue, they pressed Jose to "give them time to recover."

Jose felt cornered. "I was 31 years old. I felt I had a terrific career path in front of me and a lot of ambition.... I also didn't want to face it. I didn't want to face walking in to my superiors at Alexander Grant and saying this is what happened." Yet a year later, with losses now approaching $100 million, Jose felt thoroughly trapped. For the next five years, Jose knowingly approved phony financial statements. His own finances a mess, he began accepting loans from ESM that totaled $200,000, which he never repaid. When the Securities and Exchange Commission (SEC) closed down ESM in 1985, it caused one of the biggest financial scandals of the 1980s, costing investors more than $320 million, triggering multiple runs on Ohio savings and loans, overwhelming the state's deposit insurance fund, and causing many depositors to lose their retirement savings.

"I didn't do it for money," Jose said in an interview after the fact. "I did it because I didn't want to have to face up that I had made a mistake, that I had missed it originally." He goes on to explain how he failed to think through the decision. "Had I looked at the depositors as the ones being hurt, this would have been a different decision on my part early on. If this had been a case of somebody setting out on a scheme to defraud a bunch of people of their retirement money, it wouldn't have lasted a year because I would have stopped it. But what made it easier to accept was, yeah, ESM lost some money playing in the market—but I never looked at it as not being their money." Confronting the damage was a blow. "When in March '85 I saw the tragedy of the Ohio depositors, that really hurt. This is something I had never looked at—whose money is being played with here. That caused me a great deal of pain and sorrow. I don't think that comforts them any. I don't think it would." On the day of the article, Jose surrendered to serve a twelve-year prison sentence.[1]

The essence of unhealthy compromise is that, in retrospect, you realize you gave up something more important for something less. In Jose Gomez's case, rather than go through the discomfort of admitting a mistake, he went to prison and suffered intense guilt about the depositors he had hurt. This is similar to Julie's choice to pursue career heights that really did not matter compared with damaging her relationship with her daughter, or Mitch's losing track of his principles so he could work with people who would make him feel important.

How does this happen? Why would anyone make such a self-defeating choice?

As I alluded to earlier, it is usually because at the time you don't recognize that you are actually making a choice. For example, Jose told reporters he was not aware of crossing the line into illegality when he approved the financial statements, only that he was distorting his professional assessment.

You can also make self-defeating choices when you base decisions on misconceptions or inaccurate assumptions about your options, your alternatives, the true costs, or the ultimate outcome of the compromise. As we saw in chapter 2, unhealthy pressure can be very subtle, and the narrow, harried perspective of playing along with the game increases the chances that you will miss important cues about self-defeating behavior. "The boiled frog analogy is true," said a senior business consultant for a computer-aided design (CAD) vendor. "When you're in the water and they raise the temperature, you don't know it."

When a decision is clearly delineated, people are more likely to make the courageous choice. But when issues are vague or happen gradually, human beings are more likely to go along with actions they would otherwise condemn.[2, 3]

You could argue that these are just mistakes, not compromises. But all too often when people discover they have done something wrong, they also realize that they could have or should have known, and they go into self-protective maneuvering as Jose did. Danny Balfour and Guy Adams, two analysts of large-scale institutional dysfunction, even go so far as to say that this is often what prompts people to cross the line into misconduct: "Since it is readily apparent [at this turning point] that others are likely to react as though those involved should have known, relevant actors are likely to feel a level of guilt and shame commensurate with 'knowingly' doing harm.... This turns into a powerful psychological incentive to deny the harm or evil."[4] In other words, that's when many people start shredding papers.

If you are not savvy about unhealthy pressure and how to handle it, finding out about an unwitting compromise or even a simple mistake can trigger you to cross a line—and send you downward into the compromise trap.

This is why it is so important to understand the misconceptions about pressure, organizations, and work that often lead people into the compromise trap in the first place so you don't find yourself threatened and cornered into choices that are ultimately not in your best interest.

In this chapter we examine the ten central misconceptions about compromise at work that have surfaced in my research—assumptions that people later questioned based on their own experience or that my studies of organizations, or research in social psychology, suggest may not be accurate. (See figure 3-1.)

These misconceptions are useful because they help you recognize choice points and identify unhealthy pressure before it triggers you to make an unhealthy compromise. That way you can avoid getting into the compromise trap in the first place or break the cycle more quickly once you are in it.

I invite you to test these misconceptions against your own experience and see if my alternative propositions ring true enough for you to try them out.

Misconception 1: Compromise Is Always Healthy

Many people in business default to the view that compromise is essentially positive, probably because there is so much to be gained from the flexibility and the cooperation that come with it.

Figure 3-1 Ten Misconceptions and Alternative Propositions

Misconception	Alternative Proposition
1. Compromise is always healthy.	**1.** Compromise can be unhealthy too.
2. Good companies and leaders don't create unhealthy pressure to compromise.	**2.** Even good companies and leaders create unhealthy pressure to compromise.
3. Unhealthy pressure is the leader's fault.	**3.** Your own integrity can't depend on your leader's.
4. You have to go along to survive.	**4.** Going along can become a self-depleting trap.
5. You'll always know if you're crossing a line.	**5.** Compromise is more likely to be gradual because blinders make it hard to see at the time.
6. The company sets the terms.	**6.** More is negotiable than you think.
7. You should just say no.	**7.** You need more than a "just say no" strategy to be ready when the pressure hits.
8. Refusing to compromise means fighting back.	**8.** Fighting is one option, but there are many other ways to influence a situation.
9. You thrive when you get to the top.	**9.** You may not thrive at the top if it just brings new pressures; the key to thriving is being engaged in a meaningful pursuit that uses your talents and allows you to meet your real needs.
10. Individual integrity adds up to organizational integrity.	**10.** Organizational integrity is much harder to accomplish than individual integrity and is much rarer—and has a larger impact on the world.

Yet, hopefully, by now you can see that in certain circumstances compromise can be unhealthy—in the sense that compromising security, health, or values is negative. As discussed in chapter 2, it is not only compromising your ethics that can be unhealthy but

> **When not to compromise** Don't compromise if it involves giving up something that matters more to you for something that matters less—given a full understanding of your options, alternatives, true costs, and payoffs over the long term.

compromising any important commitment that is part of being true to yourself.

So which is which? When should you compromise and when shouldn't you?

If you were negotiating a deal, you would want to compromise—or, more precisely, give something up—only if you gained something more valuable in return. For example, you might give up an extra week's vacation to be able to work shorter hours if you had a young child and it was important to you to pick her up after school. Yet expert negotiators know that compromise can end up being a lose-lose situation where nobody gets what they really want if you don't fully investigate all your options and opportunities for collaboration or, worse yet, find yourself accommodating and making one-sided concessions.

Translating this to our more general discussion of compromise, we can create a simple rule: don't compromise if it involves giving up something that matters more to you for something that matters less—given a full understanding of your options, alternatives, true costs, and payoffs over the long term.*

For example, let's say you are being pressed to collaborate with a new team on an important project for your company. It involves

---

*To be precise, a compromise can also be unhealthy even if you get more than you give, if there is a better alternative available—the negotiations concept of *BATNA* (best alternative to a negotiated agreement). This is assumed throughout the text.

setting aside projects that might have earned you a lot of personal credit but less value for the company. For most people this is a healthy compromise because you are giving up personal glory to share in team rewards that are more important for the company's success. By contrast, imagine you are being pressured to work more hours to earn a promotion, and working those hours could mean causing long-term harm to your family relationships. For most people this would be an unhealthy compromise because family relationships far outweigh the promotion. (Remember, this all depends on which of your personal values takes precedence.)

If we draw a simple graphic of these trade-offs, you can see how the unhealthy compromise leads to a shortfall, the debt I described in the previous chapter. (See figure 3-2.)

But what about the gray area, where you sacrifice something very important for something even more important—like sacrificing spending time with your family so that you can provide for them? (See figure 3-3.)

On the surface, this looks like a healthy, albeit very difficult, compromise—a necessary sacrifice—because survival and provid-

Figure 3-2 Healthy Compromise and Unhealthy Compromise

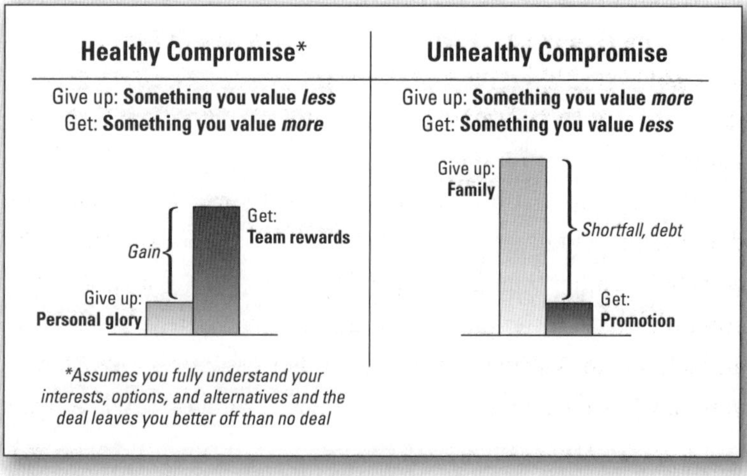

Figure 3-3 The Gray Area

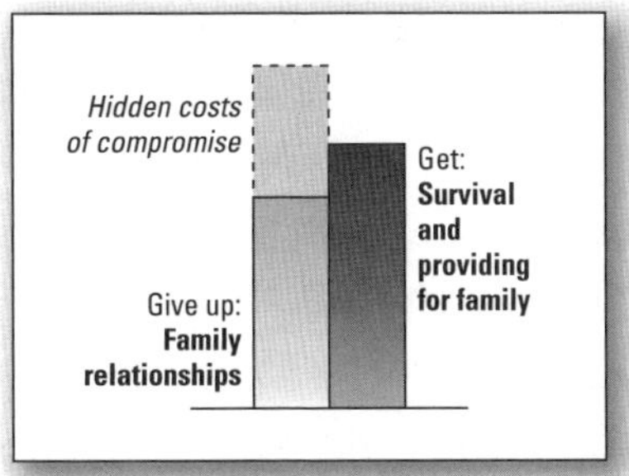

ing for your family are more important than having the closeness of relationship you might want. But from a wider perspective, this could be an unhealthy compromise. Once you factor in how the compromise would affect you and others over the long term (the "costs of compromise" discussed in chapter 2), test your assumptions about negotiating more-reasonable hours with your employer, consider other jobs, check out what providing for your family really means and what they really want and need, and whether working harder is actually going to increase your chances of survival, you may find there are better ways to get what you really want.

If you recognize up front that *compromise can be unhealthy,* you are more likely to take the time to sort out which compromises to make and which would leave you worse off. (I share a specific process for walking through this in chapter 6, "See the Larger Field.")

If you discover on reflection that what you really value most does require a big sacrifice, you will simply be dealing with a difficult choice rather than the guilt and the self-doubt of an unhealthy compromise. If times are really tough and you have a sick spouse and a kid who is struggling or some other extreme circumstance, you may just have to do work you are not proud of. (Still, you are highly unlikely to find that it is really aligned with your values to betray your basic ethics for a comfortable economic life.) In any case, you will know that your choice is aligned for you, which relieves you of the inner conflict of betraying your values, allows you to express the pain of the situation with less ambivalence, and frees you to ask for help and support as you rise to the occasion.

Misconception 2: Good Companies Don't Create Unhealthy Pressure

Many people, like Jim, the carpeting sales manager we met in chapter 1, subscribe to the "play for the good guys" philosophy. Put simply, that philosophy is this: when you work for a company with which your values are aligned, you do not confront the kinds of dilemmas we have been discussing here.

Unfortunately, it is closer to the truth to say that while some companies *are* better to work for and pursue admirable values, the fact is that all companies have blind spots. Therefore even good companies can create unhealthy pressure to compromise, sometimes in ways that cause serious harm.

For example, Jerrie was a seasoned executive who had recently joined a widely admired values-based food business that was almost an icon among inspirational companies:

> They were so dedicated to improving people's quality of life by improving their health. They were incredibly conscious about how their marketing contributed to a certain attitude about health. The problem was that they had a complete blind spot about their production processes and quality. I handled the complaints, and customers would actually mail me letters with things *in* them that had gotten into the product! I was very uncomfortable that people were getting sick. I raised the issues with plant management, the CEO, and the entire executive team, but they brushed me off.

> One day, on a particularly bad issue, I brought the corporate attorney with me to convince the CEO of the risks. Reluctantly, they recalled the product. But they just could not seem to see the root of the problem and how they were creating it. The CEO even expressed interest in systems thinking, but he was not thinking about systems on the factory floor. You expect this kind of thing at a big corporate monolith, but it's so sad when it happens in a company out to do good. They were just so convinced they were the "good guys" that they were completely blind to how they could cause harm. It's a good lesson for all of us.

If you draw too stark a line between "the good guys" and "the bad guys" and assume that unhealthy pressure occurs only with sleazy, unethical, or poor leadership, two things are likely to happen. First, when you do come across unhealthy pressure, you will exaggerate the discomfort of recognizing it and likely tune it out (because it means indicting someone as a bad guy) and, second, you may get disillusioned too easily.

For example, a midlevel manager in a growing consumer products company was quite upset one day after a leadership retreat with her company's executive team, during which her division's vice president had told a story about humiliating a member of his team before firing her. "I really thought this company was different, and I loved that its values aligned with my own. But when the VP humiliated this woman and then laughed about it later, it really got to me. I started to wonder if we're just like all the other organizations out there. Are our values just a joke?" Yet despite the vice president's behavior at that retreat, he led his unit in creating remarkable products, which attracted a passionately loyal following among consumers.

So, rather than see weaknesses and count the whole company as a fraud, you might do better to expect that *even good companies can create unhealthy pressure.* Knowing this, you are likely to respond more proactively and constructively, be more willing to see the discrepancies, and see how you can help the company evolve. You will realize that you are uniquely situated to see a certain part of the organization, and you can start asking how you can help the rest of the company see and act on what you see—without necessarily antagonizing anyone.

For example, when a young product manager finally understood that the project he was leading was structured in a way that took advantage of the customers he was so passionate to serve (despite the fact that this was one of the company's highest values), he arranged to end the project with a "failure party," celebrating what they had learned and stopping the ill-conceived direction. Apparently, his actions were one of several factors that helped a new incoming executive see that the company needed to reinvigorate its commitment to the customer.

Misconception 3: Unhealthy Pressure Is the Leader's Fault

Another common response to the question of unhealthy pressure is "That's a leadership issue." Many people believe that they cannot be held responsible for the compromises they make due to poor leadership because the leader is the one who creates or allows the pressure. I find this explanation both true and too simple.

It is more realistic to say that unhealthy pressure may be the leader's fault, but it is *your* problem. This is because part of you will hold yourself accountable for your actions, regardless of the outside pressure.

For example, in 2004 Ford was ordered to pay $75 million in damages to Mr. and Mrs. Wilson for a flawed vehicle design that led the Wilsons' Explorer to roll very easily and caused the permanent paralysis of Mrs. Wilson, a forty-six-year-old mother of two, leaving her a paraplegic. A retired judge friend of mine showed me the transcript of Ford's appeal because he was alarmed at the repeated evidence that Ford's leadership had known about the problems but was pushing to get the new design out the door, using carefully managed tire pressure and computer simulations to get around rigorous safety testing.

What interested me most was that it was the *design engineers*, not the management, who felt compelled to apologize to the woman and her family during the trial—despite the fact that they had repeatedly proposed changes to fix the design and been turned down by management. On some level they must have felt they did not try hard enough to prevent the harm they had allowed to come to this woman and even to the company. "I know it rings hollow, but I am going to say it anyway. We are sorry. We are sorry that we let you down."[5]

In the Milgram experiments mentioned earlier, people got stuck because they did not realize it was their responsibility to take back authority for their actions when the experiment became harmful. These experiments involved a scientist directing an "assistant" (the real subject of the experiment) to deliver an electric shock to a "learner" (a confederate) to improve his or her learning. Sixty-two percent of those who participated ultimately raised the shock to the highest degree—a level that they were told would cause death. If they objected during the process, the scientist directing them simply said, "The experiment requires that you continue."

When did an experiment become sufficient grounds to follow an order to kill? Yet most of those involved, from all walks of life, occupations, and education levels, often amid great personal stress, complied. Many of them were traumatized by the event for years afterward, as their own conscience held them responsible. And that is the point. The ultimate responsibility for your actions stays with you—not because others will necessarily accuse you but because on some level you will *feel* personally responsible.[6]

Every leader has weaknesses—to expect otherwise requires putting on blinders. And harm can be done by inattention as well as by bad intentions. So, given the human weaknesses of every leader you work for, what are you going to do? Truthfully, it does not work to outsource your integrity to your leader. You can save yourself a lot of regret by recognizing this up front and making your own judgments about what you will and won't do. Instead of relying on the assumption that any unhealthy pressure is the leader's fault, I invite you instead to remember that *your own integrity cannot depend on your leader's.*

Misconception 4: You Have to Go Along to Survive

It is interesting that people typically frame dilemmas about values and commitments as a choice between self-interest and "doing the right thing." Framed in this way, it seems like you need to go along to survive and meet your interests, whereas following your values may seem like career suicide. Yet as we explored in chapter 2, compromising your values can be self-depleting as well, due to the seven costs of compromise that reduce your well-being and ability to influence a situation.

How can both of these be true?

The answer lies in how broad a perspective you take. While you are in a system and give credence to whether you are doing well there, it can feel like life or death to be accepted. Then, when you are free of it, you can wonder why it was so important. An executive coach once lamented to me about a pattern he saw in his executive clients: "Over and over I've seen people caught up in the rat race in an organization, certain that they will die if they fail there. Then something happens and they leave…and it's the best thing that's ever happened to them."

Once you see the self-inflicted costs of the compromise trap, you realize it's *all* self-interest—surviving *and* living your values. This is captured beautifully by Shakespeare's famous line "To thine own self be true. And it must follow as the night the day, thou canst then be false to any man."[7]

With a narrow perspective, you can forget this and view your self-interest in terms of surviving in a job or company, forgetting that your other values are also part of what makes life enjoyable and worth living. You literally have more access to yourself—your vitality, energy, confidence, and intelligence—when you are aligned. If you take this broader view, you can weigh the costs and the payoffs of progressing in an organization with the costs and the payoffs of living your values. As one high-tech manager put it, "All you have to do is choose what is going to make you really happy—but it has to be in the long run."[8]

So, the real question is how to find a way to tap the larger perspective you have when you are *outside* a system when you are making choices *inside* it so that you include both sets of factors in your thinking.

A first step is to reframe the assumption that you have to go along to survive, seeing instead that *going along can become a self-depleting trap.*

Misconception 5: You'll Always Know If You're Crossing a Line

I think you'll agree if I say that the general operating principle in business is, unless it crosses an ethical or legal line, push things to the limit. This assumes that you will always know if you are crossing a line, whether a legal or an ethical one, or some other value or commitment.

Yet researchers in the fields of social psychology and the psychology of ethics have found that this is simply not true: you will *not* always know. According to Max Bazerman, an ethicist and negotiations expert at Harvard Business School, "Even good people sometimes will act unethically without their own awareness."[9]

How does this happen? Research in the field shows several dynamics at work that can lead to what Bazerman calls "bounded ethicality"—ethical behavior limited to clearly demarcated and narrowly framed choices. The following discussion outlines a few of the reasons why this can happen.

Perceptual issues: research on bias, limited perception, and logic errors Study after study shows that human beings are notoriously susceptible to bias, self-justification, logic errors, and unconscious faulty perception. One of the most tragic examples involves a study in which both Israeli and Palestinian negotiators turned down *their own proposals* when they were labeled as coming from the other side.[10] In another example, a review of criminal justice errors, prosecutors maintained that innocent people are *never* convicted even after eight murder convictions were overturned because the "victims" turned up alive.[11] These flaws might not be so damaging if people were not also completely confident that they see things as they are and know all the facts. For example, participants in a study were 90 percent confident they were right when they said New York was farther north than Rome (it's not).[12]

Compliance with authority: the Milgram experiments As I have already briefly described, in nineteen separate studies with nearly a thousand adults from a wide variety of backgrounds, Stanley Milgram showed how certain cues associated with legitimate authority coupled with incremental acclimatization and several other predictable situational factors triggered obedience in the vast majority of adult participants, causing them to override extreme personal distress at what they were asked to do.[13, 14]

The norms of professionalism: studies of systematic bureaucratic harm Sociologists Adams and Balfour reveal how the tenets of modern professionalism have contributed to several situations in which individuals overrode their morals (often with great personal angst) to participate in a harmful organizational enterprise, such as the German Civil Service under the Third Reich, the internment of Japanese citizens in the United States, and the launches of the Space Shuttles *Challenger* and *Columbia.* In particular, they claim that equating professionalism with emotional detachment keeps people focused on "how" to accomplish something and suppresses questions and concerns about "what" they are engaged in.[15]

The power of roles: the Stanford prison experiment Echoing some of Milgram's findings, this controversial study involving a mock prison demonstrated how powerful roles with known "scripts" could lead a group of ordinary students to barbaric and abusive behavior in an extremely short period of time. The basic theme is that when a person is uncertain how to act, the requirements of a role will trump his or her individual character. Though the design of this experiment has been challenged, the findings are echoed in several other analyses.[16] For example, Dennis Gioia, the recall coordinator for the Ford Pinto, who was partially responsible for the tragic deaths that resulted from a faulty design because he delayed a product recall, later reflected on how his role distorted his thinking, causing him to accept certain things as normal that he would not have accepted before he had the job.[17]

Group dynamics: research on groupthink Scientists Muzafer Sherif and Solomon Asch did separate research on social factors in perception and showed how the need to belong to important groups is so powerful that it causes members to unconsciously distort their perceptions to conform with the group's—even if their own perceptions are in direct contradiction. Because this happens below the level of consciousness, people are not even aware they are doing it. For example, in one study participants reported seeing something different from what was actually in front of them when others in the group described it differently. Together these studies support Irving Janis's theories about groupthink.[18]

Gradual acclimatization: studies of U.S. prisoners of war in Korea Robert Cialdini describes detailed investigations into how the Chinese indoctrination program during the Korean War was surprisingly successful in gaining cooperation from American soldiers, in marked contrast to American POWs during World War II. Apparently, their program relied on successive, slightly graduated public commitments whereby soldiers would "go on record" with seemingly innocuous concessions about the flaws of the United States or the benefits of communism, gradually leading them to adapt their beliefs to align with their actions, until they ended up supporting the Chinese agenda.[19]

The point of all this research is that it takes effort to stay in touch with reality. This is what Wall Street investors, financiers, rating agencies, mortgage brokers, real estate appraisers, homeowners, credit card borrowers, and others are currently rediscovering. Blinders help people cope with the stress of internal conflict, but they also hide risks, consequences, options, and even the choice points themselves, as they protect them from that discomfort.[20] Therefore, to see your true best course of action in a situation, you need to pay attention. The only way to do this is to have the humility to recognize that *compromise is more likely to be gradual because normal human blinders make it hard to see at the time.*

Misconception 6: The Company Sets the Terms

Given the intense pressure to be "on board" at work, it is not surprising that it seems very risky to push back. You may have seen people around you ostracized or effectively silenced because they challenged a company policy or a leader's direction. You may have had that experience yourself. In the face of such experiences, it is natural to view the organization as making the rules. From this viewpoint, if you don't like the terms of engagement, your choices are pretty fixed: adapt or leave, voluntarily or not. "You know where the door is," a boss of mine used to say.

What this view misses is the way organizations are continually shaped and reshaped by countless daily interactions and negotiations among and between departments and individuals, over and above the formal decisions and policies. According to Art Kleiner, author of *Who Really Matters,* organizations function as webs of loyalty clustered around certain individuals whom people *want* to see succeed. If you buy this view, it suggests there is much greater mutual influence between leaders and followers, and among followers, than we usually presume.[21, 22] Several recent analyses on followership and poor leadership confirm the role of followers as well.[23]

When you are in a threatening situation, however, it is very difficult to see this potential for influence or to imagine things shifting. This is why it takes so much courage to redefine the game.

For example, Julia, the department head for an IT team in a Fortune 50 computer and office equipment company, had begun feeling the walls closing in around her. As the company stumbled under the weight of a major merger, her department's budget had been cut multiple times, hurting her ability to support the product development teams who were supposed to turn out a brand-new suite of products that would make the merger a success. Though she raised concerns several times, her boss brushed her aside. "We all have to suck it up in times like these," her boss told her. "Figure it out." Julia knew she was expected to be a good soldier, yet she saw that the company was risking its entire new product release, billions of dollars in revenue, and potentially its future, for lack of a few $3,000 pieces of equipment. How would her boss look if that happened?

So, she spoke to her boss again: "I consider myself your ally, which means I have a responsibility to advise you about risks and opportunities I see that might affect you. And right now I see a significant risk that you could end up holding the bag for a short-sighted policy that could jeopardize the entire product launch." Needless to say, this got her boss's attention. Together they worked out several solutions, including a budget cap for each product line instead of a flat dollar amount for her department. The company met its launch deadlines, and when the boss needed someone to head a larger department a few months later, she tapped Julia. "I need someone who can figure out another mess for me," the boss told Julia when she asked her to take the promotion.

Contrary to popular wisdom, many people have made politically risky moves or pushed back on company policies and lived to tell the tale. A sales director renegotiated commission structures that were causing dysfunctional behavior on his team. A frontline loan officer held his ground on refusing to make a bad loan, even as his bosses pressed for a different answer to please the chairman of the company five levels above him. A novice accountant at a Big Six firm called the head of the audit department at 2 a.m. on a Sunday morning to check on audit procedures when he saw a problem. "I was sure my career was toast after I called the guy. I knew it was risky, but I was more afraid *not* to do the right thing," said the accountant. "Then I went to the office on Monday morning—and nothing happened! The story started going around, and I gained a lot of respect. They knew they could count on me, that I wasn't going to 'pencil-whip' the numbers as was sometimes done."

These examples illustrate that *more is negotiable than you think,* especially if you are engaging at a higher level, pursuing something worthwhile. It only seems like there is no room to negotiate because it is uncommon to see others doing it visibly. In fact, one of most significant variables in the Milgram experiments was whether people observed another person pushing back.[24]

Misconception 7: You Should Just Say No

"Just say no" is a pretty apt description of the conventional prescription for handling unhealthy pressure to compromise, and many people argue that that is all it takes. While effective in its clarity, I find this too simplistic to be a real strategy.

On the one hand, you cannot be true to yourself if you are not always ready and able to say no. "You have to be willing to put your job on the line all the time," said Maria, talking about the pressures and the humiliations she faced as an executive assistant. To return to the Milgram experiments, some analysts say that one of the primary reasons why people did not refuse to comply was that they did not have an exit strategy readily available.[25] Or, to quote Howard Gardner discussing "ethical intelligence," "If you are not prepared to resign or be fired for what you believe in, then you are not a worker, let alone a professional. You are a slave."[26]

On the other hand, "just say no" is not really a strategy. Recall that the reason why playing along with the game becomes the compromise trap is because it leads to feeling smaller, which leads you to believe you cannot afford to say no; it is a vicious circle. If you allow your sense of independence to erode, you set yourself up to not have the will, the courage, or the clarity to make the hard choice when the time comes.

So the real moment of choice is far upstream, when you build up your personal foundations. You *do* have a choice to redefine the game and engage at a higher level, but *you need more than a "just say no" strategy to be ready when the pressure hits.* "It was only after taking six months off and getting some perspective that I was able to make the decision that I was no longer going to cave out of fear," said Andrea, a high-tech marketing manager. Later, when this decision was tested, she was ready. This is the justification for focusing on personal foundations—so you feel prepared and are less likely to be overly influenced by catastrophe scenarios of what will happen if you push back.

Misconception 8: Refusing to Compromise Means Fighting Back

When people are inspired by the idea of redefining the game, they often rediscover their courage and a new source of power. They become more willing to take risks and fight back against what they think is wrong, standing up where they see harm or an abuse of power. "You've got to rock the boat regardless of the effect on your performance review! They just won't respect basic morals if no one stands up to them," said a passionate young pharmaceutical employee.

Refusing to capitulate in the face of unhealthy pressure may require a fight, but once the adrenalin is flowing it can be easy to forget that this is just one option. If you get stuck in rebelling or opposing in a knee-jerk way, you end up engaging at a lower level because this approach pits you against the other in a battle of egos. It becomes more about being right rather than helping the right thing happen.

The main reason why people retaliate when you say no to them is because it usually comes across as a personal attack rather than a commitment to something important. You are forcing them to consider whether they may have contradicted their values; and as we saw in the compromise trap, this is an incredibly painful process. In response they are likely to dig in their heels and counterattack rather than truly see your point of view and implement change in any foundational way.

This does not mean you never use power to influence change. Knowing how to use power skillfully is important to getting others' attention, being taken seriously, and getting them to the table to address concerns they may not previously have considered significant.

But it is important to remember that *fighting is just one option; there are many other ways to influence a situation,* and you have multiple options in the face of unhealthy pressure to compromise. I have identified at least five (which we review in chapter 9, "Make Positive Plays"): healthy compromise, candid conversations, positive limits, skillful influence, and constructive exit. (You may want to revisit figure 1-4.) By studying and adapting your response based on what actually works in terms of your goals, you can have a greater impact while reducing any unnecessary risk of retaliation. The paradox is that knowing you do not automatically have to take an antagonistic approach if you see something wrong increases the chances that you will recognize and respond proactively when the need arises.

Misconception 9: You Thrive When You Get to the Top

I chose the subtitle for this book, *How to Thrive at Work without Selling Your Soul,* after a longtime business colleague told me, "Yes, *thriving* at work—that's what I want. Not just making a living." Isn't that what many people want? Isn't that what *you* want (once you get past all those voices telling you not to be naive)?

If you are like most people, you reconcile those conflicting voices by telling yourself that achieving wealth or financial independence will earn you freedom and independence, so *then* you can thrive, however you define it: exploring life, becoming "self-actualized" in psychologist Abraham Maslow's terms, deepening your relationships, getting involved in your community, or cultivating your artistic talents.

Yet as someone reminded me the other day, the root of the word *wealth* is well-being. In the early days of an economy's development, when survival and security truly mean physical survival and bodily security, wealth and well-being are pretty synonymous. But as individuals and societies become wealthier, the relationship between money and well-being becomes more complicated.

For example, research in positive psychology shows that what people think will make them happy is different from what actually does. Most people believe that education and money will make them happy, but beyond a certain minimal level of income it is actually strong relationships and developing your "signature strengths" that have the greatest impact on your well-being.[27] Similarly, research on consumer-oriented values, such as wealth, image, and status, shows that holding those values has a *negative* correlation with happiness and a positive link to depression and anxiety.[28]

This explains why you can continually move up and never feel as though you really arrive. Like the CEO who felt like a boiled chicken, many senior leaders feel that the competition at the top is just fiercer. So, rather than assume that you will thrive when you get to the top, I invite you to consider that *you thrive whenever you are engaged in a meaningful pursuit that uses your talents and allows you to meet your real needs.*

Ironically, the ingredients for thriving are remarkably close to redefining the game, with its focus on higher values and goals and true priorities. This is not to say that it is an easy route. It takes a lot of courage to carve out a life where there is no prescribed path. Yet according to the most famous version of the Faust legend, after sampling all the powers, pleasures, and knowledge of the world, Faust ultimately finds that the path that requires the courage to take risks is most fulfilling. "He only earns both freedom and existence who must reconquer them each day," he claims in the end.[29]

In practice this means you may or may not get to the top, but you thrive the moment you start to redefine the game so that you can engage at the level at which you really want to be engaged.

Misconception 10: Individual Integrity Adds Up to Organizational Integrity

The last misconception involves putting your experiences of pressure in a larger context. Thus far I have focused mostly on individual challenges and pressures, yet the current global financial crisis points to both individual and organizational compromise as contributing factors. In "The Giant Pool of Money," *This American Life* tells the story of several individuals involved in the subprime mortgage crisis and how every one of them went along with systems and policies that they knew were harmful and wrong.[30] At every level it seems, a large number of people played along with a shortsighted game. As discussed earlier, the rating agencies gradually moved their "lines in the sand" to accommodate pressure to loosen their rating standards, while banks and investment banks pushed them to do it, contrary to their own long-term interest. Borrowers took on loans they could not afford, mortgage brokers gamed the credit verification processes, lenders paid big commissions to get more loans from these same brokers, and, ultimately, money market fund managers begged for more securities to invest in, when they must have suspected they couldn't all be AAA quality.

How does compromise on such a wide scale happen?

One common response is that because organizations are composed of individuals, if the individuals have integrity, the organization will. Unfortunately, a growing number of people think the problem is much more difficult than this.

One alternative explanation is that organizations and industries as a whole are facing unhealthy pressure, and those distorted incentives trickle down to individuals. In *Confessions of a Wall Street Analyst,* Daniel Reingold describes analyzing the telecom industry in the 1990s, leading up to the MCI/WorldCom accounting fraud scandal, and the distorted incentives he faced as an analyst: "*I hate what this job has become,* I thought. Everything is rumor, leaks, and guidance. Is anyone doing primary research anymore? Am I?... I was embarrassed, both for how my own work had become increasingly superficial and for the investment research profession overall."[31]

In the more recent Peanut Company of America scandal, the company managers were able to bypass regulations by firing any testing lab that did not give them the results they wanted.[32] Where competition is supposed to reward value-creation, distorted incentives and loopholes like these create financial rewards for predatory or opportunistic behavior and penalties for building capacity and value-creation for the longer term. Not surprisingly, such systemic pressure can erode the integrity of the individuals who work within the system. In one survey of CEOs, many reported personal stress due to the disparity between what they believed they ought to be doing and what was actually expected—the basis on which their performance was being judged.[33]

Still, we expect individuals to rein in the tidal wave, and we judge them harshly if they do not. Perhaps we would do better to support one another's ability to engage at a higher level in the face of such distorted incentives. I recall a homeowner who was worried about a chemically treated wood product proposed for a deck. His architect assured him it was completely safe. Sensing the architect had given him a "standard" professional response, he asked, "Would you really feel comfortable with your three-year-old running around on this?" The architect paused and said, "On second thought, let's find another material for you to consider."

Even without these distorted incentives, organizational integrity is much harder to achieve than individual integrity. According to Lynn Sharp Paine, author of *Value Shift,* organizations do not automatically function as moral actors even if the individual members do.[34] For example, she identifies seven systems required just for organizations to keep their promises:

1. Being able to accurately gauge capabilities and make promises based on realistic assessments

2. Keeping track of promises and transferring them across the organization and as roles transition

3. Getting cooperation across departments and functions to deliver on promises

4. Having all individuals be promise-keepers

5. Having promises serve as valid reasons in decision-making

6. Educating individuals to be promise-keepers and maintain these systems
7. Maintaining systems to identify and correct when promises are missed or broken

Clearly many of these systems are nonexistent or poorly functioning in most organizations, as recent studies of medical errors and air travel accidents have shown.[35] The current fascination with individual performance—whether attracting and retaining superstars or identifying and rooting out bad apples—distracts organizations from instituting these systems, even though companies like Toyota have shown that they are remarkably similar to the systems needed to delight and retain customers, engage and motivate employees, and deliver optimal returns to shareholders.[36]

For all these reasons, dealing with unhealthy pressure is more than an individual challenge. Organizations too are faced with the choice of playing along with the game or redefining it and whether to engage at a lower or higher level—for their own benefit and to live up to their commitments and obligations in the larger world.

Thus, when you face unhealthy pressure to compromise, you can expect that it often represents some way your organization's integrity is also under pressure. Until society addresses the distorted incentives and more organizations develop the capacity to systematically keep commitments, it is individuals who are going to see the disconnects and the contradictions, and every individual is uniquely situated to see a certain subset of these tensions. This is why expanding your individual ability to redefine the game is simultaneously part of the evolution toward organizations that act with integrity as a whole.

As discussed at the beginning of this chapter, the goal is to make choices that are truly aligned with your values, based on a full awareness of your options, priorities, and alternatives and the best predictions you can make at the time. Knowing these ten common misconceptions, you are more likely to make those decisions effectively because you are prepared for unhealthy pressure—even in the best organizations—and take a proactive approach to it, rather than rely on your leader to address it. Knowing that pressure and choice points are difficult to recognize, you will be more prepared to question the simplistic explanations or threats that drive you to play along with a negative game. And when you do commit to redefine the game at a higher level, you will recognize the need to do so skillfully, not with a knee-jerk bias toward fighting or just telling yourself to say no but by investing in the personal foundations that strengthen your ability to see and act on the most constructive options for yourself, your organization's results, and the organization's potential for positive action in the world.

Before you go on, you may find it useful to explore the Organizational Pressure Diagnostic (see "Individual and Small-group Activities" at the back of the book) to gain clarity about the nature of the pressures *you* face in your current setting.

Now we'll turn from these general principles to how you can find more freedom given the specific unhealthy pressure you face. We'll look at how you, personally, might be able to expand your ability to redefine the game so that you can engage at a higher level.

KEY CONCEPTS

- **The ten misconceptions** Understanding the ten misconceptions about compromise at work helps you recognize choice points and identify unhealthy pressure before it leads you into the compromise trap. Take a moment to review figure 3-1, Ten Misconceptions and Alternative Propositions, paying particular attention to whether the alternatives might be worth adopting.

- **When not to compromise** Don't compromise if it involves giving up something that matters more to you for something that matters less—given a full understanding of your options, alternatives, true costs, and payoffs over the long term.

REFLECTION QUESTIONS

- Think of a time when you really believed in the organization you worked for. What inspired you about it? How did it change your day-to-day experience of work?
- When have you been most disappointed in an employer? Why? What experiences caused your disappointment? How did those experiences color your beliefs about the company overall?
- What is your theory about unhealthy pressure to compromise? Where does it come from? If you assumed it could happen in any organization, how would you decide whom you could work for and whom you couldn't?

4

How Do I Redefine the Game?

There is a remarkable documentary called *Citizen Václav Havel Goes on Vacation* about the Czech dissident and playwright who went on to become the first president of the Czech Republic after the fall of the Soviet Union. Both terrifying and absurd, the movie is about his vacation in 1985, trying to show what life was like under the constant surveillance and intimidation of the state police (StB). During his vacation, Havel is tailed everywhere. His little gray VW Golf is followed about 10 feet behind by a convoy of one, two, and sometimes four StB cars, traveling across the sparsely populated countryside, almost in formation. He is arrested several times and held in detention for days without charges. (Havel is no stranger to jail and seems to have mastered the delicate process of negotiating with the police and the tough guys he meets there. "When they beat others, you have to protest, but you have to phrase it so people feel ashamed for at least twenty seconds...and not so they beat you up immediately, which isn't easy.")

The friends he visits are subjected to house searches, surveillance, and interrogations related to his visits. Stories are told about a young follower who disappears. Each person recalls a prison sentence of 3, 4, 5, even 10 years. Yet amid some very real dangers and hardships, Havel and his friends show a surprising degree of humor and creativity. For example, they bring hot tea down to the StB officers sitting in their cars in the rain while keeping surveillance on the house where Havel is visiting. Havel always asks each group of officers what their assignment is and even negotiates with them, threatening to terminate his vacation if there are further complications beyond surveillance. At one point just after the vacation ends, Havel goes to stay in the mountains where it is snowing, and one day one of the police cars skids off the icy road and crashes into a ditch. Havel and his friend walk down to the ditch and push the police car up out of the rut and back onto the road. Then the police continue on their way to the house, check the friend's car, and take his license away. Still, when Havel and his friends wave to the police as they're driving away, the police occasionally wave back.

Perhaps the most moving segment of the film is a brief part after the fall of the Berlin Wall and the Velvet Revolution that brought the end of communism to Czechoslovakia, when one of the StB officers involved in Havel's surveillance recalls his first meeting with him as the new president of the Czech Republic. "We were standing by the side of the road, honoring them like soldiers [saluting]. Then suddenly the car stops and they are walking toward us [Havel and the new minister of the interior]! So the shakes started. I said: 'Don't be scared!' I was nervous....I hope they're not coming to arrest me. Then Havel says, 'Let me introduce you to your new minister.'" That was it. President Havel shakes his hand, they chat for a bit about how the new minister used to work in the bakery nearby, and then he goes on to inspect the police station. There is no retaliation, no payback—then or later.

At one point near the end of the film, Havel reveals his underlying strategy, which has absolutely nothing to do with fighting or thwarting the police. His purpose even involves them. “I was trying to enlarge the sphere of things we talk about openly. It’s one of the tenets of the [dissident group] Charter 77, to call things by their real names, to speak openly.”[1] With that commitment, he single-handedly redefined what their interactions were about.

Welcome to the Parallel Universe

With this chapter we begin a new section of our journey together, shifting from the challenges of the compromise trap to how you, personally, can expand your ability to redefine the game in a broader range of circumstances, including unhealthy pressure.

Of course, redefining the game in the midst of pressure to compromise sounds like a solution only by comparison to some pretty hard realities. On the surface, it may seem like a lot of work. It’s only when you consider where the compromise trap leads that taking the harder path that courage requires looks like an answer. If you were convinced that you could play along and come out unscathed, you might think that was your best bet. Still, who is going to tell you if you are headed into a trap? “Sometimes I’ll meet someone with a lot of energy, and they ask me for career advice,” said one recruiter. “What I really want to do is lean across the desk and say, ‘Take your résumé and *run*!’” But of course, she doesn’t say that.

Talking openly about the compromise trap is sort of like being reminded of your mortality. Though it is uncomfortable, facing the fact is actually rather freeing. I remember once getting up from a chiropractic treatment and asking jokingly, “So, am I going to live?” to which the chiropractor replied, “No! You’re going to die—just not today!” I laughed all the way home. Once you see the downsides of playing along with unhealthy pressure, you become more aware of how every one of us is stuck, to one degree or another, between the compromise trap and the risks of acting courageously. Given that dilemma, the frantic rush to get to our destinations faster does seem rather funny.

This is why there is so much to learn from those in extreme circumstances. People like Václav Havel and the other dissidents in central Europe, like Nelson Mandela and those who fought apartheid for decades in South Africa, like Mahatma Gandhi, Martin Luther King Jr., César Chávez, and even the American revolutionaries demonstrate how, when you know you are between a rock and a hard place, when there is no way to win by following the given paths, you are forced to get much more inventive.

Dilemmas make you grow by forcing you to discover a new alternative between two losing propositions. It becomes necessary to redefine the game, to reconsider what you are up to and what you want your work to advance, create, or serve. How do you *want* to engage? Is it a game, really? In what sense? If it is a game in the sense that you do not control the outcome, there are other players, and you need to be creative and inventive, what you want is a *better* game—one that engages with more of reality and focuses on goals that are truly worth pursuing.

Though your situation is almost certainly not as severe as those I described above, we can probably find ways to apply the sort of liberating creativity of Havel's dissidents to push back on whatever barriers lie between you and defining the game you most want to play.

Rather than view this chapter as an itemized list of how you can be more like Mother Teresa, I encourage you to approach this process as a deliciously wicked way to deal with a no-win dilemma and get your life back—by being creative and resourceful against whatever is keeping you cornered. Remember, the idea is to increase your ability to live the values *you* hold deep down, not become the person someone says you should be.

My interview participants told me that discovering the freedom to redefine the game on your own terms is like entering a parallel universe, similar in degree to the way those who have confronted their mortality differ from everyone else. "When you decide you are going to face hard choices creatively and realistically rather than caving out of fear, you operate in a different world that is almost inexplicable to those who have not experienced it," said one line manager in high tech.

To understand how to find and operate in this parallel universe, we start by exploring what it means to redefine the game, how you become bigger so you can engage at that level, and the new questions that help you orient toward that larger perspective.

What It Means to Redefine the Game

Recall that I described redefining the game as accepting unhealthy pressure and yet consciously choosing to engage at a higher level, trying to be a positive force to help the best thing happen for yourself and others. It is not about ignoring hard realities but deciding to act courageously in the face of them, banking on your own creative capability and the possibilities of a situation.

Engaging at a higher level is almost like approaching from a higher altitude. From this vantage point, you have a broader perspective and can see larger consequences, a longer time horizon, and more creative options. You include higher values and goals, considering other people's interests as well as your own—not because you are a saint but based on seeing your own self-interest from the broadest possible perspective.

When in the trap, you let others or historical norms define the game for you. You focus on the lure of the promised rewards and, as in any trap, this can distract you from what is at stake, what you really have to lose or even what truly counts for you.

By contrast, when you redefine the game, you recall your choice about what to pursue, what actions to take, and how you keep score on success or failure, even as you work with the reality of a situation. You are more likely to question your assumptions or the conventional wisdom and take action based on deeper insight into a situation.

The result is that work becomes a professional quest rather than a game—an attempt to live and thrive while engaged in a worthwhile challenge or meaningful pursuit. Yes, you are not in control of the outcomes. Yes, you must deal with reality as it is. But you are using whatever degrees of freedom you have to serve what matters most in a grounded and practical way.

In chapter 3 I invited you to consider that redefining the game was possible even in tough situations because more is negotiable than most people think, even though some risks are very real. As my participants discovered when they decided to free themselves from the compromise trap, they already had more freedom than they thought, once they began to question their assumptions and what external validation they really wanted. By broadening their perspective on both their own priorities and the situation, they were able to focus on the interests *behind* their goals and stop making the unhealthy compromises that cost them more than they gained.

As we have seen, this is tricky to do in the face of unhealthy pressure because situational factors and the psychological blinders

Professional quest The pursuit of a worthwhile challenge with whatever degrees of freedom you have, in a practical way that allows you to thrive in the process.

that help you cope with the stress of internal conflict can mask your own best choice by hiding the real risks, consequences, options, and even the choice points themselves.

Accessing your full measure of freedom in spite of these challenges requires self-authorized leadership: licensing yourself to take a level of initiative and responsibility that is not granted by others. You don't wait for the company or boss to make it safe to act courageously or remove the unhealthy pressure; you take responsibility for your own actions in the face of the system's flaws. If the situation is not working, is causing harm, or is putting people in impossible dilemmas, clearly leadership is needed. Given the lose-lose proposition between complying or rebelling, you choose to be purposeful.[2]

What does good leadership mean to you? Here is the best definition I know: a good leader is someone who is willing to see current reality as it really is without avoiding painful facts, while simultaneously committing to a vision or possibility that is truly worthwhile. By this definition, anyone can make himself or herself a leader wherever he or she is, at any time.[3]

There are many books describing the qualities of great leaders. One of the most respected is Jim Collins's *Good to Great,* which depicts some of the paradoxical traits of exceptional leaders, such as humility combined with intense professional will.[4] As I studied the stories of those who were engaged at a higher level, I found similarly paradoxical combinations of characteristics that allowed them to redefine the game in the face of unhealthy pressure:

- **Pragmatic *and* purposeful** People who redefine the game exhibit a deeply pragmatic concern for self-interest, situational realities, and concrete action *and* the daring to be purposeful with whatever degrees of freedom are available.

- **Committed *and* independent** They are committed to their organization and their colleagues but at the level of purpose, potential, and long-term health rather than loyalty at all costs. This can mean opposing actions that are shortsighted or self-defeating.
- **Understanding *and* responsible** They are compassionate and willing to face flaws, contradictions, and weaknesses in themselves and others. Knowing this, they take even more responsibility for paying attention to situational forces, biases, and blinders.

Dilemmas tend to set up either/or choices that are overly simplistic: go along or be fired, be committed or be a troublemaker, deliver quality or low cost, serve the customer or be profitable. Yet, as revolution after revolution in business thinking has shown, these are false choices. High quality can lower total costs. High customer service increases loyalty and can increase profitability. The same is true for your more personal choices. The most committed person is often the one who calls on the organization to change. These three counterintuitive pairs of characteristics remind you that you can redefine the game to allow many possible both/and combinations.

How do these both/and combinations and self-authorized leadership help you deal with unhealthy pressure?

Imagine you are swimming in the ocean and you start to feel an undertow. If you just ride along, which is like playing along and falling into the compromise trap, you will be swept out to sea. But if you fight directly against the force of the current, which is like rebelling, you will exhaust yourself—and then be swept out to sea because the current is far stronger than you are. The only way to get out is to *cut across* the current, so you conserve your energy but still head toward the shore. With this new strategy, you have invented a completely new option beyond the obvious ones presented, which requires leadership and questioning either/or assumptions.

When you undertake a professional quest or engage at a higher level in any way, it is as though you are swimming across the current rather than into or against it, as Havel illustrated in his dealings with the police, or Jim and Roberta did in confronting their organizations. This is why being purposeful rather than reactive or aggressive is actually a self-preservation strategy. By focusing on something higher or more important, you avoid triggering the system's defenses and minimize the retaliation directed at you. At the same time, you strengthen yourself because you get direct and immediate satisfaction from working toward something intrinsically valuable to you. This means you are less dependent on external signs of success, which paradoxically enables you to be more effective and productive.

Becoming Bigger

By now it is probably clear that redefining the game in the way I've been describing requires that you *become* bigger. To exercise leadership across the current, you cannot rely on external rewards, at least in the short run. Instead you need to switch to internal reinforcement, relying more on your personal foundations for your security, confidence, independence, well-being, creativity, and courage.

It is a significant transition to stop waiting for a leader to do the right thing and opt instead to take whatever measures you can to help the best thing happen. In psychological terms, this is part of the move beyond following rules simply because of penalties or social conventions and living a self-responsible life. It means expanding beyond a child's loyalty to a more adult relationship with authority.

And, according to the research, those who develop to this level are more likely to act in accordance with their values, less likely to cheat, and more able to resist pressure, help those in need, and blow the whistle if necessary. They raise or sustain a group's level of decision-making through their model, and they see the relationship between their behavior and its outcomes more clearly, enabling them to be more responsible in their lives overall.[5]

But how do you *make* yourself bigger?

As we explored in chapter 1, you make yourself smaller by eroding your confidence, security, and well-being. So making yourself bigger is the opposite: learning to move beyond the fear and the worry at the core of the compromise trap.

There is a saying that fear shows up whenever we run away from "what is."[6] Similarly, in negotiations one way to strengthen your bargaining power is to face your less attractive alternatives and worst-case scenarios head-on so you are less reactive to threats and can better pursue your real interests. When you dare to look at your dilemmas in an open-minded way, the challenges tend to shrink down to size and your resources, capabilities, and options seem to grow.

Based on this, one way to become bigger is to act for a moment as though the worst has already happened. Rather than wait to hit the limit, like Julie and Gary the CFOs, or Mitch the organizational effectiveness executive, you see what you can learn by going through that experience in your mind.

What would be the worst-case scenario for you? What is the fear or concern that tends to cause you to play along, to whatever degree you do?

For many people the worst-case scenario that leads to unhealthy compromise is the fear of losing their job. So, if you want to know what redefining the game feels like in action, I invite you to spend a day thinking like you have already given notice on your job or you already know you are going to be fired and there is nothing you can do about it. Or, if that seems too hard, imagine you have won the lottery or inherited billions from Warren Buffet.

Go ahead and try it for a moment—really daydream. What would you do differently? What risks might you take, knowing you had nothing to lose? What would you give up worrying about? What would really be your most satisfying alternative choice?

Within your thought experiment, you may feel more clarity and freedom. Not needing to attack or defend, you might find you know what is needed and how to do it without antagonism or resentment. Paradoxically (in real life), this increases others' ability to hear you and reduces their reactiveness as well. How many people find that after they have given notice they are able to address the issues that previously had made the job so uncomfortable?

For example, just after Deborah, a mutual fund manager, gave notice, her boss took her out for lunch. While they chatted, he admitted he was at a loss for how to really engage the women on his team. Prior to giving notice, Deborah's strategy had been to tell her boss "the intersection between what he wants to hear and the truth—usually a very small amount of data!" But now she had nothing to lose, so she said, "Boss, the problem is the department operates like an old boy's network. And I hate to say it, but you're the ringleader. I don't think you recognize it but you seem to just naturally invite the guys out for drinks or cigars or golf but never the women. I am sure you could change that if you wanted to, but it might feel a little uncomfortable for a while. Would you like some ideas about how?" Deborah didn't attack or humiliate her boss; she just spoke candidly and directly in a way that could help him if he chose. And guess what? His reply floored her: "That was so helpful! I had no idea. But why didn't you tell me before?"

Another person who worked for an aggressive and temperamental leader went to work on Monday after refusing to work the weekend when his boss had directed him to the previous Friday. As he walked into the building convinced he was about to be fired, he asked himself, *If I am about to be fired, what can I do while I'm here?* Strangely enough, this led him to tell his boss what he thought needed to change to achieve the company's goals—and he ended up getting a promotion! "This happened over and over. Every time he put me on the spot and I took the chance to say what I thought was really needed, I ended up getting a promotion—until I ended up president of the company."

Somehow, once we have accepted the worst, we feel freer to offer whatever we have to give, to risk engaging in what really matters, to show up based on what we really stand for in life. One of the most remarkable traits of those who redefine the game consistently is that they keep this perspective almost all the time. It is as if they have redefined losing—and therefore winning. In *Power Failure* Sherron Watkins tells the story of the Houston investment counselor who lost his customers' respect (and presumably some of their business) for a while because he "didn't get it" about Enron. They thought he was a loser, "old-fashioned, mired in the past," but he just calmly told them he wasn't going to invest in a business he couldn't understand.[7] When you do not buy into others' power to judge you as a winner or loser, you can focus instead on what you really want to be doing—earning enough to meet your needs and turning your attention to what really gives you satisfaction, perhaps even a professional quest.

For example, Bill, the CEO of a public alternative fuels company, told me, "I can't fail because I have no ambition." He went on to elaborate:

> I'm basically a cathedral builder…and all I'm doing is laying the bricks that will be the foundation of something that could be great

> someday in the future. I estimate it will take 150 years to transition to fully sustainable sources of energy. I'll be buried underneath ivy and grass and fallen trees by the time it's finished, but if there's a nice structure at the end, who cares? So the foundation that I'm putting together, I'm just trying to make it good enough that it can be used. It'd be great if that made us some money, but, if not, someone else will pick up the pieces of what we have created and learn from what we have accomplished. So, you see, none of this can be meaningless. There's no way to fail.

By challenging your own failure scenarios in your thought experiment, you give yourself a taste of the freedom that comes with redefining your own game, a way to reconnect with your right, and your responsibility, to lead a life that is deeply satisfying to you.

Creating Room to Redefine Your Game

Now, from the larger, freer perspective created by this experiment, I invite you to look at your actual situation. Use the peripheral vision we talked about in the Introduction to help you see what might be trying to get your attention from the margins of your awareness. (You may want to make a few notes because whatever comes up in this first reflection is likely to be the most useful later.)

- What limits your ability to redefine the game, wherever you are currently engaged? What is the pressure that drives you to play along (to whatever degree you do)? What would have to be resolved for you to engage at a higher level and pursue what is most meaningful and satisfying for you?
- How is your current strategy working? What are the hidden costs and the consequences for you and others when you look honestly over time? Who is ultimately affected by the commitments you are compromising? How?

- Is there anything telling you that it's time to engage at a higher level? What are the longings, wishes, or impulses that might suggest a professional quest waiting for your attention? Who or what would benefit from your increased ability to act on that mission? How?
- How might you be narrowing your perspective too much, perhaps out of stress, fatigue, or unquestioned acceptance of others' expectations? What assumptions have you made that it might be time to test?

In a way, what you have just identified are several key areas for learning as you recalibrate the full costs of playing along and what is really worth committing to in your life. The personal foundations we cover in the next section are what allow you to follow through on these learning opportunities.

Bigger Questions

The fundamental assumption when you dare to engage at a higher level is that people and systems can learn. The fields of systems thinking, societal evolution, and complexity theory all argue that families, organizations, teams, individuals, and even societies can grow and evolve as they gain a critical mass of awareness of what is not working and invent new options in an ongoing process of change.*

From this systemic perspective, things become a lot less personal. You can view yourself as partnering with the larger forces of change in any situation to help the best outcome unfold, instead of

*One of the most exciting ideas in organizational change is that it is possible to work with the process of evolution, looking for what is needed and helping change happen in the most mature way possible. See Action Learning Labs at *www.actionlearninglabs.com*; also see C. Otto Scharmer, *Theory U: Leading from the Future as It Emerges* (San Francisco: Berrett-Koehler, 2009).

wearing yourself out with heroics trying to prevent the inevitable or giving up and becoming a passive player in the process. With this orientation, redefining the game may simply mean lending a hand to missions or purposes others have already begun. Besides, you increase your influence when you look for trajectories that are already under way because you are less likely to be up on your high horse trying to *make* the right thing happen, which can come across as self-righteousness or an ego trip.

So, how do you partner with these larger forces of change?

At its simplest, you start by asking bigger questions.

For example, when Mary, a seasoned executive, took a new role to launch an ambitious new product line for a respected training company, she soon discovered there was very little market for the product. Yet when she tried to tell her executive committee, they thought she was trying to lower forecasts so she could look good later, when the real numbers came in. So, she asked herself, *How can I help this system learn?* Ultimately, she got approval for a small market research study on product features. When the study showed the lack of demand, the committee was shocked—but grateful to find out before they had gone all the way through development.

As Mary's story shows, conflict is one of the main vehicles that allow systems to learn. In fact, there is an emerging field that suggests that everything we call "knowledge" is actually the result of a negotiation, as individuals and groups reconcile their separate discoveries into a larger body of knowledge.[8]

When you see this, you start to see opportunities to help this conflict and learning process happen constructively rather than destructively. Rather than accept either/or trade-offs as given, you begin to view tension between opposing goals as part of the search for a new answer and start to look for both/and opportunities. And finally, with this mindset you begin to recognize that every member of an organization has an important role to play in that system's learning.

The underlying philosophy behind Václav Havel and his compatriots' actions described earlier is outlined in one of Havel's most famous essays, *The Power of the Powerless.*[9] Published illegally in 1978 and passed across central Europe, this essay had a profound effect on citizens throughout the former Soviet bloc countries, including dissident movements such as Solidarity. In the essay Havel says that there was no "head" to the totalitarian system in Czechoslovakia, only followers who had been infected with a disease, a willingness to live inauthentically, in "automatism" and fear, which led them to collude in keeping the system in place and punishing others who stood up. (His description is remarkably similar to what I've called playing along, though to a far greater degree.)

For Havel the most powerful transformative act in such a system is the decision to "live in truth"—if nothing else, naming and acknowledging the constraints that keep you from acting freely but also including the countless small transformative actions (like the ones I described) that contributed to the overturn of the communist governments and the almost bloodless Velvet Revolution that brought democracy to Czechoslovakia and, through similar relatively peaceful revolutions, to other countries. For Havel "living in truth" is the power of those who feel powerless because every person influences and reinforces those around them, including those with formal power.

To see this power in action, consider Andrew, who worked as a stockbroker. In the year when he was studying for a demanding series of financial exams, his life was not his own—nights, weekends, twenty-four-hour shifts, he could be called on at any time, as the "low man" on the totem pole. "I could just feel them 'levering' me, making all kinds of money based on my effort and exhausting me in the process," he said. It reached a breaking point when he could no longer exercise or keep up with studying for the exam. Then one day it hit him: his boss had a young family at home, too. When the timing seemed appropriate, he asked his boss, “How is this for you, having to be at the office so many weekends with a young child at home? That can't be working.” To his surprise, his boss said, no, it wasn't working well at all. So Andrew proposed that they proactively manage their schedules so everything could get buttoned down by close of Friday and minimize everyone's time spent on the weekend. It turned out to be a win-win for all and soon became standard operating procedure.

As Andrew's story illustrates, it's a myth that coercion is the primary way human beings influence one another. If you were to watch what actually happened between people, you could create a long list of countless other methods, including humor, role modeling, logic, empathy, appealing to values, begging for mercy, and so on. Once you know you have this power of the powerless, the primary issue becomes where to focus as you redefine the game. Bigger questions help you see ways to be purposeful, rather than reactive or aggressive, and how you might help the right thing happen.

Interestingly enough, it was a hallmark of the people striving to redefine the game that they used certain types of questions to reframe their dilemmas from a larger perspective. The accompanying figure is a sampling of the questions they asked, as compared with the playing-along questions people fell into when they felt more defensive or threatened. (See figure 4-1.)

As you can see from the last redefining-the-game question, taking this systemic perspective does not mean you ignore your real needs or your need to support others. The point is to make sure it is based on what really best supports you and those you care about. For example, a dentist worked hard to build a thriving practice, but once it got going, rather than raise his standard of living

Figure 4-1 Playing-along and Redefining-the-game Questions

Playing-along Questions	Redefining-the-game Questions
■ How soon can I get out? ■ How can I avoid trouble? ■ How can I/we get by without x or y? ■ How do I get mine? ■ Why don't they change? ■ How do I take care of myself/my family?	■ What do I want to do while I'm here? ■ How can I help the right thing happen? ■ What is needed here? ■ How can I help this system learn? ■ How can I/we have more x *and* y? ■ What influence *do* I have? ■ What am I uniquely situated to do or stop doing? ■ What do I/we really need to sustain ourselves?

he decided to take off one day a week to volunteer, doing dental work for homeless people, foster children, and so on. By keeping his financial needs simple, he has more time with his family, his kids are involved with him in the volunteer work, and he is much happier than if he were working the extra day.

Do I Have to Leave to Engage at a Higher Level?

Contrary to the conventional wisdom about "chucking it all" to do meaningful work, the questions in figure 4-1 show that you do not have to leave your organization to engage at a higher level.

You can redefine the game by staying, leaving, or doing something in between. After all, if the place where you work has any impact on the world, how could it not be meaningful to stay and help it improve—so long as you have influence and can sustain yourself while you are there? The very fact that there is unhealthy pressure says there is some work to be done. If it does not involve crossing your most basic values, it may be that your biggest contribution is to stay.

The difference between playing the game and a professional quest is a matter of how you are engaging, not where you work.

For example, Bill, the CEO we met earlier, started out in the auto industry. "I grew up in 'smogdom,' working for one of the Big Three automakers in the 1970s just after the emissions laws began to change. The Japanese responded aggressively to the pollution laws and the CAFE [Corporate Average Fuel Economy] standards, but all three American companies fought them. Yet through that whole process, I got to work on reducing emissions and making automobiles cleaner. I wasn't actually conscious of it at the time, but retrospectively I can see that through many different jobs that was what my work was about. I was really engaged in the whole reduced pollution movement but from inside."

So what do you actually *do* differently when you are engaged at a higher level or pursuing a quest, if you don't necessarily leave?

From the outside, engaging at a higher level may seem to be a pretty subtle shift, a slight change in what guides your decisions and how you take action as you respond to what is needed in the moment or pursue your professional quest over time. What is constant is the emphasis on acting as a positive force and helping the right thing happen. I have identified five possible ways to take this sort of constructive action.

Five Positive Plays

Healthy compromise If you decide that a compromise is worth the sacrifice and there is no better way to get what you really want, you may decide to go along. You need to make sure you are clear about what you are agreeing to, however, and clean up your other commitments so you don't set unhealthy precedents or betray others' trust.

Candid conversations Knowing that everyone occasionally avoids dealing with uncomfortable or difficult situations, one of the most important ways to help the right thing happen is to be willing to admit where you made a mistake, when you made an unhealthy compromise, or when you can no longer keep a commitment.

Positive limits When agreeing to a practice or request crosses a line for you or sets a dangerous precedent, you need to know you can say no in a constructive, effective way that does not invite retaliation or telegraph that you are not committed.

Skillful influence More proactive than simply setting limits, this involves initiating actions that contribute to addressing the root cause of the unhealthy pressure, or raising awareness of the need to do so, using (and building up) whatever influence you can while still taking care of your own real needs.

Constructive exit If the compromises required are too severe, you no longer have influence, or you cannot sustain yourself in a given setting, you may have to leave. If that's the case, the constructive approach is to leave in a way that makes as much positive difference as possible and to pursue your next engagement in a way that reflects what you have learned.

Tapping Your Personal Foundations

As we have seen through many examples now, it takes courage to make these positive plays. Even if it is in a constructive way, you are diverging from expected behavior, which is challenging in any circumstance let alone under unhealthy pressure. To carry it off, you need strong personal foundations to give you the gumption and the clarity to see openings and carry them through. These foundations are:

- Reconnect to your strengths
- See the larger field
- Define a worthy enough win
- Find your real team
- Make positive plays
- Keep your own score

Put simply, before you embark on this new venture, you need to know how to really take care of yourself, what you consider a win, how to read the larger forces at work, how to find your team, and how to keep your own score on whether you are living the life you really want instead of gauging by comparison to others. And you need the skills to make the positive plays discussed in this chapter.

Think about the college students who sat at the lunch counters in Tennessee in the 1960s to protest racial segregation. They did not just show up one day to try to change the world. They went through weeks of training in the principles of nonviolent action—both on how to sustain their action when it triggered retaliation and how not to react aggressively to racial slurs or violence.[10]

Though to a lesser degree, you need the same reinforcement.

Whether you are being pressed to choose between supporting your family and making poor loans, passing on poor investment advice, eroding relationships with customers, misleading employees, taking advantage of stockholders, or some other betrayal of trust, unhealthy pressure puts you in a bind. This is how your situation is like Havel's and his friends' in Soviet Czechoslovakia. When you are caught in no-win situations like these, you have no choice but to take some risks.

In the next six chapters, we will walk through the reinforcement you need to tap each of your personal foundations. As you explore these foundations and apply them to your key areas for learning, you will lessen the costs of taking risks. And as you practice making positive plays and begin to feel bigger, you will be able to see more opportunity and find more hidden freedom to negotiate and shape the pressures you face.

Don't worry about being altruistic. Just think of redefining the game as a way to reclaim your freedom by being generous. Try it out before you buy the whole idea. Here's a simple experiment: The next time you are in a meeting, ask yourself, *How can I help this person get more of what he wants?*

Will it make a difference? Who knows. You do it because it makes you feel more comfortable, confident, and creative—while also having more fun. And, yes, it might actually make a difference, although not likely in a way you can measure and get kudos for. As Havel put it, "When a person tries to act in accordance with his conscience, when he tries to speak the truth, when he tries to behave like a citizen, even in conditions where citizenship is degraded, it won't necessarily lead anywhere, but it might."[11]

Before proceeding to the next section, you may find it useful to explore the Self-diagnostic (see "Individual and Small-group Activities" at the back of the book) for a quick self-assessment that builds on the questions raised here and identifies which of the personal foundations might be most helpful for you.

KEY CONCEPTS

- **Redefining the game** This means accepting unhealthy pressure and yet consciously choosing to engage at a higher level, trying to be a positive force to help the best thing happen for yourself and others. It is not about ignoring hard realities but deciding to act courageously in the face of them, banking on your own creative capability and the possibilities of a situation. Your goal is to *cut across* the current of unhealthy pressure as you would with an undertow so that you can be purposeful rather than reactive or aggressive. You can do this from inside an organization, from the outside, or from somewhere in between.
- **Professional quest** When you engage at a higher level, work becomes a professional quest rather than a game, even if you stay right where you are. A professional quest is the pursuit of a worthwhile challenge with whatever degrees of freedom you have, in a practical way that allows you to thrive in the process.
- **How to become bigger** The fundamental assumption behind engaging at a higher level is that people and systems can learn. To help this happen, you license yourself to take a level of self-authorized leadership and responsibility not granted by others, asking bigger questions and reframing dilemmas from a larger, both/and perspective. Redefining winning and losing helps because it frees you from others' judgments or threats.
- **Five positive plays** Once you choose to redefine the game, these five positive plays allow you to put that strategy into action: healthy compromise, candid conversations, positive limits, skillful influence, and constructive exit.
- **Personal foundations** Your independent personal foundations enable you to make the five positive plays and sustain

your ability to engage at a higher level: reconnect to your strengths, see the larger field, define a worthy enough win, find your real team, make positive plays, and keep your own score.

REFLECTION QUESTIONS

- For a couple of days, keep a "question journal," jotting down the questions that first come to mind when something unexpected happens or you face a challenge. These might be internal "self-talk" questions or ones that you ask out loud with others. When do you ask more playing-along questions, and when do you ask redefining-the-game ones? What happens if you consciously change your questions?
- In what parts of your life are you a leader? What do you consider the real work of a leader? What would it mean to act like a leader in relationship to your organization, including those who are above you in the leadership hierarchy?
- Think of someone you know who seems to have redefined the game of what her work is about and invite her to coffee or lunch or just to have a brief chat. Ask about her philosophy of work and how she came to think in that way. If she is open to it, ask about how she approaches hard choices or dilemmas and what questions she asks to frame her thought process.

5

Reconnect to Your Strengths

I reached the low point of my working life in 1988 when I was promoted to corporate group sales manager for a beautiful four-star hotel and assigned to cover the western region. My boss, Ed, was a tall man, slightly bald, whose eyes narrowed to slits when he was angry. According to him, I was supposed to meet with ten prospects per day during my sales trips to Los Angeles, and he routinely checked my appointment schedule to make sure I did. He also directed me to travel on Saturdays to get the airline discount but prohibited me from picking up my rental car until Monday morning to save on expenses.

Aside from the boredom of sitting in a hotel room all weekend without access to a car, there was another problem with his policies. It's simply not possible to meet with ten *good* prospects in L.A. on a single day because the organizations that have any business for a hotel are spread out. So, hell-bent on actually increasing sales (and being something of an idiot), I nevertheless scheduled ten visits with dispersed yet worthwhile prospects as efficiently as I could. I then proceeded to taint all these valuable relationships by arriving late or canceling because I had gotten caught in traffic.

The other salespeople told me that the trick was to find businesses near one another, whether or not they were good prospects, and count those. I couldn't believe that was how things worked and, being twenty-five years old, thought I just needed to try harder to be able to live up to the procedures while really building customer relationships. Ed was often angry at me, and I got so intimidated when he would poke his finger in my face and glare at me that I completely lost my balance. I began reacting to every criticism, obsessing over my sales reports, fudging on my appointment schedule, and desperately trying to push customers into making bookings.

Convinced that I was failing, even though the customer relationships I had built were turning into a growing body of business, I believed Ed when he told me I was not cut out to be a salesperson. Less and less sure of myself, I found myself feeling grateful that I could just hang on to the job. Still, I was miserable, going through my days in a frenzy of activity, often catching colds and flus, and inviting even more of Ed's disapproval. It was only when a colleague, stuck in a similar cycle, actually did find a better job somewhere else that I recognized how I had lost touch with my core self-confidence and talents and was actually viewing the bad conditions themselves as proof that I couldn't expect better.

As we have discussed, when you face healthy pressure, engaging at a higher level is likely to result in rewards and recognition, from simple "attaboys" and "attagirls" to more-formal awards, bonuses, and promotions. By contrast, with unhealthy pressure such as I faced (and that others have described in the past few chapters), you are swimming upstream and may even be criticized or penalized for doing what you really *should* be doing.

Karen, a marketing communications director, described an incident with a new vice president of the high-tech startup where she worked. "He told me to put out a press release reporting false sales numbers. I refused and pointed out that I'd been letting market analysts know our general sales numbers, so it would be obvious to some people that we were faking it. The VP became furious and yelled at me that I didn't know how to do my job."

This sort of distorted feedback is exactly the reason you need to switch to the internal reinforcement of your personal foundations to avoid the compromise trap. With this chapter we begin exploring those foundations in depth.

Thus far I have encouraged you to reevaluate whether your work is actually a game and, if so, in what sense. My personal view is that it is not a game in terms of its real impact (for better or worse), the real resources involved, and the real limits imposed by the law, accounting principles, regulations, and the like. On the other hand, it can be useful to view it as a game in the sense that the outcome is not in your control, you depend on other people, decisions and actions are negotiated, skills and creativity matter, certain numbers count, and having some detachment is useful. From this perspective, work is a game in the same way that any uncertain but worthwhile endeavor is, such breaking an Olympic record, making progress on a scientific challenge, or achieving a technological breakthrough.

With that in mind, you might think of the six personal foundations as what you would naturally do to be more effective when engaging any worthwhile challenge, mission, or quest, knowing it has elements of a game. The basic idea is that your ability to redefine the game at a higher level doesn't come just from willpower but from a combination of inner competence and outer skills. The inner competence involves accessing your talents under pressure, reading the situation, and keeping the goal in mind; the outer skills include working with teammates and allies, mastering plays, and keeping an eye on the right scoreboard.

Try considering this analogy of a game as you revisit the six personal foundations and imagine increasing your capability with help from each of them.

The Six Personal Foundations

1. **Reconnect to your strengths** This allows you to access confidence and creativity and provides self-awareness to guide your choices.
2. **See the larger field** A broad perspective reveals hidden choice points, costs, and opportunities so you can be proactive and creative.
3. **Define a worthy enough win** This gives you a reason for courage and helps you weigh the hard choices.
4. **Find your real team** This provides access to added resources, validation, and support and ensures that your priorities are aligned with your family's.
5. **Make positive plays** This gives you a range of constructive actions that enable you to be true to yourself while minimizing retaliation; they include healthy compromise, candid conversations, positive limits, skillful influence, and constructive exit.
6. **Keep your own score** This frees you from comparing with others while providing reassurance of your impact and helping you learn.

Based on my interviews and informal conversations, each of these six foundations has an essential role in helping expand your ability to redefine the game and engage at a higher level. Without any one of them, you will find the going much tougher.

There are two quick notes to keep in mind as we dive into this next section of the book.

First, these foundations are scalable: you can apply each one in the moment, *and* you can cultivate each of them over time. To help you apply each foundation in the moment, I suggest any of six simple Decision Point Tools, which are also available for download (see "Online Resources" at the back of the book). And to help you build that foundation over time, I have provided a set of activities (see "Individual and Small-group Activities" at the back of the book, which are also available electronically through the "Online Resources" link).

The second thing to note is that each foundation is really just a pointer to a much larger field of study. I have distilled the most crucial elements here to help you with the compromise trap, but as you get into the reinforcing loop of redefining the game you will find them very satisfying tracks for further personal development as they continue to expand your capacity and resourcefulness. Because my simple descriptions of these rich territories are nowhere near comprehensive, I have included a link to a list of suggested further reading (see "Online Resources").

And now let's develop your personal foundations.

Reconnect to your strengths is first because it allows you to access the capacity and the clarity to invest in the others while simultaneously helping you make better decisions in the moment.

What It Means to Reconnect to Your Strengths

Redefining the game is, above all, a bet on your strengths—your creativity, courage, insight, and so on—so that you can get the most satisfying outcomes possible from even the most difficult situations and enjoy the gratification that comes from being your best self. To cut across the current in the face of unhealthy pressure and the risks of social ostracism or retaliation, you need full access to your creativity, presence of mind, and powers of communication.

Unfortunately, it is easy to lose touch with these strengths when you are under stress, so you don't make the best of even the options you do have. Stress and time pressure beyond a certain level tend to impair your judgment and make you more susceptible to intimidation or impulsiveness, so you are more likely to find yourself playing along. For example, research in negotiations has shown that time pressure consistently leads negotiators to make unnecessary concessions or accept flawed deals.[1]

According to George Prince, an expert in creativity, anxiety greatly diminishes your ability to think creatively, make connections, and solve problems:

> Everything else is instantly subordinate and because the feeling is not subject to thought, I am impelled to take whatever action promises relief....If I feel confusion, I stop thinking in that direction. When it is risky to make a connection to figure something out, I do not make that connection. I stop thinking for myself and seek help from an authority or I simply stop pursuing understanding.... Every stab of anxiety reinforces the disintegration of my self-regard and presses me away from being a learner and toward defensiveness and reactivity.[2]

When you are functioning in an overloaded state, you are less likely to recognize the cues that signal something needs your attention. For example, in *The Tipping Point* Malcolm Gladwell tells the story of seminary students who were asked to give a talk on the Christian parable of the Good Samaritan (about helping an injured person by the side of the road). As they were each sent to deliver their talk in another building, they encountered a man slumped over in an alley, eyes closed and groaning (a confederate). The single greatest factor in whether they stopped to help the person was whether they were in a rush (only 10 percent of those in a rush stopped to help).[3] This is why the Center for Law Enforcement Ethics cautions officers on too much stress or overwork, warning them that it can lead to impulsivity, loss of patience, and a lower "moral threshold."[4]

Thus, managing your stress and sustaining a work/life balance are not only critical to your health, your relationships, and your productivity but they are essential for maintaining access to the inner resources you need to recognize unhealthy pressure and act in alignment with your values. As one longtime AT&T executive put it, "A [person] with a crowded, hurried mind has neither the time nor the space for morality; he falls back into instinct and obedience, he ceases to be autonomous for lack of time and space to know his own will, let alone to exercise it freely."[5]

But there is another, more optimistic and surprising message in these findings, as well: contrary to normal assumptions, there seems to be growing evidence that you can learn to intentionally access *more* of your capabilities. For example, in one study participants were able to get scores in Trivial Pursuit that were 30 percent higher than classmates with similar backgrounds, simply by thinking about what it would mean to be a professor for five minutes prior to the test (as opposed to sitting and thinking about soccer hooligans!).[6]

This is an astounding study in a way. It means that your talents are not just a given but that you need to activate the right ones at the right time, practice them, have the presence of mind to connect to them when you need to, and disbelieve the apparent evidence that you are stuck, powerless, or not up to the task.

For example, after my compatriot left the hotel where I worked for Ed, I began using my sales trips as opportunities for personal reading, journaling, and to get out and explore the city. I even took myself to Disneyland after-hours to ride the roller coasters because the thrill felt a lot like courage and self-confidence. After about a month, I applied to business school on a faintest hope that I might do better than the dead-end job where I was. Much to my surprise, I got in. Even more surprising to me at the time, I took a short-term sales role for the four months before school started—and I outsold the next most successful salesperson by a factor of about ten.

I am sure you have been in circumstances in which it was only an act of faith that led you to reach out to change the situation or find a better one because there was little evidence in front of you that you had what it took. If you are lucky, you have a recollection of past strengths and talents to guide you and you just need to reconnect to them. For others, accessing your strengths means discovering that deep confidence that allows you to persist in experimenting, negotiating, or changing things when they are not right.

Reconnecting to your strengths means proactively cultivating and connecting to the core gifts and values that make you who you are, that allow you to face reality and make the best of whatever situation you are in. You do this in the moment by reconnecting with whatever activates your resourcefulness, where you have access to your courage, creativity, and clarity—mentally "riding your own roller coaster." Over time you reconnect to your strengths by learning more about your capabilities and adopting routines that help keep you in touch with them.

Reconnecting to Your Strengths in the Moment

If your capabilities can change based on your situation—be depleted by stress, anxiety, and fear and enhanced by supportive activities and routines—the first step in building your personal foundations is to learn to activate those capabilities when you need them. The easiest way I know to do this is to come up with your own equivalent of the roller-coaster ride.

For me, when I am riding a roller coaster (okay, most of the time when I ride a roller coaster), I am fully immersed in the thrill and the excitement. When I disembark, I am relaxed, happy, and positive, eager to see what comes next—the opposite of fear. If you are like me, just by stepping into a little car, sitting down, and putting on a strap, you have completely changed your physical and mental state. You may have other activities that do this for you, such as skiing, stock-car racing, or playing the piano, to name a few of those practiced by people I know.

Even subtle things can change your state this way, too.

For example, in one study about cheating, the majority of participants cheated by about 50 percent in a self-scored math test where they received money for correct answers. Yet when participants were asked to contemplate their own standards of honesty—recalling the Ten Commandments or signing an honor code—cheating dropped to zero.[7]

Imagine that: simply activating people's values just before they made a decision dramatically changed how they applied those values.

This has enormous implications for how you handle stress or unhealthy pressure. It means you can intentionally plant cues that help you remember what you are really up to and what you are really capable of so you don't lose track and fall into playing along with a negative game. According to the authors of "The Neuroscience of Leadership," it is the "attention density"—how much and how often you focus on something—that determines how much it will affect your action.[8]

"After I read that study about cheating, I realized I should take down all my task reminders and deadlines," said a user-experience designer. "Instead I should probably put up pictures and quotes and reminders of my priorities and deeper commitments."

One manufacturing manager did exactly that: he kept photos of his wife and children on his bulletin board at work as a reminder to have courage. "When I have to do something uncomfortable," he explained, "I look at the photos to remind me that people depend on me to do the right thing." This device helped him on several occasions when it was tempting but irresponsible to avoid a conflict, such as when a peer was misrepresenting information to others in the plant. "When your success is not just for you, it is much clearer why you need to be courageous," he added.

Putting the Idea into Action

What is the equivalent of a roller-coaster ride for you? What experiences, memories, or reminders recall your gifts, talents, strengths, and true priorities to mind in a way that feels real and compelling so that they motivate you?

During our interview one HR director walked over to her mantle to look at photos of the children she met in Papua New Guinea on her navy tour of duty. She keeps them there to remember her passion for helping children and women around the world, an avenue she plans to transition into in the future. As she looked at them, she laughed when she told me the story of how they had grabbed her hands, drawing her into a game of ring-around-the-rosy. "When I look at that photo, I don't feel so dichotomous," she explained. "I remember what my strategy is, why I am working here, and I know someday I will be ready to move on to working with the children that inspire me so much."

Don't make this just a mental exercise; find something concrete. Perhaps it is a particular memory, a photo, a quote, or a saying that puts you in touch with those strengths. Perhaps it is a physical activity—a game of tennis or a ski run—that makes you feel more powerful and capable. Perhaps it is a certain writer who reminds you of what you have to contribute and how to do it skillfully. Or perhaps it is a memory of a particular accomplishment, or the birth of your child, or a trip where you experienced something that changed you.

To help you activate your strengths when you need them, I've included a short process you can use anytime you are facing a difficult situation. (This is the first of six tools that are available as a download; see "Online Resources" at the back of the book.)

DECISION POINT TOOL #1

Activating Your Strengths

This simple activity is one you can use anywhere at any time to increase your resourcefulness. It works by having you alternate between activating the stressful situation in your mind and then activating your strengths.

☐ **Think of a situation.**

Think of the context or situation in which you'd like to have greater access to your strengths. Pick out an area on the floor a few feet away from you to represent that context. Now imagine yourself in that situation, seeing what you see, hearing what you hear, and feeling what you feel. As the experience begins to feel real, step forward into the designated area on the floor. Allow the feeling to increase and, just as it begins to peak, step back out of the area.

☐ **Activate your strengths.**

Recall a time when you felt joy—the feeling of "I'm glad to be here"—perhaps one of the peak experiences I invited you to consider above. As that experience begins to feel real, step into the area on the floor. As it begins to peak, step back out. Do the same for two other types of memories: a time when you felt warmth toward another person—the feeling of "I'm glad you're here"—and a time when you felt conviction, or "I know what I know." Once you've practiced with these memories, step into the area on the floor, access all those strengths at once, and allow them to mix like a blender. Step out again.

☐ **Bring your strengths into the situation.**

Finally, step directly into the area on the floor and bring all those strengths with you. Think about the challenging context or situation with which you began the exercise. What is it like now? What happens? Think about a time in the future when it will be useful to have access to these strengths.

You might want to take a moment right now to give this a try so the next time you feel cornered by a bad situation you can use it to remind yourself of your natural strengths, your true priorities, and your constructive options.

Or perhaps you just want to take a break and go ride an actual roller coaster, race a stock car, or take a few ski runs!

Reconnecting to Your Strengths over Time

I have described some of the more difficult people I met in the hotel industry, but I was also fortunate to meet some truly remarkable individuals. For example, during my last few years working in the hotel business, I became friends with a professional hostage negotiator. Two or three times a year, Gerald would come to San Francisco to negotiate the release of a corporate executive who had been kidnapped. The quintessential English gentleman, Gerald was a sixty-five-year-old former intelligence officer, who, over coffee or a glass of wine, could describe the critical dimensions of any conflict hotspot around the world, the most dangerous phase of a kidnapping process, and the best way to coordinate a release. He had a gift for seeing opportunity in what seemed to be hopeless situations, and he enjoyed using it. And yet, contrary to what I expected of someone so dedicated to his work, Gerald always took the time for a 5-mile run at the end of the day. Imagine an older Jack Bauer from the TV series *24* saving the world—and still taking time for a run. How did he do it? Weren't the situations he dealt with truly life or death?

When I asked Gerald how he managed to stick to his routines for taking care of himself, he told me he viewed taking care of his own sanity and capacity for clear thinking as the best thing he could do for the people whose lives he was working to save.

His perspective gave me a vivid example of what I had heard so often but not believed: investing in your own health is one of the best ways to increase the value you generate because it helps you access your strengths. And in Gerald's case, negotiating skillfully enough that no one got hurt required that he take a daily run.

Many businesspeople dream about achieving "self-actualization," one of the highest levels on Maslow's hierarchy of needs. According to Maslow and others, self-actualization is really the cultivation of possibilities that are already inside you, much as the acorn holds the pattern for an oak tree.[9, 10] If you want to access those strengths consistently and cultivate them, you need to respect yourself enough to take care of them.

Reconnecting to your strengths over time means learning more about your gifts and values and adopting the routines that help keep you in touch with them. You do this not because you view your well-being as more important than your other responsibilities but because, like Gerald, you consider it a foundational commitment that allows you to contribute at the level of your potential.

But you know all this already, right? You already know that exercising, eating right, and getting enough sleep are good for you, that they help you think better and make better decisions. Yet it is a common complaint that many people are unable to follow through on this fundamental commitment. What stops you? Are there perhaps assumptions that investing in self-care or health is selfish or irresponsible?

What I'm proposing here is that investing in your health is not an indulgence but actually a responsibility—a necessity for you to recognize important choices, identify and respond to unhealthy pressure, and live up to your commitments.

The recent financial meltdown is evidence on a massive scale of the poor decisions that result when people at every level, in a multitude of industries, make decisions too quickly, about products that are too complex to understand, without considering the risks. Recent research into economic behavior and decision-making shows that people need time to weigh the facts and make the healthiest choice.[11] Philip Zimbardo, who has made a life study of what causes people to do harm, considers this so important that he includes references to time in two of his guidelines for avoiding unwanted negative influence: being mindful and keeping a balanced time perspective.[12]

In practice this is about building in space and time for yourself—perhaps especially when you think you can't afford to. "I know I'm going to need a retreat at least twice a year," said Andrea, a high-tech marketing manager. "And if I think I can't take the time, I *know* that's when I need it most."

Putting the Idea into Action

There are many good tools for learning more about your strengths and values and for developing the routines to support them. If you have a favorite, I encourage you to follow it now with renewed appreciation for how important it is to living up to your commitments and priorities.

To help you get started, I have included a short activity that invites you to use your own story to help you explore your strengths and values and then identify the routines that support you. Please see Activity #1: Finding the Strengths in Your Story in "Individual and Small-group Activities" at the back of the book.

You may want to take a moment now to try the activity so you can build on it as we move on to the next personal foundation.

Where to Go from Here

Reconnecting to your strengths is essentially about the very direct and tangible things you can do to feel bigger, on your own, regardless of your situation. By learning to activate your strengths and values, and by committing to routines for self-care and health, self-reflection, and learning, you immediately counteract the normal effects of unhealthy pressure, which tend to make you feel smaller, less courageous, less confident, and more isolated.

Once you have familiarized yourself with Decision Point Tool #1: Activating Your Strengths, you might take it further by finding ways to put reminders of your strengths and gifts around your work area or home, as the manufacturing manager did with the photos of his family or the HR director did with the photos of the children in Papua New Guinea. And the next time you find yourself triggered by catastrophe scenarios and threats, you might try using the Activating Your Strengths tool to see if you can get a bit of your clarity and courage back.

Second, once you have clarified more about your strengths and some of the routines that help you access them, you might try picking one or two and practicing them actively for twenty-one days—long enough to make them a habit. It may be slightly bumpy at first, but the habits pay off as you continue them.

Amazingly enough, these relatively simple actions can start you on the reinforcing loop of redefining the game and making positive plays—because you feel bigger and can bring your strengths to bear in a broader range of situations, because they telegraph your deep commitment to pursuing your own potential, because you are in a better position to see the value of investing in the other personal foundations, and because they accelerate your ability to learn from your experience. When faced with difficult situations, taking these actions gives you the energy to move from defensive, reactive responses to proactive, creative ones.

As you feel bigger, you are more able to see and accept the natural flaws, weaknesses, and contradictions in yourself and your organizations, without viewing them necessarily as wholesale indictments—which is why I had us start with *reconnect to your strengths* before anything else.

In the next chapter, "See the Larger Field," we explore the hidden options that become clearer when you take a closer look at the unhealthy pressure you face.

KEY CONCEPTS

- **Reconnect to your strengths** This refers to proactively cultivating and activating the core gifts and values that make you who you are, that allow you to face reality and make the best of whatever situation you are in.

  In the moment you do this by reconnecting with whatever helps you access that resourceful state where you can tap your courage, creativity, and clarity.

Over time you cultivate this foundation by learning more about your strengths and values and adopting routines that help keep you in touch with them.

- **Decision Point Tool #1: Activating Your Strengths** This short process helps you tap your equivalent of the roller-coaster ride and activate your strengths whenever and wherever you need them.
- **Activity #1: Finding the Strengths in Your Story** This activity invites you to use your own story to help you explore your strengths and values and then identify the routines that support you. (See "Individual and Small-group Activities" at the back of the book.)

REFLECTION QUESTIONS

- When was the last time someone commented on a gift or strength of yours? Was it about a quality you value in yourself, or perhaps something you take for granted? What other gifts or talents might others appreciate about you that you undervalue?
- What's your theory about people who consistently have time for self-rejuvenation and how they find the time? How does it pay off for them?
- What's your natural way of making transitions in personal habits? Do you do better going "cold turkey," or do you prefer a gradual change? How might you use that as you adopt these routines for keeping in touch with your strengths?

6

See the Larger Field

In my early career, my nickname was 'body bag,'" said Tom, the former division head of a global snack food company who now ran a small specialty food company. "I gave a speech one time about sending our competition home in body bags, so the nickname stuck. I grew up as a competitive athlete, and everything was competition to me. Sales was about 'bringing home scalps.' I could count it; I could understand it, and it was very simple. As long as we were selling more product every day, we were doing what we were supposed to do—so 'don't bother me or confuse me with the facts' was my attitude."

Tom grew up working for this company, following in his father's and his uncle's footsteps, working every job, from the factory line to sales to the delivery trucks. As he moved out of sales into positions of greater responsibility, he became part of articulating the company's vision, inspiring his teams to greater ambition and growth. "Sure, there were critics of what we were selling," he explained, "but they seemed both irrelevant and clueless, with their exaggerated claims that our products were contributing to obesity, especially in children. We had convinced ourselves that our products offered 'one of life's simple pleasures'; that was all."

Then one day Tom and his wife were talking after work, and she challenged his simplistic framing of the issue. "She is a rigorously honest person," he explained, "and one night she said, 'Do whatever you want to do, but don't do it in an asleep fashion. Recognize your role and that you have a responsibility to yourself and to the world. Don't kid yourself. It ain't one of 'life's simple pleasures.'"

Apparently, Tom's wife had often been able to point out things he had missed, and she was able to cut to the core of the situation—so he listened to her. As he described it:

> Something awoke in me at that moment. I began to realize she was right, and part of me had been aware that there was more going on here all along. Our products were offered in schools where there were few other choices, and serving sizes had increased to ridiculous excess. A huge amount of our business was superheavy users who were eating eight high-sugar snacks a day, and the long-term effects of that much sugar...; the evidence shows increasing obesity and diabetes, and our products were probably a significant cause. At a minimum we needed to investigate what our obligation was in this situation.

From that point on, Tom began engaging his direct reports in crafting a new vision for the organization—a vision that included healthier options, environmental responsibility, and accountability to the communities they affected globally. "I couldn't go along the same way anymore. So I focused on my role as a leader, creating space for people to be more innovative, to change the culture, to engage in more corporate social responsibility," he said.

Curious about his transformation, I asked him, "Why was it so hard for you to see this larger field until your wife raised the issue?"

"Cognitive dissonance," he replied immediately. "You just can't hold two conflicting thoughts at one time in your head. It's *very* uncomfortable. So most of us just keep telling ourselves, *It's fine. It's fine. There's no problem.* But once you see it, it's really hard to go back to sleep. You can, but it's hard."

What It Means to See the Larger Field

Thus far, I have argued that developing your ability to take a larger perspective is the key to redefining the game. But that risks being a platitude if we don't get more specific about what you actually do when you take off the blinders that distort everyday perception.

In a general sense, taking a broader perspective is like learning to see more of what's happening in a high-stakes competition like the Olympics—on the playing field and beyond. With a narrow view, you might be overwhelmed by the 300-pound wrestler barreling across the mat at you or the downhill skier whizzing by your left shoulder. But as you learn to see more, you begin to see your opponents' strengths and weaknesses, you learn to predict and rely on your teammates, and you are more likely to be able to spot openings for taking the lead. Going further, you might recognize the tension between countries and the merciless pressure on all the athletes to make a good showing on their nations' behalf. And even more broadly, you may appreciate that the countries' governments; the coaches, support teams, vendors, representatives, and fans; the host city and the host nation—all are intensely engaged in a common process of building ties that surpass and encompass national borders.

The challenge with achieving this broader perspective is that, like Tom, every one of us narrows our vision all the time, tuning out vast amounts of information to make life manageable. When you are committed to a goal or metric, it is natural to focus most of your attention on the scoreboard and what will rack up points. Having a few key metrics is good for helping you cut through trivial complications to get to what matters. They create a map from where you are to where you want to go.

Yet when you start mistaking the map for the actual territory, you are in trouble.[1] If you have this misconception, when something unexpected comes along you may tell yourself, *We'll think about that later* or *We'll cross that bridge when we come to it,* when what you are tuning out may represent important risks, unintended consequences, or opportunities. "I used to think the memo *was* the reality," said Gary, the manufacturing CFO. "Now I see what a false assumption that is. Still I've known plenty of CEOs who insisted everyone drink the Kool-Aid and substituted illusions for leadership."

Being open to new information is also the only way to really take responsibility. Indeed, it is hard to imagine living with integrity without this effort to stay alert. "The spirit of honesty goes far beyond not lying—it means acting on full awareness. So for me, the golden rule is *Be interested,*" said a director of software engineering who was committed to continually learning how his actions affected those around him, inside his organization and beyond. According to one author, integrity in the Taoist philosophy can be understood as a "right relationship" with reality, and its Chinese character includes figures indicating seeing, caring, *and* action.[2]

This is why the most basic commitment of redefining the game has to do with the willingness to see clearly, to continually take off the blinders that protect your (and my) ego but hide problems and opportunities. Seeing the larger field means recognizing the ways that your work is not a game but real life. In that sense redefining the game means engaging more of reality and what gets discounted or dismissed in treating it like a game, as Tom did above. You look beyond the official metrics and scoreboard to what is going on off the field, with customers, suppliers, employees, shareholders, and other stakeholders in your business.

In the moment, this means "questioning the deal" when you are pressed to compromise, using your own dissonance as a signal to pay attention and think through your choices from a broad perspective.

Over time seeing the larger field means an ongoing commitment to recognize the inherent tensions in your business or role and to identify opportunities to redefine the game or pursue a professional quest.

Seeing the Larger Field in the Moment

Besides the general recognition that you should watch out for the compromise trap, what else becomes clear when you take a broader perspective on your work?

Seeing more of the field makes it easier to recognize choice points and suggests several specific ways to "question the deal" when you are being pressured.

As Tom found, there are very rarely any flashing lights to signal an unhealthy compromise. It isn't often something you actually choose; you're just focused on something else, and it slips by.

So the first step in seeing the larger field in the moment is to improve your ability to recognize choice points.

The single best way to do this is to accept that unhealthy pressure is very common and to have an understanding attitude about it—toward yourself and others. Paradoxical as this may sound, it actually increases your ability to live up to your values because it becomes less threatening to acknowledge mistakes or contradictions. Conversely, a harsh puritanical approach that judges yourself or others mercilessly or rushes to accuse without humility is more likely to shut down truth-telling and self-awareness than to lead to better behavior.

This does not mean you pass off responsibility—far from it. With this lens, being responsible means a foundational commitment to altering your behavior as soon as you understand what is needed, knowing that your understanding is constantly changing. And you can fulfill that responsibility only if you make paying attention your first commitment.

For example, Jim, the carpeting sales manager, recognized the need to change in his approach as he got more data about his company's lack of commitment to its sustainability story. When I asked Jim at what point his company's failure to deliver the new product became an integrity issue for him, his answer focused on awareness as much as action. "You're responsible as soon as you know," he replied quickly. Then he hesitated, and we both thought hard for a moment. "I'd have to revise that," he added. "It's too easy to push the information away when you don't want to hear. You're responsible as soon as you *should* have known."

Then, once you recognize a choice point, you have the chance to weigh out consciously whether or not you want to accept the current path or redefine your options.

Putting the Idea into Action

One way to think about unhealthy pressure is that you are being offered an explicit or implicit "deal." If you can recognize the choice point when the offer is made, you can "question the deal" to see if it is a healthy one or if it will ultimately deplete you.

Decision Point Tool #2: Questioning the Deal is a quick checklist designed to help you think through both the surface factors and the hidden factors as you contemplate a compromise. (This is the second of six tools that are available as a download; see "Online Resources" at the back of the book.)

DECISION POINT TOOL #2

Questioning the Deal

This simple thought process will help you distinguish between healthy and unhealthy compromises, weighing what you could be giving up, what you expect to gain, and any hidden costs of compromise.

☐ **What am I being asked to do or go along with?**

What is this situation really about—on the surface and in terms of the hidden factors at play?

ON THE SURFACE	*HIDDEN FACTORS*
______________________	______________________
______________________	______________________

☐ **What do I have to gain?**

What am I being offered, on the surface or implicitly? What negatives might I expect to avoid by making this compromise? (Avoiding pain counts as a gain too.) How important/valuable are those gains in terms of my core values? How credible is the offer or my expected gain, given everything I know now?

ON THE SURFACE	*HIDDEN FACTORS*
______________________	______________________
______________________	______________________

☐ **What would I be giving up?**

What need, want, interest, commitment, or value would I be giving up or relaxing if I went along with this compromise? How important/valuable is that in terms of my core values (for example, ego versus keeping a promise)? Are there less obvious factors I would be giving up or putting at risk, as well?

Consider basic moral reasoning as you answer:

- Consequences: Who is affected or harmed? By how much?
- Rights: Whose rights might be infringed? Is this within my/our legitimate authority?
- Duties: What are my/our duties and obligations in this situation?
- Values: Is this true to what I consider my core values or my character?
- Care: What are the core relationships here, and what is my/our duty of care toward them?

ON THE SURFACE	*HIDDEN FACTORS*
____________	____________
____________	____________

☐ **What are the hidden "costs of compromise"?**

Beyond what I would be giving up directly, what else might I have to lose by making this compromise? How will I feel in the long run about this?

Consider the costs of compromise:

- Greater internal stress
- Tuning out (acclimatizing over time)
- Escalating commitment to prove I was right
- Increasing need for external validation
- Setting precedents with bullies
- Loss of reputation/trust
- Neglecting a real business need

ON THE SURFACE	*HIDDEN FACTORS*
____________	____________
____________	____________

☐ **Is this a healthy compromise?**

Does this amount to giving up something less important for something more important, especially when I consider the hidden costs of compromise? Do I need to look for a better alternative?

Consider drawing a graph to weigh out your choice, listing on the right your expected gains and on the left what you would be giving up and the hidden costs of compromise. This should not be a strict quantitative exercise but a thought process to help you think through each element carefully. (An example of such a graph is shown in figure 6-2.)

ON THE SURFACE	*HIDDEN FACTORS*
____________________	____________________
____________________	____________________

If you can train yourself to walk through these five questions, you will avoid being blindsided into unhealthy compromises because you will see more of the field and you will increase your ability to recognize and commit to healthy ones.

In particular, when you stop and think about what you would be giving up, you can sort out whether the decision is an ego issue or truly involves crossing a line. This is also where moral reasoning becomes most important. Though your gut can tell you a lot, everyone can improve by becoming more aware of the ways each of their actions affects others. So, as you consider what you would be giving up by playing along, you might want to take a closer look at the basics of moral reasoning. (See figure 6-1.)

When you then consider the costs of compromise, you clarify what is at stake. Many people do this with a simple newspaper test—imagining your actions on the front page of your hometown paper or the *Wall Street Journal*—which is a good start. I would

Figure 6-1 Basics of Moral Reasoning

Ethicists generally refer to five or six different criteria when weighing the moral reasons for or against an action.[3] Among these are:

- **Consequences** Who is affected or harmed? How much?
- **Rights** Whose rights might be infringed? Is this within my/our legitimate authority?
- **Duties and obligations** What are my/our duties and obligations in this situation?
- **Values and character** Is this true to what I consider my core values or my character?
- **Care** What are the core relationships here, and what is my/our duty of care toward them?

encourage you to think beyond that, however, to all the hidden costs of compromise we discussed in chapter 2 and which I've included in Decision Point Tool #2.

Finally, when you consider what you are being offered, you want to consider not only obvious gains but also negative outcomes you hope to avoid and how credible that gain or risk is. You don't want to compromise to avoid catastrophes that aren't going to happen or minor discomforts that don't count in the long run. For example, Jose Gomez thought he just couldn't bear admitting a mistake and compromised to avoid that. But how bad would it really have been, especially if he did it skillfully?

In addition, you don't want to compromise to maintain a status quo that is no longer in the cards. For example, Deborah, the bank loan officer pressed to make unsound loans, initially believed she would be giving up her own and her team's job security by pushing back, which made it a very hard choice. Yet six months after she quit (rather than make the loans), the bank was sold and her team was dismantled anyway due to economic pressures. No amount of capitulation was going to achieve the security she had imagined.

Once you have explored each of these elements, you are ready to make an honest assessment of whether it amounts to giving up something less important for something more important and whether you are better off looking for an alternative. You might consider actually sketching this out as the costs of compromise versus the gains. For example, the accompanying graph shows how the "deal" might have weighed out for the young product manager who held a "failure party" rather than build a product that took advantage of customer loyalty. Clearly, this was not a healthy compromise for him. (See figure 6-2.)

Of course, you don't want to take these too literally, as in a cost/benefit analysis where you can strictly quantify each item. Think of it more as a weighing process to help you think carefully about the things that are easily discounted or dismissed because they are not vivid and dramatic right in front of you.*

Now that you are clear about whether the deal makes sense, you are ready to explore whether there is a way to help something better happen—for you and the other. We explore this in chapter 7, "Define a Worthy Enough Win."

---

*Now, you may be asking yourself, *Does this mean I am really free to go ahead with any compromise if the benefit outweighs the cost to me?* Put simply, I think you'll find that pursuing what you really want in the long run and with a broad perspective will lead you to avoid actions that cause harm, take away others' rights, or show disrespect for what others consider important. As experts in positive psychology remind us, developing your character is satisfying in its own right, not just as a means to some future pleasure and not as a cost to your self-interest as is so often assumed. Otherwise, why would it be so painful to betray your values? In practice this means there are certain things you won't do because the cost is just too high. For example, barring very extreme circumstances and sometimes not even then, it is almost inconceivable that lying, violence, cheating, fraud, and deceitful or illegal practices represent a healthy compromise. For more on this subject, please see Jonathan Haidt, *The Happiness Hypothesis: Finding Modern Truth in Ancient Wisdom* (New York: Basic Books, 2006).

Figure 6-2 Sample "Questioning the Deal" Outcome

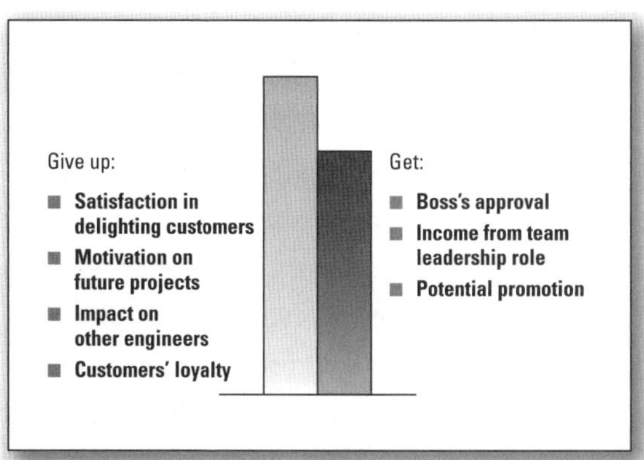

But first, let's examine what it looks like to see the larger field over time.

Seeing the Larger Field over Time

Decision Point Tool #2 allows you to respond to unhealthy pressure when it arises in the moment, but what if you could *predict* it? Better yet, what if you could turn those predictable tensions into opportunities for a professional quest?

Every business confronts inherent tensions due to the normal pressure of limited resources, attention, or other constraints. Where those tensions become unhealthy pressure to compromise is often at the intersection of what is measured, visible, and rewarded and what is important but hard to measure, less visible, or intangible (and so not explicitly rewarded).

Because the metrics used to gauge organizational performance are always partial approximations of what is really going on, companies must rely on individuals to use their judgment and "hold the line" on principles or commitments that are less visible but important in the long run. For example, many salespeople are compensated based on revenue, which means they receive their commission whether or not the product is sold at a profitable price. In companies with this arrangement, leaders have to trust the salespeople to avoid unnecessary discounting.

The unmeasured but important factors that affect long-term health are usually much harder to see and weigh in decisions because they are intangible, remote, or affected slowly over time, like the rating agencies' quality standards or the long-term health consequences of an unsafe product. And even when a company does attempt to measure these factors or a profession requires an oath or a certification, it still relies on individuals to live up to the substance of the measure rather than just try to game the numbers.[4]

So, if you want to predict likely hotspots for unhealthy pressure in any business, industry, or role, simply ask yourself: *What is important but difficult to see or measure because it is intangible, remote, or delayed?* This is where you will find the most inherent tension, as the pressure to perform in more measurable and immediate ways causes these less visible factors to be underweighted or forgotten.

Interestingly, these are often exactly the areas in which others have to trust you or your business (at least in the short run). For example, consumers have to rely on restaurants to serve safe food, employees have to depend on their bosses when they promise future promotions for extra work done today, leaders have to depend on their employees to do honest work, and shareholders have to depend on management to keep the books honestly.

Knowing that these are exactly the areas most likely to get short shrift under pressure, you can use your ability to predict inherent tensions to identify opportunities to redefine the game and, potentially, commit to a professional quest. I can think of two specific places you might look: raising the visibility of underweighted factors and innovating to shift the trade-offs.

Raising the visibility of underweighted factors The inherent tension in a business between what is more visible and what is less visible often mirrors the tension between extracting value and creating value. Engaging employees, providing value to customers, investing in the business for long-term shareholder value—all are harder to measure than profit this quarter, yet they drive profits down the road. You can help the business better weigh the trade-offs by elevating the visibility of the factors that tend to get short shrift. This is what Mary did brilliantly when she arranged for additional market research on the ill-conceived training product so that the senior executives had the information they needed to make a better decision. When you try this tactic, the key is to not try to supersede all other concerns. A business does need cash to survive. You are trying to ensure that the harder-to-measure factors get weighed accurately amid the other factors so that decisions are as rational and aligned as possible.

Innovating to shift the trade-offs A second way to redefine the game is to look for opportunities to help the business get more of both sides of a trade-off. As I said earlier, many trade-offs are false—between cost and quality, cost and speed, or revenue and customer service. By focusing on both/and rather than on either/or, you can help the business engage at a higher level. For example, when Bill worked in research and development to reduce emissions in the auto industry, he was looking for ways to comply with government regulations *and* achieve reasonable costs. A significant advantage of taking this approach is that you make yourself an ally to those you differ with by showing that you respect their concerns and by helping reduce the costs of doing the right thing.[5]

Though ethical decision-making does not always lead to a measurable business payoff, the type of thinking that focuses on shifting trade-offs rather than crossing an ethical line seems awfully similar to the creative, barrier-breaking approach needed for innovation in general. So, developing that capacity is not likely to hurt. In fact, the more I explore this territory, the more it seems that the opposite of playing along is striving to create real value.

Putting the Idea into Action

Seeing the larger field over time means an ongoing commitment to recognize the inherent tensions in your business or role and to identify opportunities to redefine the game or pursue a professional quest to help the business or role evolve.

To help you uncover the inherent tensions and opportunities in your situation, you may want to walk through Activity #2: Redefining-the-game Opportunity Map in "Individual and Small-group Activities" at the back of the book.

Or, you might just get out and engage in the world with the people and the places that have to trust your business, that depend on you and it—and then see what new commitments and opportunities become clear. For example, Derek, the dentist I mentioned earlier, intentionally took public transportation and volunteered in the community to keep his ego in check and to understand where his help was needed. As he told me, "The question is: how do you come into contact so you *can* care for other people? If we are not exposed to others in our daily lives, it becomes a fundamental barrier—and we don't even know how we could really make a difference."

Where to Go from Here

Dwight D. Eisenhower once said, "If a problem cannot be solved, enlarge it."[6] In this chapter, by learning a way to intentionally and methodically perceive the larger field, you have become familiar with a basic stance that can dramatically improve the quality of your decisions both personally and professionally. "I try to put a higher penalty on delusion than failure," said Gary, the CFO, when he realized how putting on blinders was affecting the quality of his decisions. "I used to be the answer man. Now I've learned to listen. It is amazing what you learn when you open your mind."

Seeing the larger field requires more alertness and flexibility, but you spend less time in survival mode, less time feeling indebted. As Sven, a former consumer products CEO described it, "If you feel guilt, then you feel victimized, trapped, dependent on the system...and less free to speak up. By telling the truth, you learn to accept yourself. If you accept yourself, you can stand up." This is the payoff for engaging more of reality.

Once you begin expanding your perspective, the next step is to practice tolerating dissonance without tuning out or having knee-jerk reactions. You may still have to compromise, but you will know you are compromising with reality rather than capitulating to someone or something in hopes of avoiding discomfort.

Learn to connect the dots, knowing you will revise your map again and again. Allow yourself to study where you can take action that will make the most difference—in the moment or over time. Then you will be able to define a worthy enough win, as we explore in the next chapter.

KEY CONCEPTS

- **See the larger field** The most basic commitment of redefining the game has to do with the willingness to see clearly, to continually take off the blinders that protect the ego but hide problems and opportunities. Seeing the larger field means recognizing the ways that your work is not a game but real life and attempting to engage and address more of that reality. The best way to do this is to have an understanding yet responsible attitude about human weaknesses so that you are more likely to recognize issues and choice points rather than tune them out.

In the moment you act on this by "questioning the deal" when you are pressed to compromise, using your own dissonance as a signal to pay attention and think through your choices from a broad perspective.

Over time you cultivate this ability by making an ongoing commitment to recognize the inherent tensions in your business, role, or industry and to identify opportunities to redefine the game to help the business, role, or industry evolve.

- **Decision Point Tool #2: Questioning the Deal** This checklist is designed to help you think through both the surface factors and the hidden factors to see whether a compromise is healthy.
- **Activity #2: Redefining-the-game Opportunity Map** This activity helps you uncover the inherent tensions and opportunities for redefining the game or pursuing a professional quest in your business, role, or industry. (See "Individual and Small-group Activities" at the back of the book.)

REFLECTION QUESTIONS

- When are you proudest of what your industry, organization, or product contributes to the larger world? What experiences highlight that contribution most powerfully? (You might consider stories from customers, articles in the news, or seeing a physical facility.) What are the criticisms of your industry, organization, or product? What makes it hardest to take this criticism seriously? What would you have to know for it be convincing?
- Think about what concerns you most about what is going on in the world—looking at it from the perspective of a parent, grandparent, citizen, leader, member of a community, or human being. What seems to deserve the most attention? How do those concerns affect your civic and community involvements? How do they relate to your choices at work?

7

Define a Worthy Enough Win

I thought I was being petty and territorial," said the technical program manager for a large government technology project. "They kept cutting my budget, and I found myself in argument after argument. I wasn't absolutely sure why I was making such a fuss, but some part of me just wouldn't let it go. It bugged me that they kept cutting systems without a detailed review. Yet my 'no' had come across more as resistance than as a truly effective limit." The manager paused for a moment and looked around. He was standing in a large ballroom filled with other workshop participants: managers, executives, and professionals who shared his challenge with saying no. "But now I get it," he continued. "Though I didn't realize it at first, the reason I want to say no to this sort of cut is not because I am trying to build my empire or protect my turf. I am really, seriously concerned about program safety. Without a detailed review of the impact of these cuts, we have no idea what we are compromising, and that could end up being disastrous." His manner changed, his back straightening a bit. "Knowing there's that much at stake, I feel much stronger and clearer about what I need to do."

What It Means to Define a Worthy Enough Win

The third personal foundation supporting your ability to redefine the game is *defining a worthy enough win,* which means committing to an outcome, purpose, mission, or quest that is important enough to give you a reason for courage and a guide to what is worth doing.

One of the most critical elements of redefining the game is knowing and staying in touch with what you are redefining the game *for.* Because you choose what you consider a win in any situation, for what are you going to aim? At what level do you want to engage? Having a worthy enough win—one that feels important enough to inspire your courage and passion—is a crucial counterweight to the instinct to play along. It lifts you out of the traps of fear or ego and focuses your attention on what really needs doing. With a valid purpose, you find that your life immediately takes on a greater sense of meaning and relevance and you are less focused on questions about your own legitimacy or competence.

Your "win" is simply your aim or intent in a given context. In a specific moment, say under pressure to compromise, your worthy enough win is whatever is important enough to be a reason for courage and the basis for a constructive response. Over time, you define a worthy enough win by committing to a professional mission or quest—a purpose or passion that becomes an organizing focus for your career.

Defining a Worthy Enough Win in the Moment

When you consciously look at the higher, more important values involved in a situation, you give yourself a reason for courage. You see that your voice is needed. Otherwise, without a worthwhile reason to step forward, the dictates of your conscience can seem petty, trivial, or selfish, as the technical program manager felt before he realized the link to program safety.

The quickest and easiest way to access courage is to focus on who or what needs your help. The moment you focus on something intrinsically worthwhile—helping someone else, serving something larger than yourself, creating something of value—your fear recedes and you feel more engaged and courageous. "It just doesn't *feel* like risk when you feel right about it," said Andrea, the marketing manager.

With this attitude any dangers or risks are put in the context of something that matters more, which is why redefining the game opens up more options. Ambrose Bierce once said, "Courage means recognizing there is something more important than fear."[1] When you take the time to connect the dots between a business decision and its longer-term, more remote impacts, you will find that your choices suddenly become much clearer.

Even better, by its very nature a worthy enough win is more likely to engage others.

One of the most difficult aspects of pushing back is that others tend to view it as serving your own self-interest, out of a desire for self-aggrandizement, comfort, or convenience. When that happens they don't think it's courage; they think it's an attack and feel justified in retaliating. But if your efforts are honestly for something worthwhile, it's more likely they will respond constructively to your proposals.

For example, Stephanie was an HR business partner supporting an IT department going through a major turnaround effort. As time went on, she found herself increasingly in a bind. The leaders had been talking about change but not doing much in practice. Even the senior VP went back and forth week to week. Stephanie began to suspect she had been touting a program that was destined to die on the vine, so she decided to confront it gently but directly.

"I was sitting in a meeting, hearing the leaders say they were fully on board with the need to change. It all rang false." About halfway through the meeting, she stood up, took off her badge, and laid it quietly in the center of the conference room table. "We've been talking about this change for a long time now. I think we all know it is needed. But personally, I see and sense negative behavior continuing when we leave the room. I don't want to continue talking the talk if we aren't going to walk the walk." Everyone was startled and silent, staring at her badge there in the center of the table. When they began again, the conversation shifted to be more real and honest. From then on leaders would refer to Stephanie's example when they were tempted to sidestep an issue. Even working in a completely separate part of the organization, I heard how the story of Stephanie's "laying her badge on the table" inspired other leaders. (I also found out later that she had approached her boss and asked whether her own actions might have been contributing to the IT team's inaction and whether removing her from the team might have helped.)

This was not an isolated event for Stephanie. She had been called on to handle the most challenging cases of fraud, harassment, misconduct, and workplace violence, often fraught with conflict and difficult emotions, for three different Fortune 500 companies. When I asked her how she was able to handle these situations and take such risks, she described the power of a foundational sense of core purpose, which for her revolves around valuing diversity and treating people with respect. Her approach is to watch a situation carefully for a time, then step in to engage where needed. "Though I'm a very quiet person," she explained, "I've learned over the years to be more courageous. Now I gravitate *toward* the line, *toward* the challenge, instead of avoiding it. I know that by engaging conflict directly, with good intent, something is going to shift."

As Stephanie's story shows, when your intentions are set on something worthwhile, you have far more freedom to differ, initiate, and even oppose, with much less risk of retaliation. According to William Ury, author of *The Power of a Positive No*, the secret to a positive *no* is to first be clear about your underlying *yes.*[2] When you are clear about that, you find a source of personal strength and increase the chances of engaging others constructively, at a higher level. This is why it worked for Stephanie to challenge the team, and it worked when Andrew approached his boss about long hours and weekends, not just on his own behalf but also for his boss's benefit. Indeed, this is the heart of what it means to be a positive force rather than just go along or rebel. You are redefining the game in a way that invites others to join you in pursuing something better.

Putting the Idea into Action

When you are faced with unhealthy pressure in a specific situation, you define a worthy enough win by looking for what is important enough to be a reason for courage. You can then use that touchstone to frame a both/and question, which provides a goal for your efforts, focusing your creativity and guiding your actions.

As you recall, when you are engaging at a higher level you do not automatically accept either/or trade-offs as given but view the tension between opposing goals as part of the search for a new answer. When you ask yourself a question that includes *both* sides of the tension or compromise, you activate your natural creativity and open doors for collaboration. For example, if you have been compromising on spending time with your family to provide for them financially, you might ask yourself, *How can I provide for my family* and *have enough time to spend with them?* Or, at an organizational level, salespeople who feel pressed to lie to win sales might ask, *How can we win more customers* and *be honest in the process?*

Decision Point Tool #3: Defining Your Worthy Enough Win is a quick worksheet to walk you through the process of identifying a reason for courage and a both/and question to provide a goal as you move into action. It is best if you have already done Decision Point Tool #2: Questioning the Deal; but even if you haven't, this can help you respond constructively and courageously under pressure. (Decision Point Tool #3 is the third of six tools that are available as a download; see "Online Resources" at the back of the book.)

DECISION POINT TOOL #3

Defining Your Worthy Enough Win

You can use these two questions whenever you are under pressure and want to make sure you are focused on a worthy enough win.

- ☐ **What is important enough here to be a reason for courage?**

  What really matters to me here and why? What is important but not necessarily getting enough attention? What are the potential consequences and risks in this situation? Who could be harmed? What is possible if we act wisely?

- ☐ **What's the both/and question?**

  Use your answer to the first question to frame a new question where one side is your reason for courage and the other side is the source of the pressure to compromise. For example: *How can we have more of x* and *y? How can we effectively weigh long-term important factors* and *short-term urgent drivers in our decision-making? How can we protect important values* and *minimize costs?*

  Your both/and question becomes your worthy enough win, your goal as you move into action.

To answer the first question, consider what is really at stake in the situation, what it means, and what might be the consequences for those involved. (You might want to revisit your answer to "What would I be giving up?" in Decision Point Tool #2 in chapter 6.) Try to get a vivid, firsthand understanding of the potential consequences and any symptoms that are showing up now, internally and externally. Check your assumptions wherever possible.

Whatever might be lost in a situation becomes the heart of the win—what needs to be protected or advanced by your courageous action. For example, the technical program manager identified program safety as what was really at stake in the budget cuts, just as Julia had identified the new product launches that were at risk. For Stephanie, at stake was her own credibility as well as the opportunity for the change program to achieve its real potential. These are typically those less visible factors we discussed in chapter 6 that are underweighted or forgotten in making decisions.

You need not have a solution in place when you frame a both/and question based on this reason for courage; the question is just a focal point for finding and inventing solutions, and it helps reconcile conflicting interests along the way. For example, a company that asks, "How can we save money *and* increase customer satisfaction?" is bound to find new options that reduce the need to trade off one for the other and thus the need to compromise.

As you will see in chapter 9, "Make Positive Plays," your both/and question can help you frame a counteroffer if you must set limits or say no, giving you a way to offer others something better when they press you into an unhealthy compromise. It also gives you a direct way to take action yourself because you can use it to guide your efforts to be creative or improve processes without going overboard in one direction or the other.

Defining a Worthy Enough Win over Time

Over time defining a worthy enough win is about exploring your unique professional quest—the outcome, purpose, or mission that serves as a focal point for what you want to do with whatever degrees of freedom you have in your life as well as an organizing focus for your career.

The dictionary defines *quest* as "a search or pursuit made in order to find or obtain something" or "an adventurous expedition undertaken by a knight or knights to secure or achieve something," as in the quest for the Holy Grail.[3] Building on this, I have defined a quest as the pursuit of a worthwhile challenge with whatever degrees of freedom you have, in a practical way that allows you to thrive in the process.

A certain kind of energy becomes available when you discover something about which you are truly passionate. "I am a man on fire. It was being convinced of an opportunity that was motivating," said Walt, a packaging director who is pioneering approaches that use less waste. Steven Covey describes this power in *The Seven Habits of Highly Effective People,* and there are even elements of it in Mihaly Csikszentmihalyi's *Flow.*[4, 5]

For many people, though, committing to something as idealistic as a quest seems like a luxury, something you do once you have "made it." It may seem a bit vulnerable, even a little unprofessional, to care about something that much. This is such a deeply ingrained assumption that books about personal purpose and those about ethics seem on the surface to be in two completely separate categories. Yet this perceived separation is based on a very limited view of values, as strictly as guardrails to keep you in bounds rather than also serving as guides to what is worth doing, what goals are important to achieve, and what is intrinsically worthwhile to you.

From this point of view, far from being a luxury, purpose actually unlocks strength.

When you know you are engaged in a meaningful quest, you gain the immediate rewards of doing something you value for itself. For example, Josh, a young quality engineer who works for a much-admired medical devices company during the day, is also setting up a social venture in his spare time. Like Walt, the "man on fire" above, he is overflowing with ideas and enthusiasm. "I just have a lot of energy. I get jazzed about this stuff," he explained. "My friends were telling me one day that I shouldn't put so much effort into it because it might not pay off. My answer was: 'Who cares? So I find out I've wasted my time. Even if just my family uses this program, we'll be able to build an entire school! Just with four of us! How can that be anything other than a win?'" Notice he didn't say he'd get rich, earn fame, learn a new skill, or add to his résumé. It was just satisfying to know he was making a difference somewhere, potentially a big one if it did take off.

Being fully engaged in a meaningful pursuit also means you are much less susceptible to unhealthy pressure. According to Peter Block, this is *the* antidote to fear and dependence on external events, putting you back in charge of your own choices.[6]

"You *need* a mission. It becomes life and death on the little things if you have no mission," said Beth, a process excellence manager for a large consumer software company, who focuses on how experiences at work ripple out into civil society. "Having it gives me a different yardstick to measure the risks and issues against." When I asked her for an example, she told me this story:

> Recently, I proposed an event where each new product development team could share what they were working on and what they were learning. People were very skeptical, including my boss. "What's it going to look like? What value are we going to get?" they asked. So I put in a lot of time coaching each team about how to get ready and

> kept reassuring them it would be worth the work. Well, it happened the other night and it was *phenomenally* successful! People went, "Wow, wow, wow! We're connecting all the rest of this work with our own!" My boss said, "I didn't get it, but you showed me, and now I see the connection." This is where the action is for me. This is where we can push the frontier on how people make use of their collective intelligence, which is why I went into process improvement in the first place. To the extent that we can clear away the crap that gets in the way of getting the work done, as well as connecting with each other, then, isn't that a sort of practice for democracy?

As you can see, Beth's sense of a quest serves as a guide for what is worth doing, an ongoing focal point for learning, not just a set of rules about what *not* to do. To use Bill George's concept, it is the "true north" by which you navigate.[7] As a software engineering director put it, "Human beings tend to squabble if we don't have something higher that we're pursuing."

The range of possible professional quests is infinite. Here are just a few of the passions people have told me about:

- What if shared decision-making at work could serve as practice for a more active democracy?
- How can we build relationships of mutual respect in a hierarchy?
- How can I help surface "more of the truth" in organizational decision-making?
- What if software could increase the level of entrepreneurship around the world?
- How can we help business really become self-regulating?
- How do we design products that are infinitely recyclable?
- What sort of environments actually accelerate healing?

You will notice that all of these are phrased as questions. This fits the nature of a true quest—that it is uncertain, more of a question than an answer (indeed the words *quest* and *question* share the same root[8]). It is something so meaningful it is worth pursuing despite its uncertainty.

Paradoxically, this sort of quest is far more sustainable than willpower. It does not require that you self-sacrifice to the point of martyrdom but allows for your tangible needs and responsibilities as well. It is simply what you want to do with any spare energy or capacity you have—which will vary over time.

In fact, if you are pursuing what really matters most to you, it is likely to be complex and long-term, like Bill's contribution to the 150-year project of achieving fully sustainable fuel. The great thinker Reinhold Niebuhr once said, "Nothing that is worth doing can be achieved in a lifetime."[9] Pretending that the challenge isn't there is what makes a mission seem sappy or naive. But if you both recognize the challenge *and* decide, *Yes, I see the reality, and I still want to contribute to something better than that,* you can tap into the real power of personal purpose—and sometimes inspire others to do the same.

When you make that sort of open-eyed commitment, your goals and needs become less frenzied or driven because you are not using them as a vehicle for proving anything. As one former investment banker explained, "I know the man I want to be—the father, the leader, the husband—and I've decided I am going to be that person *today.* I don't have to wait until I am independently wealthy to do it. It's not a question of wealth."

According to Viktor Frankl, the noted psychotherapist who wrote about his experiences in the concentration camps in Germany and developed an entire school of therapy based on the human drive for meaning, a quest or mission cannot be about just self-expression; there has to be some sort of pull from outside you, something you are answering for in your life, a connection to what is needed in the world around you. He wrote, "It has to be unique, single, something only we can fulfill. For one man, it was a child who was waiting for him, for a scientist, it was a series of books that only he could complete."[10]

For this reason pursuing a professional quest does not have to look different on the surface. Your existing goals may have the seeds of a meaningful pursuit buried in them if you dig a little deeper.

For example, Kimberly had made a commitment to achieve a vice president title before she turned forty. But in our private conversations, she expressed some hesitation: "It feels a little greedy and shallow. I don't know why it's so important to me." Still, as we talked further, it turned out that she had made that promise to herself because her mother had never been able to break through a certain glass ceiling in her career. So for Kimberly achieving that goal would mean a significant symbolic breakthrough on behalf of women in the workforce. Realizing this, the goal took on a whole new meaning for her.

Organizations can also pursue quests, making it their mission or purpose to step up to a particular need or challenge in the world. More and more values-based businesses are explicitly committing to this level of engagement, and their actions are redefining the game in many industries. To find opportunities for quests in your field, you might take a look back at the Redefining-the-game Opportunity Map discussed in chapter 6.

Putting the Idea into Action

Defining a worthy enough win over time means exploring or reconnecting with your unique professional quest: the independent outcome, purpose, or mission that unlocks your strength because it guides you to what is really worth doing.

There are many worthwhile programs and books to help you uncover a sense of purpose. Activity #3: Discovering Your Professional Quest leans toward finding one that links your unique character to the particular situation and opportunities around you because this tends to make your efforts more sustainable (see "Individual and Small-group Activities" at the back of the book).

Once you know what you are pursuing, you can use this to develop and clarify a set of professional guidelines that help you make decisions day to day.

Given that every industry has inherent tensions and the potential for unhealthy pressure, and almost every professional job involves the use of knowledge and discretionary judgment, it is important that you clarify for yourself the principles, interests, and values that will guide your professional decisions.

One of the people I most admire for his ability to do this is Jim Lehrer of the *NewsHour.* In an era when many journalists struggle with the pressure to give short shrift to serving the public interest as well as the bottom line, Lehrer and his team at the *NewsHour* have consistently stayed the course in balancing informative, well-researched stories that credit the viewers' intellect while running a successful show.

To stay clear on what he stands for, Lehrer created his own "code"—a set of guidelines that represents his commitments as a professional. (See figure 7-1.) This simple list elegantly captures the inherent tensions in the industry and provides practical, actionable guidance on where to draw the line day to day in a way that reflects the public's need to trust his reporting and his commitment to serve the public interest.

Activity #3: Discovering Your Professional Quest will also help you translate your mission into a set of professional guidelines akin to Jim Lehrer's. I encourage you to take a moment now to skim it and schedule a time to complete it soon so that you can

Figure 7-1 Jim Lehrer's Personal Work Guidelines

- Do nothing I cannot defend.
- Cover, write, and present every story with the care I would want if the story were about me.
- Assume there is at least one other side or version to every story.
- Assume the viewer is as smart and as caring and as good a person as I am.
- Assume the same about all people on whom I report.
- Assume personal lives are a private matter until a legitimate turn in the story absolutely mandates otherwise.
- Carefully separate opinion and analysis from straight news stories and clearly label everything.
- Do not use anonymous sources or blind quotes except on rare and monumental occasions. No one should ever be allowed to attack another anonymously.
- And finally, finally I am not in the entertainment business.

Used with permission.

get the satisfaction that comes with that greater sense of personal alignment (see "Individual and Small-group Activities" at the back of the book).

Where to Go from Here

Professional quests serve as a sort of "learning edge," the junction between what is comfortable and what is important but slightly risky. You don't want to shoot too far out or play it too safe. For example, a consultant who worked with very senior leadership teams in several companies told me, "I find that the sense of being on a quest is a very powerful orientation. It prompts me to look for what I can do *in the midst* of all the dichotomies and how I can cultivate the conditions for others to create what they really want to create, given the realities they face. This stance naturally leads you to ask: 'What sort of compassionate challenge might make a difference?'"

Once you have your description of your professional quest, you might want to post it somewhere and let it sink in. Try it on. There is no need to rush off and make drastic changes today. In fact, just "owning" your priorities is a powerful step that may lead to greater clarity as you go through your day. You may find that your quest is something as simple as trying to help the best thing happen in the situations you encounter.

When you feel ready, you might try using it as a new lens for learning about the root causes of a larger issue. For example, Jim, the carpeting sales manager, dedicated every Saturday morning to educating himself about environmental sustainability. Second, you can try applying your professional guidelines to a few practical decisions and resolving the challenges and the clarifications that requires. That way, when you engage others, you will be more credible (and humble!). For example, in Robert Fuller's work on "rankism," the first step is to see how we ourselves engage in rankist behavior and learn to reduce it.[11]

When you take the time to define a worthy enough win, either in the moment or over time, you identify the challenges that really count for you. As one marketing executive asked, "How can you have integrity without being committed to anything?"

In a paradoxical way, this may mean reconnecting with values you have held for a long time but perhaps dismissed in an effort to fit in or get ahead. For example, at the very end of our interview Roberta, the young sales director we met in chapter 1 who had since become an HR business partner, summed up her reflections on her career in this way: "You know, Elizabeth, for a long time, I thought that the things I believed when I was young were stupid. But now I've been through everything—I'm probably going to retire next year—and I'm realizing that the values I held, the things that I believed were truths twenty years ago—they weren't stupid things. Not at all. They were real."

What a relief to be able to own those again. To be able to live your worthy enough win to its fullest, you'll want to *find your real team* so that you can cultivate relationships that give meaning to your pursuits and further reinforce that your professional quest is real, valid, and important enough to act on. We explore this in the next chapter.

KEY CONCEPTS

- **Define a worthy enough win** This means recognizing that whatever is important enough to give you a reason for courage and a sense of purpose is what unlocks your strengths. Making this commitment lifts you out of the traps of fear or ego and focuses your attention on what really needs doing, helping you weigh hard choices as you take action.

  In the moment you practice this by taking whatever might be lost or harmed in a situation and making it the win, then using a both/and question to activate your creativity. A both/and question asks how to improve both sides of a trade-off.

  Over time you put this into action by committing to a professional quest or mission that becomes a guide to what is worth doing and an organizing focus for your career, a place to contribute with whatever degrees of freedom you have.

- **Decision Point Tool #3: Defining Your Worthy Enough Win** This worksheet walks you through the process of defining your worthy enough win in a specific situation, including how to frame a both/and question.

- **Activity #3: Discovering Your Professional Quest** This activity helps you uncover the mission that links your unique character to the particular situation and opportunities around you; it then walks you through identifying professional guidelines for making day-to-day decisions based on that quest (see "Individual and Small-group Activities" at the back of the book).

REFLECTION QUESTIONS

- Think of a time when you had a reason for courage. What was the situation? How did having that reason affect your thinking and your actions? How might you intentionally *look* for a reason for courage in tough situations?
- Have you had periods in your life when you felt a sense of passion or purpose? What happened? What lessons did you learn from the experience that you might apply to sustaining a professional quest over time?
- What kinds of professional quests does your current organization naturally invite and support? Which are most needed?

8

Find Your Real Team

In August 1941, J. C. Penney, the founder of the retail giant; Lew Mobley, a senior executive at IBM; and Weyman Huckabee, a minister, met for lunch in Long Island, New York, along with eight or nine other businesspeople. Each of them had been privately troubled by the fact that they were asked so routinely to do things in their business roles that they would never do as individuals. Now, sharing their experiences and concerns over lunch, they found such valuable encouragement that they agreed to meet again the following week to provide mutual support in living their values at work.[1]

This small group continued to meet every week *for twenty-seven years* and gradually blossomed into a growing community of business and professional people dedicated to the idea of deepening their part in building spirituality into the life of the world. First called the Laymen's Movement and then the Wainwright House, this pioneering community, which included some of the most innovative and daring leaders in business at the time, offered management courses in listening, innovation, change, learning and development, and accounting approaches that aligned with the true economics of a business. This was in the 1960s, long before these were widely accepted business topics. Though the members were thoroughly human with plenty of human weaknesses, the Laymen's Movement/Wainwright House provided them enough reinforcement that they were able to stay truer to their values and sustain lifetime efforts to transform management practice within their firms and across entire industries.

One of their members was Robert Greenleaf, an executive from AT&T who crystallized many of their ideas in his writings on servant leadership—the concept that being a leader is not a trophy but a call to practice an attitude of service and stewardship. Though I knew of Greenleaf's work, I had personally never heard of the movement that inspired him, until I learned the story from Jahn Ballard, whose father had been a core member. It amazed me to discover that a small effort, initially just to provide mutual support and encouragement among a few professionals, had legitimized and reinforced the better instincts of several generations of leaders.

What It Means to Find Your Real Team

As the story of the Laymen's Movement so vividly demonstrates, one of the best ways to keep to your values is to consciously gather a support network that reinforces the person you want to be. So often, we fall into relationships haphazardly or forget that we have a choice about which ones to cultivate because they bring out the best in us. Finding your real team, the network of true allies who support the person you want to be, is one of the most direct and powerful personal foundations as you expand your ability to redefine the game because it converts what is often a source of pressure into a source of support.

Relationships often seem less important, or perhaps even a burden or distraction, when you are hyperfocused on playing along with the game. But it is closer to the truth to say that if your relationships are satisfying, it is as if you are making ongoing direct deposits to your sense of security, confidence, and courage—the very thing people tend to think playing along will get them. "True security does not come from wealth but from the strength of your relationships and your ability to access your inner creative resources," said Sven, a former consumer products CEO who had watched many colleagues let their personal selves be "colonized" by the pursuit of wealth.

Trying to do without a support system may be heroic, but it is ineffective. As we have seen, human beings are "wired" to pay attention to what their social network thinks of them. If you do not proactively choose and cultivate a network you respect, the sheer pressure of conformity will cause you to default to the culture around you—which may not include people you particularly admire, respect, or share values with. Maintaining your independence in such a setting is possible but unlikely without a group of people somewhere who "get" you.

It is your relationships that help keep you honest, so your real team has to include people who keep you real. "We need a few trusted naysayers in our lives," say the authors of *Mistakes Were Made (But Not by Me)*, "critics who are willing to puncture our protective bubble of self-justifications and yank us back to reality if we veer too far off. This is especially important for people in positions of power."[2]

This is not just about where you fall short or cross your guidelines; it is also about helping you rise to your potential and sustain your professional quest or mission.

For example, Cesar discovered the vision for his career because one person had the guts to challenge him about fulfilling his potential. He was handling career development for a very large utility when he met Carlos, whom he had contacted to help him build the organization's Latino network:

> I will never forget when he walked into my office. Here I was in this relatively nice space, downtown, with a view of the water. Well, he stood just inside the doorway, looking around him slowly, then looking hard at me, before he walked over to sit down. *What was he looking at so carefully?* I thought. We talked for a few minutes about the network and how he might help. We agreed on a first group meeting, and he promised to get me a plan the following week. As we were wrapping up, he looked around my office again. Then he looked at me and said, "I am not trying to pry, but is this really what you're up to? You know, the whole climbing the corporate ladder thing? Is that really what you most want to be doing?" I was quite taken aback by the question. I had felt I was doing quite well for myself, and now this guy was challenging my whole outlook!

Still, Cesar was intrigued. He and Carlos stayed in touch, and gradually, through their conversations and Carlos's feedback, he realized that what he really wanted to do was develop leaders, not help people make incremental changes in their careers. "It was a tipping point for me in beginning my journey of self-discovery," Cesar added.

As we turn now to the fourth personal foundation, we move from the more intangible, internal focus of *reconnect to your strengths, see the larger field,* and *define a worthy enough win* to the more tangible external support of *find your real team, make positive plays,* and *keep your own score.* Though it comes fourth on our list, finding your real team helps you with all the other foundations, such as defining a worthy enough win, as Cesar found above, and seeing the larger field, as Tom found with his wife in chapter 6.

And what exactly does *find your real team* mean? Basically, it starts with committing to your relationships as a source of strength, well-being, and perspective, looking for true allies at several levels.

You might think of your real team as made up of three concentric circles extending outward. Ideally, your family is at the heart of your network of relationships—and you are at the heart of theirs. Next, in addition to your family, you need other close relationships with people with whom you share values and a commitment to support one another's potential—what I call your "circle of allies." And, finally, in the outermost ring, you need a looser network of professional contacts, those whose respect you share but who may not necessarily be close to you personally.

In the moment, finding your real team means using all three levels of this support network to help you recognize, weigh, and respond to challenging situations. You do this by involving your family in your thinking and plans for dealing with unhealthy pressure, paying attention when they call out a problem, actively talking to your circle of allies, and tapping your professional network to test your assumptions, gain information, and help the right thing happen.

Over time you broaden these connections by actively seeking and cultivating the relationships that reinforce the values you want to strengthen, including having a new type of conversation with your immediate family about what you want from life and the risk of the compromise trap, finding and building circles of allies who reinforce that your professional quest is real and valid and who help you think independently, and growing your professional network so you can influence your organization for the better.

Finding Your Real Team in the Moment

A friend recently passed me a cartoon that captures the heart of the challenge with this personal foundation: A businessman is sitting at his desk, trying to make a decision. On one shoulder he has an angel saying, "Talk to legal"; on the other shoulder, a devil is telling him, "Talk to accounting." Whether or not you consider your legal or accounting departments as part of your real team, the point is still relevant: whom you talk to during an important decision makes all the difference.

If you are struggling with unhealthy pressure at work, it is important to bring your family and loved ones in on it. If you can do this early enough, you don't have to trigger huge alarm bells but can strategize together about your options if things come to a crisis. Your family and close allies can even help you recognize choice points and signs of the compromise trap because they are likely to be most affected when you are struggling with inner conflict.

Your family and closest friends are also probably best able to help you find a reason for courage—perhaps even better than you can on your own. Those closest to you are the ones who best know what you really believe in and can reflect back those principles, values, and passions when you need reinforcement.

Your circle of allies is another source of courage, ideas, and support. They can "have your back" if you are cornered, helping you sort through decisions, test your assumptions, challenge your fears, and remind you of your priorities and options. For example, during one support group for professionals that I used to lead, the operations and accounting manager for a large computer magazine came in late one evening and sat very quietly and tensely for most of the meeting. Finally, she told a very emotional story about how she had been burning the candle at both ends, trying to live up to ever-increasing demands at work while sustaining her after-hours volunteer work at a grief center for children; she said she had almost quit the volunteer work. With the group's help and support, her priorities came back into focus. "I see that my work with the kids is too important to give up," she said. "I am going to have to renegotiate my position so I can keep my commitment to my volunteer work." She went on to work out a stress reduction plan with her company's employee assistance program so she could continue to volunteer. Several years later she left to establish a new grief center for kids, which she now manages full-time.

Your family and close relationships and your circle of allies help you achieve clarity about your motivations and choices and bolster your resolve. But as far as making a practical difference when you face unhealthy pressure, there is no substitute for a strong professional network.

According to ethicists Linda Trevino and Katherine Nelson, having relationships throughout an organization makes it much easier if you need to push back on a policy or directive because you are much less likely to be dismissed as self-interested. Such relationships also enable you to test your assumptions about the logic of a policy or the seriousness of a threat. And, truth be told, this is often how important issues get addressed. Joseph Badaracco, author of "We Don't Need Another Hero," puts it this way: "The vast majority of difficult human problems are not solved by the dramatic efforts of people at the top but by the consistent striving of people working far from the limelight."[3]

Let's walk through a quick outline of how you can put the idea of engaging your support network into action when you need it under pressure.

Putting the Idea into Action

To recap briefly, finding your real team in the moment means engaging all three levels of your support network to help you recognize, weigh, and respond to challenging situations. You can use Decision Point Tool #4: Tapping Your Real Team in a Crisis to remind yourself to apply this support network when you face unhealthy pressure. (This is the fourth of six tools that are available as a download; see "Online Resources" at the back of the book.)

DECISION POINT TOOL #4

Tapping Your Real Team in a Crisis

These questions can help you improve the quality of your thinking; keep your family, allies, and professional network informed as you sort out a challenge; and help you access the support you need to handle a difficult situation.

- ☐ **With your family:**

  Have you been trying to get my attention about something? What do you need me to understand? Can you help me sort out what to do in the face of some unhealthy pressure I am facing? How can I help the best thing happen? How can we make sure your needs and concerns are addressed and you are fully involved?

- ☐ **With your circle of allies:**

  Can you help me sort out how to engage in a tough situation? Here's the unhealthy pressure I'm facing, what I think it would mean if I went along, and how I'd like to redefine the game. Can you remind me of the core values and the higher priorities I told you were important to me? How might I best apply them here? Have you ever faced a similar situation? What might I be missing? How can I best help my family through this? How should I tap my professional network?

☐ **With your professional network:**

Can you help me test my thinking about a tough situation? Here's the unhealthy pressure I'm facing, what I think it would mean if I went along, and how I'd like to redefine the game. What might I be missing? What would you need to know to be certain my diagnosis is accurate? If my assessment is accurate and I don't act, what might the consequences be? What could I do to help the right thing happen here? Would you be willing to help influence the situation for the better?

As you talk to each of your networks, you'll want to be diplomatic but responsible to avoid raising false alarms or spreading inaccurate information. Don't underestimate the value of simply asking for help, including emotional reinforcement, as you think things through.

Finding Your Real Team over Time

It is difficult to tap all these sources of support if you have not invested in them first. Even worse, misaligned expectations and destructive relationships can help push you further *into* the compromise trap.

Let's examine how you can cultivate each of your concentric circles of relationships in parallel.

Talk to your family about your goals Sadly, many people do not fully explore their mutual priorities with their families, at least not in light of the real trade-offs and costs of unhealthy pressure at work. During my interviews I was surprised to find how often unexamined beliefs about what others wanted contributed to regret and unhealthy compromise. The result, unfortunately, is that families and close relationships tend to bear the hidden costs of playing along with the game.

Recall that Gary woke up one day to see that his breakneck pace was causing serious harm to his marriage and that he and his wife did not share his goals. A former investment banker and high-tech CEO told a similar story: "I was using caffeine and food to keep going because part of me just didn't know what else to do. I didn't know how to get off the treadmill, and I didn't want to face the consequences. Of course, that was very damaging to my family."

Paradoxically, having conversations about larger goals and life choices can be clarifying and provide a new sense of support and empowerment—a sense of joint involvement in a shared destiny. You may be surprised at the support you get. One IT manager, sitting with his wife on a Saturday afternoon, said, "I can't believe she really doesn't mind if I cut back on my career goals and start playing more music, but that's what she is telling me." To this she replied, "I want him to be happy. His current career is just eating him up."

When you invest the emotional energy to stay engaged and connected, your family becomes a source of strength and perspective that you can tap when you need it, as the manager did who kept photos of his wife and children on his bulletin board as a reminder to have courage.

Even if you do get far afield, acknowledging that and rebuilding commitments with your family can help strengthen your resolve to not fall into the same trap again. For example, as I described earlier, Julie dug herself out by doing some honest self-reflection; she then went to meet with her (grown) kids and thanked them for giving her the feedback she needed. "They are my purpose, the root of my love." Gary came to a similar conclusion: "The meaning in my life is from my daughters, my family, and my satisfaction in my work. My family and I are learning each other again."

Develop a core circle of allies Your circle of allies is the group of people beyond your immediate family who keep you aligned around your real priorities and help you think independently. They may even actively support your professional quest. They come in many forms—a group of neighbors, a religious or spiritual community, a discussion or book group, a learning community, an online network, a personal coach, a psychological support group, or a group of friends. Although cultivating a circle of allies takes more conscious effort these days, as life is so busy and hectic, the payoff in terms of peace of mind, clarity, and more-effective action is dramatic.

A circle of allies can be anything from an informal group of friends to a committed organization such as the Laymen's Movement that meets regularly. The ideal group will leave you feeling both supported and challenged, remembering old principles and finding new insights. It will allow you to raise questions, have doubts, feel bad, and change your mind—as well as share victories, laugh, admit mistakes, and dare to take risks. They will encourage you to think independently and to respect your values and sense of what's worth pursuing.

The group does not need to be specifically focused on redefining the game or pursuing a professional quest to be helpful. But if it does, it can drastically accelerate your learning.

I have had the pleasure of being part of several powerful circles of allies, each of which took a slightly different form: getting together one weekend every six months to compare notes in a new field or meeting monthly to practice new skills.

Most of the circles of allies I have known exist outside of a specific organization, though it is possible to form them with people in your company. In his book *Who Really Matters,* Art Kleiner describes what he calls a "shadow core group": an alternative group without real power, a cluster of informal allies who come together out of a shared concern for their organization's future. They focus on achieving legitimacy for ideas they believe are important enough to be incorporated into the organization's operating system, helping leaders evolve their thinking while simultaneously working to change themselves. And, according to Kleiner, though much skill is required to master this subtle practice, it may just be one of the most powerful ways you can change the world.

The point is, everyone needs a group of allies somewhere as a counterweight to the gravitational pull of work life as it naturally is. As one IT engineer described it more eloquently, "With connection, we are encouraged."

Reach out professionally By seeking out principled people in your organization, even those you disagree with, you increase your ability to "help the right thing happen"—during a crisis or over the long haul.

Everyone has countless social opportunities in their work settings. The choice is whether you let them default into gossip sessions or try to connect on something more positive—whether your family, your outside interests, your volunteer activities, your personal goals, or your sense of the company's potential.

Shifting to a constructive focus enables you to connect without playing politics and can make work a lot more enjoyable. "I was skeptical about working in a predominantly white culture," said Dale, an African-American telecom executive. "I had seen some pretty bad discrimination in prior jobs, so I was on guard. People just have a way of taking care of their own. Then, at some point, it occurred to me that *I* was the one putting up the wall! I was acting very stiff and formal, and naturally no one really opened up with me. So, I decided to connect a bit more, to let people in at work. And it was really great! We actually had a lot in common, and now they know me better."

As you build your network of professional ties, you will naturally see opportunities to help the right thing happen, especially as so many organizations struggle to connect the dots across business units and functions or to share information up and down the chain of command.

Putting the Idea into Action

You might start cultivating the relationships that reinforce values you want to strengthen by first focusing on your family.

Try making a project of understanding one another's priorities and what really makes each of you happy. As you set goals together, consider the pressures and the risks at work and look for options that lead to the best overall sense of well-being. You may even want to encourage each other to consider looking deeper for your real wants, as Walt, the packaging director, did with his children: "I see how much pressure they put themselves under—to achieve, to succeed, to be the best. I know where they got it from, but I try to tell them they can relax and focus more on what is really going to make them happy."

If your family or those close to you have paid the price while you were playing along with the game or have borne the brunt of your difficult choices at work, you'll want to start by cleaning up whatever damage has been done. How you approach reconnecting after a breakdown will be highly individual to your family or relationships, but you might start by investing some time and attention to reconnect, inviting them to tell you how your work habits have affected them, sharing more about your experiences at work, making any amends that seem appropriate, and exploring what you each need and want next.

Once you have some common understanding, create protected spaces for checking in about whether you feel you are off track—for hearing if your behavior is damaging yourself or others. The activity for this chapter includes a list of dinner-table conversation starters that you might find useful for raising important topics with your family in a relaxed and engaging way. (See Activity #4: Strengthening Your Connections with Allies in "Individual and Small-group Activities" at the back of the book.)

As you move beyond your family to build your circle of allies, start by reflecting on your primary friendships. Are there some that really bring out the best in you, as Carlos did for Cesar? Perhaps there is a way to strengthen those ties or to connect your friends with one another so that you all benefit. Do you already have a group that serves as your circle of allies but with a little prompting could do more? Are you interested in forming a new group, perhaps focused on supporting one another's professional quest? Activity #4: Strengthening Your Connections with Allies also helps you identify those relationships you want to deepen and offers several suggestions for how to begin. (Please see "Individual and Small-group Activities" at the back of the book.)

Finally, you might look for ways to deepen and broaden your professional network by trying to really understand what others' goals and interests are and, when it feels appropriate, by sharing more of who you are and what you are up to—as Dale did with his colleagues at the telecom company.

Where to Go from Here

As I said earlier, connecting with other people is one of the most direct and powerful ways to expand your ability to redefine the game or pursue your professional quest. In fact, it's probably the best way to remember that you *want* to engage at a higher level, which is half the battle. It will also help you keep threats in perspective, find a reason for courage, and gain access to ideas from other creative minds.

But more than this, when you are actively looking for allies and cultivating positive professional ties, you are looking at your organization through a different lens. In a sense you are now on the lookout for other people trying to be a positive force. As you begin to notice how many people care about doing good work, maintaining professional standards, and keeping commitments, it may restore your faith in humanity and reinforce you in continuing with your own efforts to engage at that higher level. And you may even see places where you can lend your support.

For example, at the end of my second interview with Jim, the sales manager for the carpeting company with the recyclable products, I casually mentioned how hard it is for people to keep going with a sense of mission or purpose when there is no one to see and acknowledge what they are doing. His response came quickly and spontaneously. "*Hmm,* that's interesting. I bet the people I am selling to are often lone rangers in their organizations, trying to explain the importance of sustainable products. I wonder how I could help them know that their efforts are seen and appreciated?" I have to admit that it brought tears to my eyes just to hear him brainstorm how he might be more encouraging to his customers. How often does anyone acknowledge your generosity—the ways you try to help the right thing happen, whatever they are? I wonder what it would mean to you for someone you respect to really see and acknowledge that more often.

In the next chapter, as we turn to the more action-oriented aspects of redefining the game with *make positive plays,* you will see how the strength of your support network is one of the most important factors in your ability to influence your organization and to minimize the impact of retaliation when you need to oppose something with which you disagree.

KEY CONCEPTS

- **Find your real team** This means committing to your relationships as a source of strength, well-being, and perspective by consciously gathering a support network that reinforces the person you want to be, including your family, your circle of allies, and your professional network.

  In the moment you practice this by tapping all three levels of your support network to help you recognize, weigh, and respond to challenging situations. This means involving your family in your thinking and plans, paying attention when others call out a problem, actively talking to your circle of allies, and tapping your professional network to test your assumptions, gain information, and help the right thing happen.

  Over time this foundation involves actively seeking and cultivating the relationships that reinforce the values you want to strengthen. You can help this process by talking with your immediate family about your shared goals, finding and building circles of allies who reinforce your values or professional quest and help you think independently, and reaching out to grow your professional network so that you can influence your organization for the better.

- **Decision Point Tool #4: Tapping Your Real Team in a Crisis** This tool can help you as you sort out a challenge by suggesting ways to tap your support network to improve the quality of your thinking; keep your family, allies, and professional network informed; and help you access the support you need to handle a difficult situation.

- **Activity #4: Strengthening Your Connections with Allies**
  This activity helps you take stock of your current relationships, identify where you would like to form stronger alliances, and craft the first steps. It includes a list of dinner-table conversation starters to help you deepen discourse in informal settings with your family, friends, or allies (see "Individual and Small-group Activities" at the back of the book).

REFLECTION QUESTIONS

- Many of the people I interviewed described a moment when someone "tapped them on the shoulder" and invited them to consider redefining what they were up to. Who most convinced you of your potential? What did they say or do to help you imagine engaging at a higher level?
- How have your support networks and the various communities in your life evolved over time? Think back to the communities that had the most impact on your identity. What values did they reinforce in you? How did you apply those in your life?
- Imagine that an anthropologist came to study the organizations and the communities in which you spend most of your time, as if they were a foreign culture. What would the anthropologist notice about these groups' values, norms, and priorities? How closely are those aligned with your own highest values, preferences, and priorities?

9

Make Positive Plays

She told you my comment was the turning point? I had no idea," said Scott, the senior vice president for learning and development who also functioned as the customer champion for a growing nationwide chain. I had called Scott because another vice president told me it had been Scott's presentation three years before that was the turning point in the company's transition to a customer-focused, quality-oriented organization from one that had spent most of its time putting out fires.

"He stood up in front of the firm's two hundred managers and summarized his findings from his research with our field staff," she said. "Basically, he said his interviews suggested that working here was sometimes like 'setting your hair on fire and putting it out with a hammer.' When he said that, I was floored. We all were. No one had told the truth like that before." According to this vice president, that was when the company began to change, investing in frontline staff, reducing the "lightning bolt" management that took them away from serving the customer, and significantly increasing their customer satisfaction and profitability.

As I talked to Scott, the story I heard was not quite so reckless:

> I knew the findings of my interviews were going to be a little difficult to hear. So first I did the senior leadership the courtesy of a prepresentation before sharing them with the broader group. Of course, they pushed and prodded and questioned. But to their credit, they agreed that if those were the facts, they needed to be dealt with. So, I went ahead with my presentation to the broader management team, not trying to gloss over the difficult aspects. I guess it was a turning point because I actually told the truth from the field interviews. It might have seemed risky, but I find that if you tell the truth as you see it—not being an obnoxious jerk but telling it in a reasoned way—you actually build up a savings account of trust with people over time.

In the end Scott not only built trust with the senior leaders but his courage to say what needed to be said also signaled a need for change, inspiring the field leaders to take greater pride in their work and focus more energetically on staff development, customer service, and financial performance. Scott went on to lead the customer service department and provide cutting-edge leadership development programs for the field management and staff in an industry notorious for low pay, high turnover, and abysmal customer service. The result was a company with exceptional customer loyalty and profitability to match. Of course, Scott's presentation was not the only factor contributing to this transformation, but it provided a useful focal point and signaled a new level of commitment, especially when backed up by new strategies and initiatives.

What It Means to Make Positive Plays

Taking action is different when your goal is to redefine the game. When you are trying to help the best thing happen, you view what you are doing quite differently than when you are on a crusade.

The steps you take and how you pursue them are guided more by a sense of what is needed and what will be most effective in facilitating a desired outcome than a desire to be right, to win, or to punish. Scott wasn't interested in embarrassing the leaders of the company so much as pointing out a need—and backing it up with ideas once he had their attention. This attitude is easier to sustain when you recognize that unhealthy pressure is not uncommon and that, being human, others can miss their own best interests when their perspectives are narrowed. It comes from knowing that you see only part of a situation and that you have your own blind spots.

You might think of making positive plays as being "angular" to a system rather than opposed, "diverging" rather than counterattacking—similar to cutting across the current as we discussed in chapter 4. You have a distinct point of view, but you also want to bring other people along with you if at all possible; and to do that, you need their trust.

"My bar is higher than the company's," said Alex, the product manager. "I try to bring everything I learned in the past and apply it here rather than fit into the corporate norms that are a low bar. That said, there are always things you'll adjust on because of the organization's quirks or because they do it better than you. So you bring in the improvements."

The central challenge in moving to action with redefining the game is to be true to what you see needs to happen, without unnecessarily polarizing a situation—locking others into their views in defensive ways so things change little over the long term—or, perhaps even worse, disrupting things out of your own ignorance. As Scott's story illustrates, when this works well it has probably been delicately managed to avoid embarrassing people or disrupting their ability to lead, while still telling the truth.

The benefit to you, besides reducing the risk of retaliation, is that this approach allows you to act more proactively and intentionally, so every experience of unhealthy pressure doesn't automatically become a life-or-death situation.

In this chapter we walk through the options for constructive action, what I call the five positive plays. Rather than group them in terms of what you might do "in the moment" or "over time," as I have in other chapters, I present them as a menu that you can draw on to respond creatively to whatever situation you are in.

The Five Positive Plays

Let's think for a moment about your options. At the most basic level, the question is whether you are going to leave, fight, or stay (and compromise). Economist Albert O. Hirschman described these three fundamental choices as *exit, voice, and loyalty* (if we view fighting as a sort of voice).[1] Yet clearly there are many more options with voice than fighting. I think this is where there is the greatest opportunity for creativity.

Do you recall the scene in *Pirates of the Caribbean* where the beautiful young heroine, cornered by two desperate pirates demanding she hand over her gold, stymies them by insisting on a "parley" with their captain?[2] This is what you are looking for: the unexpected move that shifts the interaction toward a more constructive outcome. (Interestingly, the word *parley* is a play on the French word *parlez,* "you speak.")

Thus far, I have found five positive plays that have this potential to shift the interaction, allowing you to help the right or best thing happen while taking care of yourself—which is just another way of saying redefining the game. Not surprisingly, three of them are primarily about voice. Here is a brief summary, in reverse order from Hirschman's list. (See figure 9-1.)

To illustrate, let's imagine for a moment that you are a bank loan officer and you are evaluating a loan application from a highly

Figure 9-1 Overview of Five Positive Plays

LOYALTY-ORIENTED	
Healthy compromise	Adapting to pressures or constraints by sacrificing *lower* values, wants, or priorities for *higher* ones—in a way that pursues a worthy enough win, addressing potential side effects or precedents in the process
VOICE-ORIENTED	
Candid conversations	Being willing to take responsibility, speak candidly, admit where you are mistaken or made an unhealthy compromise, or renegotiate when you can no longer keep a commitment
Positive limits	Setting a limit or saying no when something needs protecting or changing in a constructive, nonantagonistic way that does not invite unnecessary retaliation and offers the other parties a way to meet their interests as far as possible
Skillful influence	Initiating actions that help redefine the game at a higher level over time, using whatever influence you can, while taking care of your own real needs
EXIT-ORIENTED	
Constructive exit	Leaving in a way that makes as much positive difference as possible and pursuing your next engagement in a way that reflects what you have learned

prestigious customer, someone who has personal and political ties to the chairman of your bank. As you review the loan, which is for a small shopping center, you see problems with the owner's forecasted revenue, which will determine whether she can make the payments. You have professional guidelines that say you won't make a bad loan. But now you are getting pressure from your manager and four levels above him because the customer has talked to your bank chairman. In fact, you've just received a memo marked all over in red pen with comments such as, "What's holding this up?" "Let's make this happen...*now.*"

What are your options?

Let's take a look at each of the five possible positive plays.

Healthy Compromise

When it contributes to something more important and is the best way to get what you really want, compromise may very well be your best option.

It may be that there are larger stakes than you see or information you are missing. For example, perhaps this shopping center is the spearhead deal in a city program to revive a declining neighborhood and will attract other, more profitable projects in the future. Or you may find the compromise actually fits with your values, it's just a painful choice. For example, if you have a child with a serious illness that requires your spouse to stay home, you may reluctantly decide that in this case your obligation to your family outweighs your professional guidelines.

The key to weighing this accurately is to make sure you are seeing the larger field, including the hidden costs, risks, and opportunities, and are in touch with the personal values that help you define a worthy enough win. This is where you bring together the support of the other foundations, including reconnecting to your strengths and tapping your real team for help.

So, after a good night's rest, let's say you do some honest thinking and talking with your family and friends, as you walk through the Questioning the Deal worksheet (see Decision Point Tool #2 in chapter 6). Looking at the overall picture, you may decide that what is really a worthy enough win here is to help the bank make the best possible business decision, for now *and* over the long term, that creates the most value for its customers while taking care of your family's needs. And let's say you do discover that there is a neighborhood revival program, in which case you agree that this is a healthy compromise.

To make this a truly positive play, you would not just sign off on the loan but would take other measures to minimize the side effects or the risk of dangerous precedents. For example, you may decide that you need to document the concession being made on this loan and talk with the department responsible for the loan's payback performance so that you're not setting them up to look bad if there are problems. You might also use this documentation to give the chairman a way to quantify the value of the bank's concession to this customer (while also confirming that he understands what he has agreed to!).

By making the choice consciously and taking these additional steps, you avoid some of the hidden costs of compromise—the stress, the need to justify what you've done, negative precedents, or distrust from those who depend on you.

And if after walking through this process you discover that the choice really is unhealthy, that is it leaves you *worse off*—perhaps there really is no mitigating circumstance—you will see that you have no rational choice but to take a different tack.

Candid Conversations

Often there are things directly within your control that can help prevent or clean up an unhealthy compromise, places where you contribute to the issue or have the power to resolve it. This is where candid conversations come in.

For example, let's imagine that as the loan officer, during an initial casual conversation, you encouraged the customer to believe that the loan would probably go through; then, on further analysis, you realized its weaknesses and communicated your doubts. When senior management responds to the customer complaint, you have the choice of whether to admit your contribution to the problem.

Could you do it?

It has been said that the price of freedom is courage.[3] Being willing to admit your mistakes can free you of all sorts of unhealthy pressure after the fact. And you might be completely astounded by the response. People, particularly bosses, are so accustomed to others trying to get out of uncomfortable situations that a clear gesture of responsibility may take them completely by surprise. Finally, when you step up to take responsibility, you lay the foundation for strong relationships that can handle more-challenging issues, including the ones where you have bad news or a differing opinion.

For an example, an executive coach for a manufacturing company told me this story:

> This new leader had just transferred in, and in his first few weeks handled a dilemma in a way that raised doubts about his judgment and integrity. When I asked him about it, he flat-out lied to me. I was disappointed, but I decided to hold my tongue for a day. Then around 9 p.m. that night he called on the phone. He had been trying to read a bedtime story to his kid and couldn't do it; he had broken down crying. This is a forty-five-year-old man, but he couldn't go on, knowing what he had done. "I stood up there and did my presentation: 'I'm your new leader, you can count on me for honesty, and so on,'" he said. "Then I broke every one of those rules. And I lied to you about it." Well, we cleared it up between us and everyone else who knew he had lied. What I am sure he did not count on is that now our relationship is closer because he came clean."

As this story illustrates so well, the positive play of candid conversations means taking responsibility for keeping your relationships and commitments clean and current.

Beyond admitting your own mistakes and errors, this means proactively renegotiating expectations and agreements when needed and sharing important information and perspectives you have to offer, constantly renegotiating as you become clearer about what you can and cannot promise in good conscience.

Carrying this out means getting more comfortable with honesty and candor in general, not just when there's an issue. If you invite others to give you feedback, address problems and bad news proactively, or even let others get to know you a little more and how you might think differently from others, you set a tone of honesty and respect from the beginning. The goal is to set the expectation that you and others *are* going to differ—and can do so productively and creatively. In fact, I once heard a business coach suggest that when you get a new boss it is important to ask, "How do you want me to disagree with you?" Notice the question isn't *whether* but *how.*

Other than compromise, candid conversations is the positive play that is most in your control. By coming clean and accepting consequences, you remove the hooks that keep you feeling small and trapped—which is why con artists always say, "You can't con an honest man."

Positive Limits

When you have come to the conclusion that a compromise is truly unhealthy and you cannot clear it up with a candid conversation, the most direct response is to say no, to set a limit on what you will and won't do. Especially when something crosses a line or sets a dangerous precedent, you need to know you can refuse. Being able to say no and set limits is the only way you can ever truly take responsibility for anything, including your most important values and commitments.

So, as the bank officer, let's say you are convinced that this *is* a bad loan that is going to cost the bank money. How do you say no in a constructive way?

According to William Ury, author of *The Power of a Positive No,* the secret is to sandwich your no between two yeses in a yes-no-yes pattern:[4]

> **Yes:** What you are standing up for, your worthy enough win. With this positive focus, you convey that you are not *against* the other or his needs but *for* something important, which reduces the need to retaliate.
>
> **No:** A simple statement of a limit on a demand or behavior. If you have thought it through, this does not need to be antagonistic, just clear and firm, which helps avoid offending or provoking the other.
>
> **Yes:** An offer or proposal that honors your limits but helps the other meet his needs, wants, and interests as far as possible.

Basically, you are making a counteroffer to a bad deal, attempting to help the other meet his interests and help the right thing happen overall.

For example, a colleague of mine, Warren, once worked for a very talented and well-recognized senior consultant, Moshe, who was both passionate and occasionally terribly abusive. He had a reputation throughout the consulting firm for "going off" on people when he was frustrated, attacking their intelligence and worth as people and belittling them in front of peers, superiors, and team members. One day relatively early in their relationship, Warren and Moshe were working on a project that was not going well. Looking up from the charts they were reviewing, Warren saw the early-warning signs of Moshe's temper in his face. Before he could gather enough steam to launch into an attack, Warren quietly held up his hand in a warning gesture to stay *stop.* "Moshe," he said, "we're not going to go there. You and I are not going to play that way. We are going to get through this, and we're going to get the best outcome we can. But you don't need to do that with me. I am already committed to getting this right." Then he stopped, breathed, and gave Moshe a moment to calm down. Without saying a word, Moshe turned his attention back to the charts. He never blew up at Warren in the years they worked together after that.

By taking a nonantagonistic but firm approach that set a limit on the abuse (his *no*) while demonstrating his commitment to the project (his proposal), Warren was able to shift the interaction to something more constructive than a battle of egos.

What Warren was taking a stand *for* (his first *yes*) was a more mutual, mature relationship with his boss.

According to Ira Chaleff, author of *The Courageous Follower*, one of the most critical elements in your ability to support your boss is to realize that you do not serve him but rather the two of you are focused on a common purpose. In my view the same holds true with customers. You create far more value, and help others achieve their goals far more effectively, if you are a true partner offering your intelligence and judgment.[5] This means thinking about the other person's true best interests, not just their demands or emotional triggers.

So, what does this look like for our banker? For the real person on whom I based this example, his first *yes* was to making the best business decision for the bank. This led him to a simple nonantagonistic *no*, which was, "I'm sorry, but I am not willing to make a bad loan." And, finally, his second *yes* was, "I'd be happy to walk through my analysis with you to show you in detail why I think this is a bad loan and see if I missed anything." In the end, for the person involved, this meant going to several review committees with his detailed files. All the reviews came to the same conclusion he had: it was a bad loan, and the bank should not make it.

To do this well, you need to have your alternatives lined up in advance, including being ready to quit if need be. If the issue is a serious ethical one, you need to know your organization's official procedures for reporting misconduct to a hotline or up the chain of command. Being familiar with these and using them gradually if you must—not as punishment or retaliation but as the natural progression required to pursue the right or best thing—puts you in a position to enforce your limits in a positive way. Of course, involving your family in your decisions is crucial before you get to this point, so you know where you stand together and how to take the next step.

If you do this successfully, you may find that the other people involved thank you in the end. And even if they don't, you will have avoided a compromise that simply cost you too much.

Skillful Influence

Most of the time, redefining the game is about practicing the art of skillful influence while taking care of your real needs.

Recall from our exploration of a worthy enough win that there are usually two main opportunities to redefine the game: (1) increasing the visibility of consequences, risks, or opportunities that are out of sight and out of mind and (2) pushing the envelope on the inherent tensions in the business by trying to get more of both sides of a trade-off.

As the bank loan officer, let's say your worthy enough win is helping the bank better balance the trade-off between keeping customers and making good loans so there is less unhealthy pressure to sacrifice loan quality when a relationship is at stake. You see several opportunities to improve on this, such as reforming how problems with a loan are communicated to customers, helping customers evaluate their own business deals more realistically, and creating a more rigorous process when bank management disagrees about a deal due to relationship considerations.

But as a simple loan officer, how can you have an impact on practices and processes that are set by senior leadership?

Admittedly, this is a very large subject, and skillful influence is one of the positive plays you should be most prepared to continue developing well beyond what we can cover together here. (I have listed several of my favorite resources for further reading; see "Online Resources" at the back of the book.)

That said, there are several constructive ways to get started right now. I've outlined some basic principles for influencing without formal power that show up in most of the writings about organizational and societal change. (In fact, some say you need these just as much when you do have formal power.) They are based on the idea that an organization is a network of relationships, power, information, and resource flows and that change happens by influencing these relationships and flows.

Build your equity Demonstrating your ability to deliver in whatever currency counts in your organization makes it more likely you will be heard and trusted when you have something to say. Art Kleiner, in *Who Really Matters,* lists several specific ways to build equity, such as attracting customers, putting together deals, handling crises, developing new solutions, and executing reliably.[6]

Try it yourself first Experimenting and trying out an idea on a small scale allows you to test your thinking and provide a vivid demonstration when the time comes. For example, as the banker, you might develop your own checklist for weighing relationship considerations against the profitability of a specific loan.

Explain the risk, need, or opportunity Make your case by connecting the risk, need, or opportunity to others' underlying goals and interests so that they see the impact on something they care about. As one marketing manager put it, "It is awfully easy to get on your ethical high horse, but it isn't effective. I've learned that I can get better responses if I lay it out as 'just a decision,' with all the pros and cons. Then I'm not putting them on the defensive."

Let the risk, need, or opportunity reveal itself As we saw with Mary's story earlier about the marketing study, a strategic effort to bring in more information can be more credible than ranting. What independent data or experience would demonstrate the need most powerfully? What convinced you? How can you help others have that experience, too, if they are open to it?

Connect people Observe how influence works in your organization, who trusts whom—who are the "mavens" or "connectors" in Malcolm Gladwell's language.[7] Then see if you can imagine connecting those who see the risk, need, or opportunity with those who have the power to act differently. Debra Meyerson, author of *Tempered Radicals,* shows how forming steady, purposeful alliances "under the radar" may help you gradually shift the organization's awareness and habits, though it is crucial to do so without polarizing.[8] In *The Soul in the Computer,* Barbara Waugh describes how connecting authentically, even with those you oppose; scaling down the initiative; and amplifying those who model the future you envision—all build momentum.[9] According to Philip Zimbardo, three is the minimum number for shifting majority opinion, as it is less likely to come across as self-interest or a conspiracy—but only if you are rational, consistent, and steady, focusing on the worthy enough win.[10]

Make a proposal You need to be ready with a specific idea that others can say yes to—even if it is just an experiment or research about a problem. To know what to propose, ask yourself: *What small test would I like to ask people to make so that they can see the benefit of acting differently or become more informed about the risks and the opportunities? What could I propose that would make these risks or opportunities more visible to those who could actually act on them?* The key is usually to start small and incorporate ways for those involved to test for themselves how it works.

Negotiate for substantive change Finally, you may want to take the more dramatic step of negotiating for change. Debra Meyerson's *Tempered Radicals* suggests looking at crises as opportunities to negotiate for a new direction, such as responding to a diversity issue with a request for an information session with the entire staff.[11] As you get more experienced, you may be able to negotiate for policy changes and take more-explicit collective action, if that fits with how you are aiming to redefine the game.

To do any of these skillful influence strategies well, you need to take a both/and approach to both people and issues, adopting a bias toward being angular rather than opposed. You will get nowhere if you dismiss the other side of a trade-off, pretending that short-term or financial concerns should be ignored, or draw lines between "us" and "them." One committed internal change agent declared, "We've been wrong, trying to fight the traditional business folks. We need to talk to the CFO to understand the financials." What you want is more of *both* sides or at least minimum side effects on one as you improve the other.

I will always remember listening as Peter Senge signed copies of his book *The Dance of Change* during a conference. Each person told a story about his or her struggle to change an organization, especially how the leaders were reluctant to change. Finally, after a particularly frustrating account of a leader who was driving his organization into the ground and just didn't "get it," Peter responded with a simple question: "Is there anyone he trusts?" His attitude of concern for the leader, respect for his judgment, and constructively looking for ways to connect completely reframed my thinking.

Engaging in skillful influence requires steady patience—a committed intention with detachment about specific outcomes, almost as if you are in a prolonged conversation with the organization as it works its way to the next better solution in a progression of better solutions. You will be most effective in this if you are willing to be influenced as well, without letting go of what really needs attention. Remember, the groundwork that sets the stage for a tipping point is often invisible.

Constructive Exit

The last of the five positive plays is constructive exit, which means leaving your situation in a way that makes as much positive difference as possible and pursuing your next engagement in a way that reflects what you have learned. This might mean transferring to another position, leaving your organization, or opting for another career or way of life.

When you get to the point that you do not have sufficient influence, you cannot sustain yourself and your family in a healthy way while working in an organization, or the compromises are just too severe, this may be your best option. At times, exiting may actually be the way you can best help the right thing happen.

For example, someone else's exit caught my colleague's attention in a long-lasting way: "I remember when our consulting firm initiated a very large contract with a South African company during the days of apartheid. Our African-American director of personnel left just then—without a lot of fanfare but quite clearly in response. That really made me think."

Though this director of personnel did not explain, normally the key to making a constructive exit is helping others understand why you are making that choice. It is even better if you can make a proposal that contributes toward a worthy enough win before you go—as Jim, the carpeting sales manager did before leaving one company for another.

This is very similar to positive limits except that you ask yourself, *If I am on my way out, what can I do while I'm here?* You may find that what you propose on your way out actually has the most influence. This is why, tempting as it may be to lash out and burn bridges, constructive exit invites you to vent somewhere else and keep a cool head in your interactions with the organization.

When you get to the point of a constructive exit, you may have to consider whether the issues are so severe that further measures are required. For example, for Sherron Watkins the decision to simply leave Enron would not have been enough. If you are in a position to know about illegal or seriously harmful behavior or fraud, you have obligations beyond ending your own participation. These are very challenging situations, and you will need to prepare yourself by talking with your family, a lawyer, and others who can offer moral reinforcement. Unfortunately, it is often very hard for others to understand when an individual feels compelled to report an issue, even a serious breach of ethics, and they will often assume the worst about your motives.

Fortunately, now there are more legal protections and support systems for whistleblowers, internal and external. (I have listed a few for further reading; see "Online Resources" at the back of the book.) The first caution is not to panic and go to the press—you may cause more harm than good. Roger Barnes, a former accounting manager with Fannie Mae who went through a typical experience after finding significant irregularities in the company's financial reporting, suggests several key tips, which are echoed by experts in ethics.

First, talk with your family and involve them in your decisions and next steps. Second, document what you are finding and be as rigorous and objective as you can. Follow the chain of command, patiently and reasonably, explaining the issue, risks, consequences, and how it affects others' interests. Explain your motivation and why you are concerned. In the meantime do stellar work and make sure your employee file is completely up-to-date. Be prepared that doing the right thing might interrupt your career, and learn how to handle ridicule without emotion as much as possible so that you can navigate the system calmly. Finally, escalate only incrementally, using every internal recourse available and progressing gradually with external regulators that pertain to your industry, with the advice of an attorney. In Roger Barnes's case, his testimony before the Securities and Exchange Commission and Congress (after many internal efforts to raise the issue) led to confirmation of his findings and resulted in $0.5 billion in fines and a $6.3 billion earnings restatement.[12]

Constructive exit is a positive play that you and your family always need to be prepared to make in case you are ever cornered into an extreme situation. Part of this preparation is how you manage your financial obligations, which we discuss in the next chapter, "Keep Your Own Score."

The last piece of a constructive exit is making a commitment to learn from your experience, as Jim did in moving from the first carpeting company to the second. You do this by choosing your next organization and your next leader carefully and setting expectations and agreements up front, including expectations for how you will disagree.

Putting the Five Positive Plays into Action

Now that you know the five positive plays, the next step is to help you recognize when it is time to act.

"How do I become a good physician?" a medical resident recently asked Robert H. Fisher, MD, a senior clinician and now a leadership adviser and thought strategist. His answer was surprisingly simple:

> Make your own diagnosis on every patient that you see. Make up your own mind based on what you see and what questions you ask. Then test your ideas to either confirm the current diagnosis or question it. When you make your own diagnosis, you are engaged and observing and responsible. You don't close your eyes because it appears that someone else has already done the thinking. You may be the most novice person in the room, but with that status comes the potential to raise an important and new question. Do not be afraid to be wrong. Do be afraid to be silent.

By developing your own personal diagnostic process, you will stay ahead of the curve of unhealthy pressure and be able to recognize opportunities to make preventive, constructive plays—which is much more fun and much less stressful than reacting to unhealthy pressure unprepared. Decision Point Tool #5: Which Positive Play? is a thought process that brings together what you have learned in the past few chapters and helps you identify which positive plays make the most sense in the moment. (This is the fifth of six tools that are available as a download; see "Online Resources" at the back of the book.)

DECISION POINT TOOL #5

Which Positive Play?

This tool helps you identify the most effective positive play in response to whatever unhealthy pressure you face.

☐ **What is my worthy enough win?**

What risks, costs, or opportunities are important enough to be a reason for courage? What is important but not necessarily getting enough attention? Where would innovation help? What is the both/and question I am pursuing?

Refer to: *see the larger field, define a worthy enough win*

YOUR PLANS: ______________________________

☐ **What is within my control?**

Is this a healthy compromise after all? If I agree to this, what side effects do I need to help manage? Are there ways I need to take responsibility, admit mistakes, or renegotiate commitments or expectations? Where might I need to set a positive limit, either because of a bottom line or because it is the best way to influence?

Refer to: *healthy compromise, candid conversations, and positive limits*

YOUR PLANS: ______________________________

☐ **Where do I need to influence others?**

Who could act differently for the best or right thing to happen? What would I propose or negotiate for? Who might also see the need or help raise the visibility of important considerations? Who might be able to help push the envelope on inherent tensions and trade-offs?

Refer to: *skillful influence*

YOUR PLANS: ______________________________

- [ ] **What are my alternatives?**

  At what point would it be better to exit? How can I make the most positive difference as I go? If more-drastic measures are called for, how can I do so responsibly and support myself and my family in the process?

  Refer to: *constructive exit*

  YOUR PLANS: ______________________________

- [ ] **How can I back myself up?**

  Whom of my allies shall I tap? Who deserves or needs to be involved? What support do I need?

  Refer to: *reconnect to your strengths, find your real team*

  YOUR PLANS: ______________________________

For more-involved efforts, you might find the Redefining-the-game Action Planning activity a useful complement to this tool, as it helps you choose the right action over time. (See Activity #5 in "Individual and Small-group Activities" at the back of the book.)

You may want to take a moment now to try these thought processes in the context of your current situation and identify one or two actions to experiment with as you move forward with your efforts to redefine the game.

Where to Go from Here

This chapter is about lifelong skills. I have no doubt you already know a lot about setting limits and healthy compromise, candid conversations, influencing skillfully, and exiting when needed. The question often comes down to when and how much—and whether you can cultivate the skills to apply those plays for a worthy enough win in the same way you do for increasing profitability or reducing costs, which sometimes seem like less vulnerable causes.

So the central message about where to go from here is to experiment, practice, and invest in yourself. Every time you add to your ability to navigate the complexity of an institution, you increase your ability to be true to what matters and help bring the game to a new level.

More than any other chapter, "Make Positive Plays" stresses that redefining the game is a negotiation, a dance. You are neither completely in control nor powerless. Because each person has a window on a distinct part of a system, each is uniquely qualified to exercise leadership from that vantage point. No one else has quite the unique observational perspective that you have. As one master corporate change agent put it, "You get to be you if you want to! They *need* you to be you. Sharing what you observe and acting on it is really why they pay you." When you engage at a higher level in concert with others, you may end up jointly redefining the game in a way that turns out to be better than the original path.

Will your efforts make much of a difference? That is a paradox. On the one hand, you may or may not achieve the goal or fix the problem in a way that is directly identifiable as your work. Yet the fact is that there is no other way to make a contribution than to try to influence, especially where you lack positional authority—and maybe even when you have it. According to Joe Badaracco, "Successful leadership is essentially voice."[13]

"Are you willing to forgo having your name attached as the hero and just let the problem be solved? That's the question I think we need to answer," said Lisa, a director at a Fortune 50 public high-technology company.

The payoffs are many, especially in terms of your sense of personal alignment and autonomy. But you do need ways to get feedback and reinforcement and to feel a sense of achievement. You just have to look to other scoreboards than the typical definition of "winning" or the drama of "taking a stand."

That is the final personal foundation and the focus of the next chapter, "Keep Your Own Score."

KEY CONCEPTS

- **Make positive plays** This foundation is about learning to help the right thing happen while taking care of yourself, by taking a stance that is angular rather than harshly opposed to your organization. At its core is a menu of five positive plays: healthy compromise, candid conversations, positive limits, skillful influence, and constructive exit.

  In the moment this means making your own diagnosis of what is needed in a situation and acting accordingly rather than letting the thinking be done for you.

  Over time you practice this foundation by developing your skills and refining your sense of when to apply each play in concert with the other forces shaping your organization.

- **Decision Point Tool #5: Which Positive Play?** This thought process helps you quickly identify which positive plays make sense as preventive moves or responses to unhealthy pressure.

- **Activity #5: Redefining-the-game Action Planning** This series of questions helps you identify which action to take when, especially in more prolonged and challenging efforts. (See "Individual and Small-group Activities" at the back of the book.)

REFLECTION QUESTIONS

- Think about the last few changes, programs, and new initiatives that have swept through your organization. Where did they come from? Who initiated the ideas? Who advocated for them? If you trace the history of a few of those changes, what does it tell you about what strategies and positive plays work in your company?
- Many people are relatively attentive to negotiations when they exit one firm and enter another but fail to negotiate much when they get a new boss or role in the same company. How about you? Do you negotiate differently when you join a new organization versus transferring within your existing firm? Are you clearer? More daring? If there is a difference, why do you think that might be? What would happen if you took the same approach of clarifying agreements and expectations when you made an internal transfer?

10

Keep Your Own Score

In 2006 George Foreman did an interview with the *Wall Street Journal* to discuss his personal investment philosophy after two boxing careers, becoming a minister, founding a series of youth centers, and launching several successful business ventures. I laughed out loud as I read about his investment goal: He wants to pay $1 billion in taxes.

As it turns out, Foreman defines investing slightly differently. "My approach now is to invest in society," he told the reporter. He considers his best "investments" to be the money he has put into universities to fund scholarships. (Apparently, he never calls them "donations.") Just after 9/11 he put money into U.S. stocks to deliberately counter the atmosphere of fear. Of course, he also pays attention to balancing his portfolio and keeping a cushion, but basically he shoots high because he wants to give a lot back.

"Lyndon Johnson took a lot of us boys in 1965 into his Job Corps program [where Foreman discovered his skill at boxing]. We had nothing to offer society but trouble, and he took a chance, investing a lot of government dollars into it. I told my wife I would never be satisfied until I'm able to pay back $1 billion in taxes. Then I can say I've done something."[1]

I recently wrote to George to find out how he's doing toward his goal. He told me he is still on his mission of repaying the U.S. government for all that was done for him and, thanks to his business ventures in pay-per-view and the sales of his grills, he has gotten pretty close.[2]

What It Means to Keep Your Own Score

George Foreman's goal is a perfect declaration of independence. What can you say when a person *wants* to pay more taxes? And why the heck not? If he's paying $1 billion in taxes, he's pretty well earning enough to live on, no? His choice to "invest in society" reflects a liberating and paradoxical combination of generosity, independence, and self-interest.

I think you'll agree that, like Foreman, everyone wants to be able to "put points on the scoreboard." You want to know that you have made an impact and that you can accomplish what you set out to achieve. Psychologists refer to this desire as the need for "efficacy," and some even go so far as to say our identity depends on it. "There are a lot of things I've taken on with a big component of 'just to see if I could,'" said Beth, a process excellence manager.

In Western cultures this attitude is particularly encouraged. We generally buy into the idea that market success is the most reliable indicator of value, and we make heroes of the entrepreneurs who achieve these successes, pushing past their own limits to achieve some measurable result.

Yet one of the challenges with this system, as we are currently discovering with the market's recent phenomenal underpricing of risk and ongoing inability to incorporate the true cost of energy, is that neither markets nor organizations are very good yet at rewarding efforts focused on the long term.[3] And as we have seen, contributing to anything worthwhile is likely to be a long-term venture and may not even be traceable directly back to you.

So, if you are going to pursue what counts, rather than just what can be measured, chances are you may spend some time looking to others a bit like a loser or like you are treading water—like the Houston stockbroker I mentioned earlier who was criticized because he just didn't "get it" about investing in Enron.

If the essence of engaging at a higher level is redefining winning and losing, keeping your own score means choosing your goals and sources of feedback so they fit with your true values and your professional quest or mission. Like George Foreman you need to consciously choose goals that complement your intentions and desires rather than default to goals based on values you may not share or, worse, that assume your value, intelligence, or contribution can be measured by your status or wealth. It means choosing to move beyond a Pavlovian response to rewards and punishments designed *for* you, to acting like an adult who has more-complex goals and an interest in how the whole "game" is functioning overall.

In the moment, then, this means learning to gauge your effectiveness in terms of your intent, which may *include* status, respect, and approval but not as the primary or only concern. And over time it means aligning your goals with your professional quest and developing independent ways to gauge your success and reinforce your efforts.

If you can do this, this last personal foundation could be the only one you need because it frees you to navigate by what you really value. (Truthfully, you probably need the others as well, to help you remember and to put it into practice—but they all follow from focusing on this end.) Keeping your own score will leave you both freer and more secure because you will not be confusing your current social status—which is changeable and relative—with your actual security or worth.

Keeping Your Own Score in the Moment

We live in an era of particularly pronounced emphasis on status. According to Robert Fuller, author of *Somebodies and Nobodies,* in the drive to be "somebodies" people tend to make themselves subservient to those in power in the hope that one day they will get their own chance to be at the top.[4] One startup CEO I spoke with noticed this in his behavior with his board: "I got myself into real trouble deferring to people who had only a piece of the picture, thinking that because someone had a billion dollars they must be smarter than me."

We are all attuned to status and how to read it. Concern over status is a common reason why people conform or get caught up in comparisons and hypercompetition. "It feels like a social death if you don't measure up," said a former public accountant.

Status is also the stuff of theater. In fact, there is an entire set of improvisational theater skills focused on mastering status "tilts"—making a game of building up status and reversing it suddenly. "I drive a Lexus," says one character, trying to establish his superiority. "You *do*?!" says the second character, wrinkling her nose, as the first speaker shrinks in embarrassment.

These trends point out that the social interplay of rank is always there, though the currency of what is cool is constantly shifting. The problem is believing it to be a reliable assessment of your or another's real worth. In fact, Robert Fuller defines it as the "halo" we attribute to someone because they excel in one area, so we assume they have positive traits in another—or vice versa.

The solution to the status question is twofold.

First, you can learn to play with status. You can respect its role but take it less seriously. As Eleanor Roosevelt once said, "No one can make you feel inferior without your consent."[5] You can also become more flexible and watch for how "what counts" is negotiated and shifted in every social interaction. You can pay attention to how people raise (or lower) their own status and the types of moves that create an environment of respect that honors everyone's dignity.[6]

Second, you can learn to reinforce your own efforts more firmly, assessing outcomes in terms of what you think needs to happen more than by what leads others to pat you on the back. This means focusing more on the drivers of future results than on current impressions.

Surprisingly enough, there is a growing body of research that shows that paying too much attention to outcome measures and targets can actually be counterproductive. Carol Dweck's studies at Stanford show that children who focus on achieving an outcome don't perform as well as those who set their sights on developing their capabilities.[7] H. Thomas Johnson and Anders Broms's analysis of the Toyota production system compared to U.S. automakers' methods shows that focusing on results in the form of numerical targets is often detrimental to achieving the results. Instead, they demonstrate, Toyota has achieved profitability over many decades because it focuses most of its staff's attention on the "means" that generate results.[8] Radical as this might seem, this data suggests that you are likely to have more of an impact if you focus on the drivers behind the outcomes you want to achieve rather than on the outcomes themselves. You also avoid becoming discouraged and feeling like a "drop in the bucket" if you learn to recognize and respond to the immediate indicators of your effectiveness in any given moment. "We believe the world can change only as we experience ourselves changing," say Frances Moore Lappe and Jeffrey Perkins in their book on overcoming fear.[9]

How do you do this?

One way to implement this is to adopt a simple "after-action review" process after an important effort or interaction. This way you learn from what actually advances your goals (and what doesn't) and you shift your focus away from status and approval issues. For example, when Stephanie laid her badge on the table, her intent was not to earn points or win her boss's approval; she had a much more strategic vision of what was needed. In such a situation, it was critical that she evaluate her success based on her intent—or she might never have taken the risk. "You are already having more of an impact than you can imagine. If you can start noticing the direct effect of your actions more, you will feel much greater control over your life...*and* more humility!" explained a global executive coach.

Putting the Idea into Action

Most of the time, there is significant misalignment among a person's intentions, strategies, goals, actions, and the outcomes he or she is getting—which is why there is always room for improvement (and why coaching helps)!

A quick after-action review reminds you to learn from your own experience. This has the added bonus of helping you recognize a positive impact and giving you occasional cause to celebrate. You may have a favorite version of an after-action review, or you may like to try out the elegant and simple model from Bill Torbert and his colleagues, outlined in the book *Action Inquiry,* which I've adapted below.[10]

To give this after-action review a try, simply walk through the questions briefly after any important effort or interaction to help you bring your intentions, strategies, goals, actions, and outcomes into greater alignment. Gradually, you may use the questions to guide your choices in real time, while you are in the midst of an effort or interaction. (Decision Point Tool #6: Mini After-action

Review is the last of six tools that are available as a download; see "Online Resources" at the back of the book.)

DECISION POINT TOOL #6

Mini After-action Review

Use these five questions after an important effort or interaction so that you learn as much as possible from your experience and improve your impact going forward.

- ☐ **What was my intention for the situation?**
- ☐ **What was my strategy? My goal(s)?**
- ☐ **What did I actually do? How did I behave?**
- ☐ **What outcome did I get? Was it what I expected, or was it something different?**
- ☐ **What do I most appreciate about how I used my strengths in this situation? What could I change to move toward greater alignment and impact next time?**

A simple ongoing practice like this, multiplied over weeks and months, can do more for your professional growth than a hundred leadership development programs. As you practice reflecting, you will see where you are inadvertently undermining your own effectiveness—stepping on the gas pedal and the brake pedal at the same time, so to speak—so you can bring greater congruence to your actions as an individual and as a leader.

Keeping Your Own Score over Time

Being on a quest always involves learning, adapting, and making course corrections as you encounter new terrain on the journey, discover new allies and threats, and learn more about what you seek. Thus the central task of keeping your own score over time is continually ensuring that your goals are aligned with your core values and your mission while developing independent and creative ways to gauge your success and reinforce your efforts.

Let's look at each of these in a little more depth.

Ensuring that your goals are aligned When you are caught in the compromise trap, your goals are affected as well. As you get more and more depleted, you are likely to escalate your commitment to a narrow set of targets that justify your prior choices but do not necessarily satisfy your real wants or needs.

Aligning your goals may be as simple as modulating how high you aim so that you don't outpace what you can do and still enjoy life. Joe, an HR vice president who advised many up-and-coming line leaders and was concerned about their larger sense of well-being, echoed this philosophy: "At times it's appropriate to tell people to 'shoot for the middle.'"

In some sense questioning your goals happens naturally at a certain stage in your career. For example, Beth, who earlier described taking on roles just to see if she could, began shifting her focus as she got closer to forty. "Now I think I can shift the conversation to what do I *want* to do," she said.

But why wait? If you are going to want to "put points on the board" wherever you are and the group you are in determines your status, you might as well choose a scoreboard and a setting that fits with your values from the start. For example, one senior executive told me, "I've always looked for jobs with a sense of purpose, where I can benefit those who don't have all the advantages—and I've always found them. It's not a Don Quixote thing; it's how I've made my living for twenty years."

Developing independent ways to gauge your success By definition, if you cannot experience a feeling of "enough," you will stay stuck, fighting for survival no matter how much you earn. If at some point you are going to move up Maslow's hierarchy beyond the survival and security levels, you need a way to know when those basic needs have been satisfied. Otherwise, if you let yourself be continually triggered by threats to your survival, you will miss the chance to pursue your real gifts. "The system keeps us in perpetual survival mode. Even those with millions of dollars in the bank feel and act as though their survival were literally at stake every day," recounted a leadership development expert who works with senior executives in numerous firms.*

Lately, a lot of people are talking about greed, which can be confusing in an economy that runs on self-interest. Where is the line between greed and self-interest? I once asked this of a cab driver whose earnings supported a wife and three children. He gave me a very interesting response: "Greed is relentlessly pursuing a need that cannot be filled." The authors of *Affluenza* and *The High Price of Materialism* agree. According to repeated research studies, pursuing wealth and possessions beyond a certain point

---

*Just to put our definitions of "survival" in perspective, household incomes of $150,000 or more in 2005 were in the top 6 percent for incomes in the United States. *Source:* U.S. Census Bureau, Income, Earnings, and Poverty from the 2005 American Community Survey, series ACS-01; and 2005 American Community Survey; B19001—Household Income in the Past 12 Months; B19013—Median Household Income in the Past 12 Months (in 2005 inflation-adjusted dollars). U.S. Census Bureau American FactFinder Web site. *http://factfinder.census.gov.* Accessed January 9, 2007.

can become a self-defeating and ultimately addictive substitute for what really makes you happy.[11]

Actively cultivating an independent sense of what you really want and need that is not overly swayed by social pressures allows you to be more realistic in preparing for real risks *and* recognizing when to relax and enjoy life. For example, for many people "go-to-hell money" is what most gives them a sense of security. The former CEO who had twice quit for moral reasons drew a direct link: "I could be true to myself those two times I needed to quit because we kept our expenses low. Before we even bought a car or a home, we saved a year's worth of living expenses."

Gary, the CFO, found that money took on a completely different role once he reevaluated his goals and priorities with his family. "I see money now as a way to get somewhere rather than as a way to keep score." Interestingly enough, that leads him to tell his kids not to postpone the life they really want. "I tell my kids, 'This is really it; live it like you mean it.'" In other words, it is okay to move up those rungs on Maslow's hierarchy.

Developing an independent gauge of your success and financial well-being has to start with a deeper understanding of what really gives you and your family satisfaction in life and using that to set goals together. The conversations you began in chapter 8, "Find Your Real Team," are a start. The more you explore, the more you can go directly to what you want without having to "pass go" or having made it on someone else's terms. For example, in *Your Money or Your Life,* the authors describe countless people who basically go "off the grid" and find themselves much happier.[12] How much more fun could you have if you realized you had that freedom—especially if you are still earning a salary?

Without money as the gauge of your impact or success, it becomes all the more important to check out creative ways to reinforce your efforts that are more aligned with your values and the mission you are pursuing.

Finding creative ways to reinforce your efforts One of the main reasons why people keep score on their efforts is because they need the reinforcement that what they are engaged in is valid and real. As we have seen, external rewards are not the best place to look for validation for long-term ventures, but there are other ways to find it.

There are several ways to reinforce your efforts that are likely to be more aligned and will help you keep going toward a worthy enough win and sustain your professional quest.

One way is to spend time with your allies, with those who "get" what you are up to—not as an indulgence but as a crucial sanity check. Seeking out groups in which what "counts" is as aligned as possible with the person you really want to be can eliminate a lot of stress and provide much-needed reinforcement, if you stay in close enough contact. For example, one software entrepreneur found that his local Young Entrepreneurs Organization became the one place he could be "real"—where his success was appreciated but did not give him a mystique. Attending the group's biweekly meetings gained him respect and status around priorities he really valued. And when he sold his company, they were the first to ask him what his calling was, what he felt he was meant to do with his wealth.

Another way is to develop a "leading indicator" of your contribution, as George Foreman did. Progress on your professional quest is akin to contributing to the breakeven costs for a business—anything positive is progress. So, rather than choose an indicator that lets you claim to have single-handedly conquered a challenge, look for a number that will simply help you keep going. It might not even be a number but some other way to gauge progress. For example, one woman whose mission revolves around recognizing others' gifts and helping them develop finds that a quick phone call to stay in touch with them in their new jobs helps remind her that she is doing something worthwhile.

Finally, research shows that you can reinforce your efforts and sustain your ability to engage at a higher level by practicing the art of appreciation, gratitude, and acknowledgment. Hokey as it might seem, if you pay attention to what actually gives you a background sense of well-being, you may find it has to do with getting into the right side of your brain, which appreciates beauty, art, simple pleasures, and other people. For example, a *Harvard Business Review* article on executive effectiveness says it is crucial to stop every once in a while to talk with people who generally make you feel good. (This leads me to a pet theory about why a friendly receptionist or security guard makes such a difference to an organization.)[13]

Whatever your beliefs about such practices, there seems to be data that indicate you'll be happier and more creative if you give yourself a break once in a while. For those I interviewed, practicing appreciation brought them a greater sense that they could trust life even with its harsh realities.

Derek, the dentist I described earlier who volunteers in the community, was very clear that taking time to savor what was going well in his life contributed to his ability to stick with his professional quest. For example, when I asked how he could afford to take a whole day to volunteer every week, he said, "The key is the belief that you will be cared for, which you get from the support of your family and an inner sense of well-being. Once you have that, you can afford to make decisions with a more long-term focus. Of course, you do have to live within your means along the way."

At first it may feel awkward to spend time "appreciating" what's working in your life, but all it really means is letting yourself actually feel the sense of well-being that this whole process of climbing the ladder was supposed to be about—by noticing the parts of life that are working along with those parts that are not.

Putting the Idea into Action

If you like the idea of keeping your own score and ensuring that you have independent ways to gauge your success and your progress, it might be time to do a quick review of your goals to see which are aligned with your values and professional quest and which you might want to adjust. For example, it might be a good time to see if your financial goals reflect a complete understanding of your real priorities and needs. You also want to ensure that you have included other ways of reinforcing your efforts.

To help you with this, I have included a Personal Goal Review (see Activity #6 in "Individual and Small-group Activities" at the back of the book).

Where to Go from Here

In some cultures work is viewed as an expression of a person's place in a natural order, something worth pursuing and an important element to happiness. In Western societies, by contrast, work is assumed to be a sort of punishment or "necessary evil."[14] Under the former view, work is not something to get through but rather part of "living it like you mean it," as Gary put it.

Our focus in this chapter, and indeed throughout the past six chapters, has been to gradually shift from one view to the other, so work becomes more intrinsically satisfying and not just a means to an end. Near as I can tell, all it takes is reconsidering how much you buy in to the idea that external measures of your work accomplishments reflect your worth, effort, or intelligence. According to Marcia, director of a global socially responsible business consulting firm, "This isn't about winning or having a guaranteed impact. It's just a question of *What else do you want to be doing while you're here?*"

Noted psychologist John Welwood puts it this way: "When we no longer secretly try to win love through our work, we become much better artists, businesspeople, politicians, students, or teachers. We are freed to do what we do as a form of creative play rather than as a form of self-validation."[15]

This is why I suggested that this last of the six personal foundations could be the only one you need—if you can remember it amid all the pressure to do more, have more, and be more that goes along with modern Western society.

Clearly, this is difficult to put into practice because you will be swimming upstream against some of the core ideas of our culture. That's why we have walked through these past few chapters on the personal foundations, to give you all the backup you can get: the ability to reconnect to your strengths and to scan the larger field for hidden risks and opportunities, to be clear about how you define a win, to be able to recognize your real team, and to skillfully execute the plays that move you closest to your real goals.

When you can bring all these together, there is no way you can lose. In fact, you are not fighting the culture at all. You are just trying to remember and help others remember how things really work, trying not to fall into the reactive stance of self-protection and winning in the short term that undermines the real source of your strength.

If you don't try to justify your existence by measuring your impact, you can thrive by doing what you are here to do—and, paradoxically, have a greater impact though you may never actually know how much.

For example, Frances Moore Lappe tells the story about several women standing with protest signs in the rain in front of the White House in the 1970s, trying to raise awareness about the risks of nuclear weapons. They had been standing there every day for months. They had no idea if what they were doing made any difference. "We felt like idiots," said one of them later in an interview. Yet years later, when noted expert Benjamin Spock, MD, who had a significant influence on legislation to control nuclear weapons, was asked how he got interested in the issue, he described driving through Washington, D.C., one day and seeing several women with protest signs standing in the rain. He thought to himself, *If this is an important enough issue for them to stand in the rain, it is at least important enough for me to educate myself.*"[16]

As we move into the closing chapters of the book, let's take a look back at the original promise: that switching to internal reinforcements by building your personal foundations would enable you to thrive in a greater range of circumstances, even amid unhealthy pressure. In chapter 11, "Thriving at Work," we take stock of how that all comes together.

KEY CONCEPTS

- **Keep your own score** This means choosing your goals and sources of feedback so they fit with your true values and your professional quest, freeing you from comparing with others, providing reassurance of your impact, allowing you to navigate by what you really value, and helping you learn.

  In the moment you do this by learning to weigh your effectiveness primarily in terms of your intent, including concerns about status, respect, and approval but alongside many other factors.

Over time you implement this by gradually aligning your goals with your professional quest and developing independent ways to gauge your success and creative ways to reinforce your efforts.

- **Decision Point Tool #6: Mini After-action Review** This quick self-assessment reminds you to learn from your own experience. It has the added bonuses of helping you recognize a positive impact and giving you occasional cause to celebrate.
- **Activity #6: Personal Goal Review** This activity guides you in reshaping your goals to more closely align with your true priorities and what creates a sense of "enough" for you and your family. It also invites you to craft a uniquely personal celebration to acknowledge this work you have put into achieving greater alignment. (See "Individual and Small-group Activities" at the back of the book.)

REFLECTION QUESTIONS

- Where did your current goals originate? What motivates you to pursue them? What desires, needs, or wishes do they fulfill for you? What do you imagine about the moment you achieve them? See if you find any clues to the underlying interests they represent, and ask yourself whether your goal is the best way to fulfill that interest.
- Find an old budget and look it over, perhaps with your family. How have your expectations and standards changed over time, especially regarding financial security and material wants? Which increases have led to more well-being? Which have not?
- Think back to one or two periods in your life when you felt the most self-acceptance, the greatest sense that your life was okay as it was. What was that like? How did that feeling change your focus, your goals, or your behavior? Does that tell you anything about the best way for you to keep your own score now?

11

Thriving at Work

Oh, no, I don't consider myself an idealist," said Jim at the end of our second interview. "There are people who do much *much* more than me. This is just the part I can do."

"And what got you started doing this part?" I asked.

"I was hanging out with some friends, and one of them, Lisa, just casually asked me what I was working on that really mattered to me. At first I didn't have an answer, but her question got me thinking—and you know the rest."

Nearly every person I spoke with who was engaging at a higher level also referred to what I call a "tap on the shoulder": some contact with a peer, friend, or mentor who inspired them to think about their true priorities or sense of purpose.

It turns out that the story of redefining the game is one of mutual encouragement. It is about people influencing one another for the better in nonobvious ways, up and down the hierarchy, in and out of organizations, and across generations. For Cesar it was Carlos who asked if he was doing what he really wanted. For Roberta, the sales director who confronted her boss, it was a "hippy, pot-smoking friend" who lived a very different lifestyle but connected with her on values and priorities.

How do these moments work? Who are these people doing the encouraging?

After I talked with Jim, I decided to find out about at least one of them. He gave me Lisa's e-mail address, and she agreed to meet me for an interview.

It was a bit surreal, the two of us meeting for the first time in the boardroom of a slick Silicon Valley hotel, complete with Asian fusion décor and a fountain running down one wall, the digital recorder placed strategically between us on the huge lacquered table. The strength of the relationship with Jim carried us through, though, and we were able to connect.

"The concept of right livelihood* is very important to me now, but it wasn't when I was growing up," Lisa began. "I am an attorney, and when I started out it was all about the cool suit, the great car. I am really glad I went that route because I hated it *so* much that now I am very clear that's not what I want. At some point I realized that work is a big chunk of your day and really fast you're going to wake up and ask yourself, *What did I do?*"

She continued: "The great thing about human beings is that we are creators. So at that point I had to figure out, *What am I going to create?* Soon after, I went to work for a Fortune 50 company and got involved in an unusual project, using technology to cross the 'digital divide' and help the poorest of the poor."

I'll let Lisa tell the rest of the story:

> Our approach was to make technology available to people in rural villages with little or no electrical service but in a way that gave them a say over how they were affected. The whole thing was

*Originally defined as avoiding certain specific harmful occupations and practices, "right livelihood" is a Buddhist concept now interpreted to mean work that makes a difference, benefits the community, and is personally fulfilling. See Claude Whitmyer, "Doing Well by Doing Good," in *Mindfulness and Meaningful Work*, ed. Claude Whitmyer (Berkeley: Parallax Press, 1994), pp. 9–15.

inspired by the work of the folks at Haas Business School and C. K. Prahalad, who had proven that providing services to the bottom of the pyramid—people who make very little income—can make a huge difference to their standard of living and still be profitable to the provider.[1] It was tricky staying true to that mission; it was just so foreign to our normal way of thinking. For example, in one meeting the team opted to go into a certain geography because the infrastructure was already present. I said, "Of course it's easier to go in where things are already established! But that's why the poor are *not* served, and that is our challenge—how to get to them."

The fact that I'm a lawyer gave me more latitude to say things like that, comments people might think were crazy. When you're pursuing this sort of mission, it's important to know your spheres of influence. It doesn't help to polarize. Instead try to connect to the usual ways of doing things—talk to the CFO; consider the financial side.

In our case the project was breaking such new ground it didn't fit easily with the company's schema. We started out in corporate philanthropy. But then we started to make money, so we were moved to a division where we had more leeway to grow the idea into a thriving business.

Meanwhile, our company came under fire from Wall Street, which is a true litmus test for any institution. What move do you make when your back is against the wall? You can retrench, but they'll pummel your stock anyway and you'll just end up breaking the company apart. Or you can pull a product innovation, passion-based, love-based move. You're on the precipice either way. The move that gets the public trust—the love—is the one that takes a chance. And there are people who see now that the qualities of public trust with a company are very similar to the qualities in a good relationship: both trust and passion have to be there for it to thrive. Just look at what Apple has done, and they were almost destroyed a few years ago.

> Unfortunately, in our case, the company took a conservative approach and retrenched. They split off product lines and laid off thousands of people. Our initiative was shut down because, while it was profitable, it wasn't profitable enough.

I must have looked a little downcast because Lisa jumped in quickly to follow up: "Look, it's really okay that this project died because it ignited so much public interest that the kernel lives on. And personally, I've decided to go cross-country to meet with all the people I met working on this project and see how I can advance the effort in some other way. One way or another, this deserves to happen."

"Yes, but how do you bring yourself to make the effort?" I asked.

Lisa continued:

> I have a rather simple philosophy that captures the choice the company made and the choice I think individuals make every day: you get to evolve if you've conquered your fear. The question is how much did you act out of love for yourself, for others, for something you believed in? Or were you too afraid to take that chance, to look like an idiot? And yet here's the kicker: We spend all this time in the fear-based camp, trying to feel safe, feel trust, and all these things before we venture out. And yet in the end it never motivates you to do the things you really want to do! Only love motivates you.

The Heart of the Choice

It is always a little tricky when someone raises the notion of love in a business context. Are things going to get all mushy now? Yet the French word for heart—*coeur*—comes from the Latin root for *courage,* as in "to take heart." And I think that is the sense in which Lisa is referring to love in this context. We might think of it as vitality, daring, passion, the impulse to create value—a sort of generous, purposeful courage.

It is very interesting that Lisa lays out two main choices: the path of fear or the path of love (or "purposeful courage," using our terminology). In a sense this is the simplest and most elegant way to describe the choice between playing along with the game and redefining the game.

As we begin to wrap up, let's take a step back for a moment and see how this elegant summary might apply. To recap briefly, we started out with the question of how to engage in the face of unhealthy pressure to compromise at work. We found that while it's tempting to play along with the game, that choice leads to the compromise trap. Instead, I suggested you expand your ability to redefine the game so that you can engage at a higher level regardless of the circumstances and that you could create your own internal reinforcement system for doing so by investing in six personal foundations.

Hopefully, you now have a sense of expanding your ability to redefine the game and engage at that higher level. Perhaps you have tried some of the activities and begun putting the ideas into practice.

If you have, you are likely to recognize that choosing to redefine the game is fundamentally optimistic. Even in the face of intense pressure and hard choices, it asks you to use whatever degrees of freedom you have to turn things toward the better—as poet Wendell Berry said, "Be joyful, though you have considered all the facts."[2] By contrast, playing along with the game is a sort of defection, a pessimistic option individuals take when circumstances overwhelm their ability to be generous or creative.

So, in this sense, the heart of the choice about how to engage *does* come down to choosing between fear and purposeful courage or, to use Lisa's term, whatever it is you love. And if that's the case, it's no surprise that redefining the game is also a good strategy for thriving at work.

What It Means to Thrive at Work

This book has been mostly an argument for courage—and the practices that support your ability to act with courage and daring on behalf of what you truly care about.

But as it turns out, that recipe—redefining the game so that you can engage at a higher level—has many of the same ingredients as the one for thriving at work.

Over the past twenty years or so, researchers have made great strides in understanding what actually makes people happy, especially in their work. And, as I alluded to earlier, many of the findings are counterintuitive, at least on the surface.

Martin Seligman and Mihaly Csikszentmihalyi and others in the new field called "positive psychology" have conducted thousands of surveys and many lab experiments, often using emerging neuroscience techniques to measure brain activity, trying to understand what contributes to happiness and well-being. They sum up their research with a simple "happiness formula":[3]

$$H = S + C + V$$

(**H**appiness = **S**et range + **C**ircumstances + **V**oluntary activities)

Let's take a quick look at each key element and how it relates to redefining the game and engaging at a higher level.

Set range Apparently the biggest determinant of your day-to-day happiness is your inherited orientation toward either a pessimistic or an optimistic outlook on life, which continually returns you to a certain "set range" regardless of your circumstances. This effect is so strong that in one study lottery winners and accident victims who became paraplegics both returned almost all the way to their original state of happiness within a year of these life-changing events.[4] Luckily, Seligman has found that you can shift this set range through a sort of "learned optimism" that comes from challenging your habitual thinking patterns. Redefining the game cultivates this optimism by encouraging you to question catastrophic scenarios and refocus on your true priorities.

Circumstances This is where most people pin their hopes. Yet surveys with thousands of people in many countries, at all levels of income and education and all states of health, show some surprising results. It turns out that income does correlate with well-being but, beyond one's core needs, not by very much. This is because income also tends to correlate with increases in conspicuous consumption, which does not lead to any lasting increase in happiness (because people soon adapt their baseline expectations to the new level and their peers often catch up). What actually has the single biggest impact on your happiness due to circumstances is the quality of your relationships, particularly whether you have a good marriage. Hence, the redefine-the-game approach of investing in your real team and relationships, actively protecting your commitments to your family, and keeping your own score—all reflect a more effective approach to increasing your well-being than doubling-down on your drive to climb the ladder.

Voluntary activities At the end of the day, according to Seligman and his colleagues, the most direct way to improve your happiness and well-being is through voluntary activities of two types: pleasures and gratifications. Pleasures such as food, rest, and physical intimacy have an immediate and direct effect, though it is short-lived. Gratifications, by contrast, are activities that challenge you to rise to the occasion, calling you to use your "signature strengths." This type of activity can have far longer-lasting and more-pervasive effects beyond the time spent, creating a state of very high well-being similar to what Csikszentmihalyi describes as "flow."[5] The best way to increase your gratification, according to Seligman, is to craft your life and work to enable you to exercise your signature strengths as often as possible.[6] Now here's the clincher: the effect seems to be even more powerful if you are exercising your signature strengths in service of something larger than yourself. For example, studies of extraordinarily creative individuals by Gardner and Csikszentmihalyi suggest that people get to the highest levels of satisfaction and fulfillment when they move to the level of "vital engagement" in their work—where there are both moments of flow and a sense of meaning, purpose, and significance, connected to a web of relationships and traditions.[7]

If this is true, thriving has less to do with getting to the top than with a meaningful pursuit that uses your talents and allows you to meet your real needs along the way—including the need for pleasure and enjoyment.

As you can no doubt see, these findings seem like a tailor-made prescription for adopting a professional quest as the focal point for your engagement.

Many companies are now attempting to provide opportunities for this vital engagement at work. Studies by the Sirota Group show that employees are more effective and exert greater "discretionary effort" and creativity when they are highly engaged. Data from thousands of employees in countless fields surveyed over four decades show that three conditions are required: equity, camaraderie, and achievement—the chance be proud of one's work and what the company does in the world.[8] Yet there's a twist.

> **Thriving at work** You thrive when you are engaged in a meaningful pursuit that uses your talents and allows you to meet your real needs.

Sirota's research further shows that the problem is not usually engaging employees when they start but *avoiding the ways companies disengage them over time* with frustrating work conditions and dysfunctional systems.

When you redefine the game, you are taking control of the ingredients of this vital engagement for yourself rather than relying on the company to change. You are developing the skills and the confidence to negotiate for greater equity. You are anchoring yourself in a community and a purpose that goes beyond the organization (though it may include members of your organization). And you are actively practicing and sustaining the standards that make you proud of your work. As Viktor Frankl pointed out after his own harsh experiences as a prisoner, redefining the game in terms of what is most meaningful for you helps you retain the sense of choice and impact that is the secret of inner freedom. "It's not sacrifice, it's simple mathematics," said Frankl.[9]

You cannot do this and thrive in any and all settings. Unless you are extremely altruistic, you need to choose settings in which you find at least some level of connection and mutual respect, where your values and your professional quest are angular and not diametrically opposed to the direction the organization is going.

Yet even in a recession where job choices are fewer, redefining the game may be the recipe for sanity because it recognizes your responsibility to craft the conditions for your own engagement. It challenges the myth that capitulating and kissing up is the best way to ensure your security or even help your organization, and it suggests that you contribute far more as a full citizen who takes on responsibility than as an indentured servant. It reminds you that you have to make some hard choices but you don't have to make compromises that leave you worse off and you don't have to stop trying to help the right thing happen. And, even better, engaging at a higher level, as you do in redefining the game, provides a more direct way to achieve satisfaction from your work.

For example, Joe, an HR vice president, told me that as we head into very difficult times the managers he works with are now more concerned about their kids' approval than their bosses'. "I am finding that people are giving up on the notion 'my boss will take care of me if I do a good job.' Those days are over, and people realize they must own that themselves. I see more people reverting back to 'I just want my family to be proud of the work I do.'"

The bottom line is that redefining the game is about trying to be a positive force in whatever conditions surround you. Perhaps the best way to explain why this works comes from eminent psychologist and student of human nature Carl Jung, who said, "The greatest and most important problems of life are all fundamentally insoluble. They can never be solved but only outgrown."[10] In other words, by becoming bigger.

You may thrive when you get to the top, or you may not. One thing that's certain is that your problems are going to change. The key is how you approach the challenges along the way. In what problems do you *want* to be immersed? Which problems best allow you to tap your signature strengths and experience a sense of gratification as you confront them?

That is the perspective of redefining the game. And, as I suggested in chapter 1, it begins with a decision.

It Begins with a Decision

As we have seen, the whole world changes when you decide not to cave out of fear. Still, it may *feel* like life or death in the moment because you are breaking the taboo on being different. Indeed this taboo may be the biggest single barrier to living your values in the face of unhealthy pressure. "It's not a lack of a moral compass that's the problem; that's not what's missing," said a former purchasing agent. "It's the willingness to stand apart. That's as terrifying for many of us as adults as it was in high school."

His comment hit a personal nerve for me. I remembered it took a *lot* of pushing to get me to stand apart during my school years.

Growing up, I was a nerd—the embarrassing type. I liked *Star Trek* and fractions and Shakespeare's plays, even in the fifth grade. And this of course attracted a lot of bullies. I usually tried to play nice, giving them my jewelry and my money, then walking the long way home from school to avoid more confrontations. But all this did was attract whole cadres of bullies with friends.

One day two tough girls, Irene and Michele, teased me about being a fool. "One fight and it will be over," they said. So I decided to fight. I was tired of playing small. I still remember standing in the school stairwell, with my back to the door, while Irene and Michele told me how far away my latest nemesis was from arriving at the door to pummel me into submission. Still, I kept my back turned, no matter how much I was shaking. Then, suddenly, the moment arrived and Irene and Michele said, "Now!" I turned around and there was Mary, big and angry and winding up for a punch in the face. I ducked and grabbed her legs so she would fall over, but she just yanked my hair and swung me around in front of her. I don't remember much after that except the enormous relief of finally being able to stand up for myself and the authenticity of making a stand for my right to exist. After about three minutes, Irene and Michele broke it up, took me to the dean's office, and explained. Words cannot express the sheer joy in my heart as I got on the bus toward home that day amid cheers and teasing laughs, sitting with the kids in the back of the bus who already knew that the world changes when you decide not to cave and were pleased to find out that I knew that now, too.

A few weeks later, I got a message from Mary, who had been transferred to another school. "Tell Elizabeth I said hi," was the word. Oh, how things change.

Knowing that you are not going to cave out of fear if you can help it creates space for being true to yourself. It lets you choose to pursue whatever it is you love, as Lisa suggests. It leaves you feeling bigger, so you are more likely to be able to redefine the game the next time and the time after that. And in the process, you call out the courage in other people; you "en-courage" them, so your personal redefine-the-game loop becomes multiple reinforcing loops as you encourage others and they encourage you.

As it turns out, "en-couragement" is catching. Jon Haidt, who has studied the experience of "elevation"—witnessing someone else's good deed—shows that there is a very measurable physiological effect when we see someone else do something admirable. It leaves you feeling more trusting, more likely to act trustworthy, and wanting to do good yourself in a way that influences how you interact with other people afterward.[11] As I found with Mary, this may affect even those with whom we disagree.

This suggests that your actions can activate courage in others up, down, and across the hierarchy where you work.

Imagine organizations with room for standing apart based on foundations of respect—where people take stances that are angular but not opposed, where you differ openly but not based on a knee-jerk reaction.

Imagine a team culture that enables constructive conflict without personal attack. "Come on in here and sit down," one of my favorite bosses used to say. "I have a bone to pick with you." Why couldn't we build the sort of relationships where that was possible among peers and colleagues as well?

Imagine followers who do their leaders the favor of working out how to disagree with them or who serve as honest thought partners in pursuit of a common purpose. A line leader told me a story that captures the spirit of this vision perfectly. One day she went for a run with a senior manager several levels up. He asked her some questions about an upcoming initiative, and she was quite candid about some risks that might get in the way of reaching his goal. When they returned from the run, he stopped her and said he was blown away by her comments: "You were so gentle with me. It's like you're really in my corner." To which she replied, "Yes, I *am* really in your corner, but, more importantly, I really want us to be successful." You can bet she had his respect after that interaction. And perhaps it even helped the initiative succeed.

Surprisingly, it may take some work to invite staff members to step up to this level of candor. As a leader, you may have to put some effort into letting your team know that you really want their honest assessments. Eric, a director of software engineering, found this to be true. "It took a long time to convince them," he told me. "I think they grew up believing you don't bring bad news to the top. Now they see that bringing in new data and contributing to the decision-making is not only crucial for avoiding disaster but how we actually get anything worthwhile done. I needed to show my team that I *wanted* to hear their perspective, even bad news."

Of course being honest and candid works only if you first commit to a worthy enough win. According to Dave Packard, co-founder of Hewlett-Packard, "The difference between insubordination and entrepreneurship is intent."[12] Eric echoed that perspective: "Honesty is not really that hard if you are clear about your intentions. I just ask myself, *What am I trying to have happen by saying this?*"

So, if you want to encourage, if you want to help the right thing happen, the first place to focus is on your intent, your commitment to be of help.

One teacher I respect defined *encouragement* as "coming alongside" a person, almost as if to run the last few miles of a marathon together. It is only after we commit to someone in this way—to staying with them rather than firing a shot and leaving—that we have any right to hold them accountable or call them to something more important.[13]

Each of the scenes I painted above demonstrates people coming alongside their organization, leader, or team, differing with them out of a commitment to their highest potential. This is the subtle shift of redefining the game—differing, but staying committed. Still you may ask: Is this really possible in today's intensely competitive work world? Can you differ and survive?

I believe the answer is yes, and it happens more often than you know. It's just not often visible, partly because it is by definition less antagonistic and does not generate the fireworks of rebelling. But there are traces of it, even in situations of terribly unhealthy pressure.

For example, in the story I told earlier about Standard & Poor's pressure to inflate ratings on subprime mortgage products, Frank Raiter never went along with management policy to ease standards, despite the political risks. "I didn't see it as part of the superior analytical pledge that we all took." Clearly, it was possible to survive and differ, though perhaps not while waving flags about it.[14]

Similarly, in his interview for the movie *Wal-Mart: The High Cost of Low Price,* a longtime manager describes the widespread but illegal practice where managers shaved payroll by altering timesheet records for their employees. In a telling quote, he says, "Every manager I had under me except one engaged in the practice."[15]

Who was that one person?

Perhaps that is the person to aspire to be. At a minimum you can keep your eyes open for signs that people are living with courage, even though it is subtle, and let that encourage you to make your own decision.

This is a daily choice. You have to keep rechoosing to redefine the game as the pressures and the seductions change. To remind us to choose purposeful courage and the pursuit of whatever it is we love, we might consider inscribing Faust's epiphany at the top of our daily to-do lists: "He only earns both freedom and existence who must reconquer them each day."[16]

And, yes, when you stand apart you often do become more visible. You may be labeled a boy scout, but perhaps that visibility awakens and supports others who are redefining the game or who want to. Perhaps it attracts those who are looking for just that quality—in all the senses of the word.

KEY CONCEPTS

- **Happiness formula** H = S + C + V (**H**appiness = **S**et range + **C**ircumstances + **V**oluntary activities). Redefining the game helps with all three elements of the formula. You develop "learned optimism" to raise your set range as you practice broadening your perspective beyond immediate threats. By investing in relationships and keeping your own score, you stay focused on the biggest circumstantial drivers of happiness. And striving to be a positive force or pursuing a professional quest leads you to exercise your signature strengths and experience the gratification that is the longest-lasting type of voluntary activity.

- **Ingredients for personal engagement** By expanding your ability to redefine the game, you are taking greater control of the three ingredients required for personal engagement at work: equity, camaraderie, and achievement—the chance be proud of one's work. You do this by developing skills and confidence and by anchoring yourself in a community and a purpose that go beyond the organization.
- **Thriving at work** You thrive when you are engaged in a meaningful pursuit that uses your talents and allows you to meet your real needs—including the need for pleasure and enjoyment—which is basically a prescription for adopting a professional quest. You probably do this best in settings in which you find at least some level of connection and mutual respect, where your values and your professional quest are angular and not diametrically opposed to the organization.
- **It begins with a decision** At the heart of the decision to redefine the game is the choice between fear and purposeful courage or love. The most difficult element of this decision is the willingness to stand apart. Making this choice can feel like life or death, which is why we need to rechoose to redefine the game over and over. Yet as you continue to engage at that higher level, your actions in turn can encourage others up, down, and across the hierarchy.

REFLECTION QUESTIONS

- Who is the person you could be that would make your kids proudest? Of what aspect about yourself are you privately proudest? What signature strengths does that reveal, and how might you recraft your work to allow you to express those strengths more often?
- What is your definition of thriving? What are the key ingredients? How would you describe the core choice that enables

you to thrive when there is pressure to play along with the game? Is it fear versus love? Is it avoidance versus courage? Comfort zone versus stretch?

- Have you ever had a moment of "elevation"—of being strongly affected by someone else's good deed or effort for something larger than himself? What was the situation? How did it affect you? Consider sharing that story with someone.

12

It's Bigger Than a Game

"As a leader, my actions are amplified," said Eric, the director of software engineering for a midsized public company, whom we met in chapter 11:

> There is a chain of impact from how I treat myself, to how that affects my team, the organization, the customer, and even society. Working in institutions as powerful as corporations, all our actions are amplified out into the world—even if we are not at the very top. We have a huge impact; the way business operates is shaping society these days.
>
> That's why I said the spirit of honesty goes far beyond not lying—it means acting on full awareness. And that's why the golden rule is *Be interested.* I need to care how the products we create are being marketed. I need to pay attention to the customer's concerns, even when they don't fit my timeline. I need to tell my bosses and peers what I think is needed to deliver for the customer.

I lean back and take a closer look at Eric, as we sit in the small snack kitchen near his office. He's in his midforties, has light brown hair, and is wearing a denim shirt with the company logo, jeans, and hiking shoes. I feel a little disoriented because, aside from a remarkable calmness, he looks like a familiar type in my mental cast of corporate characters, someone whose comments at a meeting I'm sure I could predict. And yet clearly, from the philosophy he is describing, I couldn't predict him at all.

"Why is it important to pay attention at that larger level?" I ask.

"One thing that concerns me is that while business is so powerful, its lens is actually quite narrow," he says. "Business operates in a culture of action, which does a lot of good, but it also creates a lot of harmful unintended consequences which are hard to see. It is opportunistic, more short-term focused. Societal concerns are more long-term. Even if business does something socially oriented, it can change directions the next day. How is the need for long-term health voiced? As a society, how do we sustain attention to longer-term issues over time?"

Larger Forces at Work

Through most of our journey together, we have focused on how you can expand your ability to redefine the game to improve your own health, sanity, and well-being—and quite possibly improve your organization's effectiveness in the bargain. But if we step back and look at the larger forces behind the dilemmas you face and the ripple effects that result when you succeed in engaging more of what matters, it lends even more importance to how you choose to respond to unhealthy pressure.

As the headlines of 2008–2009 have shown, we are living in a time of unprecedented economic challenges and uncertainty, from the systemwide distortions that led to the subprime lending crisis to the incredible damage caused by individuals such as Bernard Madoff. As the financial crisis shifts into a severe economic downturn, pundits and cab drivers alike are debating whether this is a cyclical adjustment or a painful structural shift with completely new rules of the game.

Amid all the bad news of the past year, perhaps nothing has been so intellectually destabilizing as former Federal Reserve Chairman Alan Greenspan's testimony to Congress in which he admitted he was "partially wrong" in his economic ideology and felt "shocked disbelief" that banks had not acted in their own self-interest during the mortgage boom.[1]

With his admission it became clear that some of the most foundational assumptions of our current Western capitalist approach need to be refined. For example, like Greenspan, many people have put their faith in the "invisible hand"—the idea that individuals and businesses will automatically pursue their self-interest and, in a free market, this will automatically lead to the greatest societal good. In other words, greed is ultimately good.

This is a very helpful assumption as far as simplifying decisions because it means you do not need to manage every complex nuance; you simply need to orient toward what the market rewards, and in so doing you can trust that this is also what creates the most value for society. It is at the very heart of the idea that you can "do well while doing good"—the proposition that with the same work you can provide for your family, challenge yourself, and create something of value in the world.

But what if, as Greenspan is realizing and behavioral economists are finding in their research, people and organizations do not always act in their own best interest? And what if, as Eric reminds us, businesses are precluded by their very nature from considering the long term or seeing the unintended side effects not measured by financial returns?

Many of the criticisms of the economy over the past few years are examples of what are called "market failures" in the economics textbooks. For example, economists have recently been referring to "information asymmetries"—where one party knows more than another about the true value or risk in a transaction—which lead people to act contrary to their best interests, as Bernard Madoff's clients did in investing with him. Economists also increasingly refer to "externalities," in which a company reaps the full benefit of producing a product and society pays the costs of any pollution or damage; in such cases the company has an incentive to produce more of a product even if it is harmful for the citizens overall.*

One of the major responses to these crises has been to look at the "rules of the game" that drive economic behavior, to try to reduce these distortions so that market incentives realign self-interest with societal good. In *Walking the Talk,* three prominent global business leaders argue that addressing these flaws is crucial for markets not to cause harm, impoverish future generations, and attract a civic backlash.[2]

In the meanwhile these market failures create unhealthy pressure in the industries they affect. Mihaly Csikszentmihalyi and Howard Gardner did a study that showed that when doing well in a field *did* line up with doing good, people were satisfied and engaged by their work; but when these were at odds, working in an industry felt like selling out. For example, the journalists they spoke with felt intense unhealthy pressure to sacrifice serving the public interest in favor of increasing market share.

What this trend means, in my opinion, is that it matters to the entire world how people in large organizations choose to respond to the incentives in front of them—and whether they opt to be part of redefining the game. Given that large public corporations currently have such capacity to shape public policy, make or break cross-sector collaborations, and lead or resist efforts to change

*To be precise, externalities also occur in reverse, where the company bears the cost and society gleans the benefit.

the rules of the game, it seems crucial to support all professionals in thinking through the most responsible ways to contribute to their organizations' ability to act with integrity—knowing that the incentives in the market are malleable and often distorted.

I think you will agree that much of the time when you face unhealthy pressure to compromise, what is at stake on some level *is* the organization's integrity—its ability to fulfill its commitments and meet its responsibilities to customers, employees, shareholders, or outside stakeholders.

In the last few weeks of editing this book, I met with Amrita again, the former petrochemical industry senior vice president whom I introduced in chapter 2. We attended a conference on sustainability, the field where she is now applying her technical and business knowledge to help whole industries reduce waste. Just after a particularly powerful presentation about the laws that determine what a corporate board can consider in its decision-making, including whether it is illegal to consider things like future generations, she passed me a note. "It's *bigger* than a game," she wrote, underlining the words to emphasize her point.

As we have seen throughout our exploration together, work *is* bigger than a game: it affects real lives, actual resources, and possible futures. Your individual dilemmas are the theater in which the larger forces of free-market alignment or misalignment are acted out. And when you choose to engage at the highest level you can manage, you are not only stepping up on behalf of your individual values and your organization's ultimate goals but simultaneously helping your organization evolve toward integrity on a larger scale.

This doesn't mean changing the world single-handedly; it is more about recognizing your part in a system of shared responsibility. In fact, you may find you are joining a growing cadre of professionals committed to redefining the game. For example, 50 percent of Harvard Business School's 2009 graduating class, plus more than four hundred MBAs from other programs including Northwestern's Kellogg School of Management and Oxford University's Saïd Business School, have taken an oath to "seek a course that enhances the value my enterprise can create for society over the long term" and "guard against decisions and behavior that advance my own narrow ambitions but harm the enterprise and the societies it serves."[3]

Moving toward Organizational Integrity

Given the effects of market distortions and the power of large organizations, it is not surprising that there are growing demands from all quarters that organizations take responsibility for their actions as a whole, as "moral actors" who are expected to keep commitments like individuals and take responsibility like citizens.

Yet as we discussed in chapter 3, our current understanding of organizational integrity—as the sum of the individual parts—does not add up to this moral-actor standard. Reaching the moral-actor standard is very challenging, requiring at least seven systemic functions for making and keeping commitments that don't typically exist in most organizations, as we discussed earlier.[4] Without these functions you have organizations that effectively talk out of both sides of their mouths. For example, according to Marcia, director of a global socially responsible business consulting firm, "Some of the companies I work with are playing both sides of an issue without knowing it. It's so ironic that government affairs, where they lobby for favorable legislation, is often just down the hall from corporate social responsibility, and they don't talk."

Her observation, along with nineteen years of diagnosing complex recurring organizational problems, has convinced me that the same systemic dysfunctions that hurt an organization's bottom line—frustrating attempts to improve employee retention, quality, cost-effectiveness, and customer loyalty—also limit its ability to act with integrity in the world. For example, how often do leaders and followers assume that the leader has all the information he needs to make a decision and accept the leader's judgment when the follower actually knows more? Or how often do departments set contradictory policies that hamstring the customer or some other stakeholder group without realizing it? Or how do we expect organizations to keep commitments over time when few organizations have systems for transferring promises when leaders transition to new roles?

Such organizational integrity "loopholes" mean you can have flaky, unreliable, even harmful organizations without a single villain. For example, consider Nike's efforts to address its suppliers' abusive labor practices. Over and over the company announced that it had solved the problems, and over and over the activist groups provided embarrassing proof that the harmful practices persisted. Ultimately, Nike shifted its attention from its program on labor practices to its procurement policies and bonus systems and saw how it was unintentionally undermining its own stated goals. Without the external feedback holding their feet to the fire, the leaders at Nike would never have confronted the fact that they were simultaneously making a commitment and preventing its fulfillment.[5]

If we view an organization as a moral actor, the elements of a high-integrity decision lie in multiple people's heads, often in different departments. In the absence of systems for overcoming this, or leaders who actively and constantly intervene to prevent disconnects, there is a natural entropy in organizations that leads to forgetting agendas and commitments over time, creating contradictory policies in different departments or overriding promises made by someone lower down.

This is why it troubles me that we devote so much of our attention to bad apples (or even bad barrels), narrowing our diagnosis to include only decisions made by a single individual, completely missing these larger, shared decision-making processes that can have such negative unintended consequences. It troubles me even more when I realize that to the degree any organization does act with integrity, it is because individuals and leaders are proactively intervening to correct for the system's weakness. But if they miss something, they are crucified, especially the senior leader.

When a system is pockmarked with inconsistencies and unreliability, there will always be room for individuals to defect for personal gain without being detected (for a time). On the other hand, I wonder what would happen to individual misconduct when the system as a whole is more coordinated and coherent. Wouldn't it reinforce those who might waver under pressure and make it easier to detect those who are out of bounds? Even better, wouldn't you get more of what you really want in the first place—organizations that create real value and are rewarded through financial means and/or the trust and loyalty of their stakeholders?

There is much more to explore in this area. As a start, in *Corporate Integrity* Marvin Brown proposes five dimensions of organizational integrity that go beyond consistency of word and action to include cultural openness; relationships that respect stakeholders, civil society, and the natural world; and a worthwhile purpose.[6] These are all reasonable aims, but they are far beyond what we are capable of achieving today with any consistency.

As challenging as it may be, building the capacity for integrity at an organizational level is critical or people will lose faith in even values-based businesses, for they too often miss the complexity of shared decisions and shared responsibility as much as more-traditional businesses—yet they commit to acting with more integrity.

Let's Make This Real

All models aside, at its core living with integrity is simply the decision to keep things real. As psychologist Scott Peck has said, "Mental health is an ongoing process of dedication to reality at all costs."[7] This is why it is so damaging to play along and why we have to redefine the game to stay true to ourselves. And it is why seeing the larger field is a more foundational commitment than defining a worthy enough win.

Conversely, the essence of the compromise trap is the natural but shortsighted desire to avoid confronting some difficult aspect of reality—a negative outcome, an uncomfortable situation, or bad news—as an individual or as an organization. Indeed, the gist of a devil's bargain is the choice to lie to yourself—splitting off part of your awareness, compartmentalizing your thoughts, suspending or postponing the values or principles that make you who you are—so you can fit into a mold of whom you'd like to be. For Faust, it was the desire to avoid mortality and the limits of human knowledge. For a modern professional, it might be the desire to avoid confronting the limits of her intelligence or the fear of not being a "winner," of not being able to provide the life she promised to her children. Yet a part of the mind knows the debts being incurred and dreads the moment when there is "hell to pay" and reality reintrudes on the delusion.

In many corporate scandals, there is often some comment about losing touch with reality: "They were insulated," "They forgot it wasn't their money," or "I didn't think about who it would impact." We even might say that the current painful corrections in the global economy, and the ones that may be to come, are the result of dropping certain elements of reality from our decision-making processes. It's very seductive to believe that one can accomplish the impossible, to try to be superhuman. In fact, this drive is very similar to the daring and the courage required to achieve a tough goal or a technological breakthrough. Yet if you get detached from reality in the pursuit of that goal, it takes more and more effort to continue living as if there were no tomorrow—as an individual, an organization, or a society.

One reason why I have used examples from Czechoslovakia is that Václav Havel has been so articulate about the personal psychological costs of kidding oneself. But one evening while I was searching the Web, I discovered that he too had confronted a Faustian bargain. Apparently, he had fallen into a period of discouragement and doubt during a prolonged imprisonment, and the state police offered him a chance to leave the country, to go to New York for the premier of one of his plays and be done with interrogations and surveillance, to live a free life. He admits he was tempted, almost haunted by the prospect of freedom. Yet, after a visit with his wife, he decided to stay and live out the path he had chosen with his friends in his own country. He later wrote about the experience in a play, *Temptation,* where a scientist sells his soul without knowing it, in the moment when he decides to lie to himself.[8] In fact, Havel viewed this sort of inner split as the heart of what maintained the totalitarian society. "We were all morally sick because we got used to thinking one thing and saying another," he said in a speech in 1990.[9]

It is ironic and paradoxical that there is so much to learn from former totalitarian countries about freedom under pressure. For example, during the Cultural Revolution in China, faced with arbitrary and ridiculous targets, a group of peasants came up with an ingenious solution. Given an unreal production goal, they delivered unreal results: a huge papier-mâché pig that took up the entire cargo area of the delivery truck. Unsure what to do, the government inspectors who received it behaved as if it were real.[10]

Luckily, you and I do not live with anywhere near the level of oppression of those societies at those times; we have choices and rights and many options for how we earn our living. Yet we sometimes confront similar pressures toward unreality. How often do we find ourselves delivering, or having delivered to us, papier-mâché pigs?

This is why redefining the game is as simple and as difficult as the choice to make things real.

But real about what?

In the end, all the stories and examples I've shared boil down to three essential dimensions of being real: seeing, caring, and action—the three elements of integrity as "right relationship to reality." Let's briefly look at being real along each of these dimensions, in reverse order.

The first part of being real is keeping your actions connected to your promises and commitments, individually and as part of your organization.

Like Stephanie laying her badge on the table to encourage the team to "walk the talk," you can sometimes counteract organizational entropy by gently challenging people to take the first step to acting on a commitment that has already been made. For example, an executive in a values-based company described the turning point in a product development effort: "We said we were going after this vision, we had a product specification, but we were not acting on it. Then one day at a meeting, someone said, 'Hey, let's make this real.' And that turned it around."

Similarly, when things have gotten unreal, false, or dishonest, this dimension involves getting back to reality.

For example, a sales manager who took over a new team in a remote office was alarmed to discover that salespeople had been providing inappropriate perks to potential customers in an industry where that was illegal. "This has to be keeping you up nights," she said to the sales staff at a team meeting. "I need you focused. This is unacceptable, illegal behavior. So we're going to have to clean it up." She set up an amnesty program, promising the salespeople that if they came forward, she would look at each case and determine what they needed to do to come clean. "It was a sizeable amount," she said. "Almost every single salesperson was involved—and it was eating them up." True to her instincts about the effect on morale, the team went on to record sales after that.

As this example shows, you don't need to be ridiculous about it or rigid and puritanical. You are simply looking for ways to bring your own and others' actions into alignment with their commitments and obligations.

The second dimension of being real is caring. This is about acknowledging and taking ownership of what feels important to you personally, the elements of "living it like you mean it" in your own life and in your organization—especially pursuing a business you truly believe in.

For example, the Google engineer who first proposed the company's informal motto *Don't be evil* explains on his personal blog that what he was proposing, among other things, was the radical and demanding idea that they should create and sell only those products and services that they really believed in.[11] What a concept.

Over time this second dimension of being real is what leads you to adopt a personal or organizational quest—but in an authentic way that does not overstate the level at which you currently operate. It is hard to tell at a distance which companies are truly pursuing quests; you have to be up close and personal to tell (which is one reason why I have hesitated to hold up specific organizations as models). But when a company is truly committed to something larger than itself, it can be electrifying.

For example, one leader told me about the exact moment his longtime employer became an inspiration. "The CEO introduced our new strategy by saying, 'There are three major challenges facing humanity today that we are positioned to help with....' How can you not get passionate about something focused at that level, whatever the specifics of the strategy are?"

And, finally, the third dimension of being real is seeing more of the reality of the world around you, which is the precondition for the other two.

You may have noticed that every management renewal comes in the form of some new method for getting out and seeing the reality on the ground—from "customer anthropology" and "customer experience management" back to "stapling yourself to an order," "managing by wandering around," "reengineering," and Total Quality Management. This is because it takes effort to stay in touch with reality. And yet it is only by staying connected with reality that you and your organization can learn.

This means facing the true costs and consequences of your actions though they are so easy to tune out. For example, Fred Reichheld of Net Promoter describes how often companies meet their revenue targets by relying on "bad profits"—profits gained by sacrificing a customer relationship.[12]

It also means having the humility to realize that there will always be important factors we miss because they are too remote or obscure to weigh as heavily in our decision-making as they should. Because no one can be in all places at all times, you need to develop relationships in which you trust each other's observations about external reality—so you can form a more coherent picture jointly and make better decisions.

Rick, a retired midlevel executive of a petrochemical company, described how his own learning process led him to try to bring "more of the truth" into his organization's decision-making:

> At first I thought all the protesters taking action against our company were freaks, bums, and immature kids whining because they

> didn't get enough attention growing up. But they kept at it, so I decided to check out their complaints. What I realized over time was that inside the company we were ignoring the enormous externalities created by our industry. On the other hand, the activists had their blind spots, too. For example, they insisted on an additive that was good for the air but bad for the water—and they wouldn't trust us when we told them so. (Now, twenty years later, the data shows we were right.) The point is that no one has the whole answer, but we have a greater chance of a better answer if we constantly try to bring more of the truth into our decision-making. And that's what I did for the remainder of my years with the company. They kept trying to give me a larger assignment, but I said, "No, this is what I want to do." So I went around the company, coaching teams on how to handle "more of the truth" in their decision-making.

As you can see from Rick's story and the many others we have heard, redefining the game is a demanding path. It requires great persistence. You may have to make some hard choices. You probably have to invest considerable effort in building the personal foundations that allow you to stay true, to be real.

But to be reunified with one's self is absolutely priceless.

It is hard for most of us in Western democracies to imagine what it was like to be part of the almost entirely peaceful revolution from totalitarianism to democracy in central Europe in 1989. Timothy Garton Ash was one of the very few foreign journalists to actually be present, indeed involved, during the critical days of the transitions in Poland, Hungary, East Germany, and Czechoslovakia.

Garton Ash was in Prague's Wenceslas Square when five hundred thousand people gathered in the freezing cold to hear members of the Czech resistance speak about the future they were going to create together around truth, objectivity, productivity, and freedom—after communism. He describes utterly incomprehensible moments when the crowd spoke back in unison to the speaker on the balcony, a call-and-response dialogue of hundreds of thousands of voices yelling, "Turn up the volume," "Shame, shame!" and "Now is the time."

Reflecting on the experience, Garton Ash tries to describe the significance of these dialogues in societies of such controlled language:

> To understand what it meant for ordinary people to stand in those vast crowds in the city squares of central Europe, chanting their own spontaneous slogans, you have first to make the imaginative effort to understand what it feels like to pay this daily toll of public hypocrisy. As they stood and shouted together, these men and women were not merely healing divisions in their society; they were healing divisions in themselves. Everything that had to do with the word, with the press, with television was of the first importance to these crowds. The semantic occupation was as offensive to them as the military occupation.[13]

The truth is, I think we all know a little bit about what this sort of public hypocrisy feels like. I know I do. And we also all know a bit about the courage to say what needs to be said to help the right thing happen.

When you take that risk, what you get back is soul.

It has been said that soul is the capacity to give to something greater than yourself—as an individual, an organization, a society.[14] Perhaps this is what we are protecting by being true to ourselves. After all, as we have seen, thriving seems to require contributing to a worthy pursuit.

Perhaps, in the end, this increase in soul is also how we become bigger when we redefine the game.

Thank you for taking this journey with me to explore the dynamics of the compromise trap and for considering the idea that you can expand your capacity to redefine the game and engage at a higher level.

As I said in the beginning, often what prevents people from fully acknowledging a challenge or dilemma is not knowing that solutions are possible. My hope is that now you have a far greater sense of the possibilities for redefining the game in even the most difficult circumstances and will be more equipped to recognize unhealthy pressure when it arises. Now you know that though they may not be visible in your next meeting, there *are* professionals who are guided by generosity as well as self-interest. It *is* possible to play that way and live, if you keep your own score.

Your priorities, your professional quest, may not be the same as mine. Clearly, from the examples I have used throughout this book, I have a concern about the side effects of our current economic system on the natural environment and how that will affect human life in the next few decades. Your principles, values, and concerns may be altogether different. Still, I am convinced that if you consider them to be important, they need to be spoken for.

You will decide at what level you want to engage, how big of a professional quest to pursue. If you want to keep your promises at work and be a person your kids are proud of, these ideas will serve you. And, hopefully, they will be of help if you decide that something more ambitious is calling you.

In any case, my hope is that the stories, principles, and foundations that support your ability to redefine the game give you greater trust in yourself. With that and a sense of humor and humility, I hope you become more willing to engage, to fully participate in the systems where you work, in the ongoing negotiation of what is possible and what matters, and you are able to contribute to helping the right or best thing happen. I hope you will have the satisfaction one day of discovering the ripple effects from your life into others' lives, through your children, your grandchildren, your neighbors, your colleagues, your bosses, your employees, or someone you spoke to in an airport. Perhaps one day you and I will meet, and I will get to hear the story of the part of you that wants to "live it like you mean it," and we will both have the presence of mind to have that sort of real conversation.

Until then, all the best to you and your journey, however it unfolds for you.

KEY CONCEPTS

- **It's bigger than a game** Your individual dilemmas are the theater in which the larger forces of free-market alignment or misalignment are acted out, creating healthy or unhealthy pressure on organizations. When you choose to redefine the game, you are not only stepping up on behalf of your individual values and your organization's ultimate goals but simultaneously helping your organization evolve toward integrity on a larger scale.
- **Organizational integrity** Organizations are increasingly expected to keep commitments like individual moral actors and fulfill responsibilities like citizens. This is difficult to achieve due to external unhealthy pressures and the organizational integrity "loopholes" that can create inconsistency internally. New thinking is emerging about the dimensions of organizational integrity and the systems needed for fulfilling commitments at an organizational level.
- **Making things real** At its core, redefining the game is the choice to engage more of reality, individually and as part of your organization. The first dimension of being real is keeping your actions connected to your promises and commitments. The second dimension is caring—acknowledging and taking ownership of what feels real and important to you, especially acting in alignment with what you truly believe, including regarding the products and the services you make or sell. The third dimension is seeing more of the reality of the world around you, knowing it takes effort to stay in touch with reality—and yet that is what

it takes to stay sane or learn. These three dimensions are the elements of integrity as "right relationship to reality": seeing, caring, and action.

REFLECTION QUESTIONS

- What commitments in your work environment would you like to see become real in terms of action? Where and when might you invite others to "make it real"?
- Where might you need to take greater ownership of what feels real and important to you while staying open to other perspectives? What realities from the world around you might you need to explore or investigate?
- Looking back on your life from somewhere long into the future, what are the ripple effects that would be most satisfying to trace from your life out into others' lives and the world?

Individual and Small-group Activities

This section is meant to help individuals and groups, as well as the coaches and trainers who work with them, explore and apply each of the personal foundations in fun and engaging ways so that you can expand your ability to redefine the game and engage at a higher level. Each activity can be used by both individuals and small groups.

Before you get started, you may want to take two diagnostic questionnaires: The **Organizational Pressure Diagnostic** allows you to take stock of the type, source, and strength of healthy and unhealthy pressure in your organization. The **Self-diagnostic** helps you identify the constraints that may be limiting your ability to redefine the game and the personal foundations that are likely to be of most use.

To access these two diagnostics or electronic versions of the Individual and Small-group Activities, please see "Online Resources." As I update the exercises, I will put new versions online, so please check the Web site often to see what's new.

One way to use these activities is to schedule yourself to complete one every two weeks for twelve weeks, gradually cycling through all six foundations.

ACTIVITY #1

Finding the Strengths in Your Story

Foundation: Reconnect to your strengths

Purpose: To help you discover the strengths and the values embedded in your life story and clarify the routines and the habits that help you stay in touch with them

Timing: 1 to 3 hours (2 hours minimum for a group)

Number: Can be done individually, with a partner or coach, or in a group of seven to twelve participants

This activity invites you to use your own life story as a resource for discovering your strengths and values and for clarifying the non-negotiable routines that support you.

Step 1 Draw your "emotional journeyline" Working individually, lay out a piece of paper with "Emotional Energy and Engagement" along one side and "Time" across the bottom. (See figure A-1.) Then, reflecting back on your life from childhood to now, draw a line to represent the ups and downs of emotional

Figure A-1 Sample Journeyline

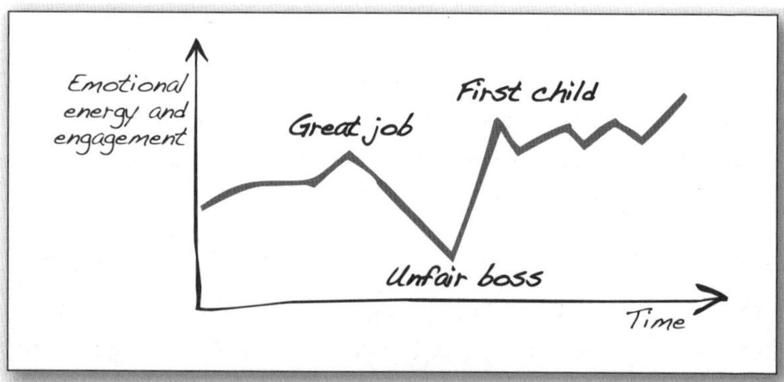

Adapted from Noel M. Tichy of the University of Michigan, who created the concept of "emotional journeylines" as a way for leaders to formulate their leadership storylines out of their past experiences. To learn more about this powerful tool, see Noel M. Tichy, *The Leadership Engine* (New York: Collins Business, 2002), pp. 58–78 and 332–47.

energy and engagement over time—when you felt good about yourself and when you were having a hard time. Label the most pivotal events, including those where you felt most engaged, capable, and courageous. Take a moment to reflect on the key moments of your journeyline, reliving them with all five senses if you can. *Allow 15 to 20 minutes for this step.*

Step 2 Tell your story Now, working with a partner, briefly tell the story of your journeyline, focusing on the pivotal experiences that most shaped you—using your judgment about which details feel comfortable and appropriate to share. Then, with your partner, reflect on these self-discovery questions:

- What are the main themes and lessons weaving through your experience? What is your story "about"?
- What strengths have shown up when you were most engaged and committed? What gifts or talents seem to give you energy?
- What does your story tell you about your values and priorities? What's core to your identity and what's peripheral? When you are most engaged, what principles or values do you find yourself embodying or advocating?
- What does your story tell you about the conditions that best support you? What are the routines and the habits that help you access your physical, emotional, mental, and spiritual energy?[1]

In a small-group setting, you may want to take a few minutes for each pair to share their key insights with the group and see if there are any larger themes at the group level. *Allow about 20 to 40 minutes total for the pair activity and 5 to 7 minutes per pair for group discussion.*

Step 3 Summarize your insights To help you put your insights into practice, take a moment to capture them in three lists:

- **List #1: Your Core Strengths** Write a short list of the core strengths that make you most who you are, based on your story. To go further here, complete the online VIA Signature Strengths Questionnaire, which measures twenty-four character strengths, using your story and notes as guides when you answer the questions. (See *www.authentichappiness.com.*)
- **List #2: Your Core Values** List the values you identified as core to your identity, those that are important but not core, and those that are more peripheral. (You might like to draw a diagram similar to the one in figure A-2.)

Figure A-2 Sample Values Scheme

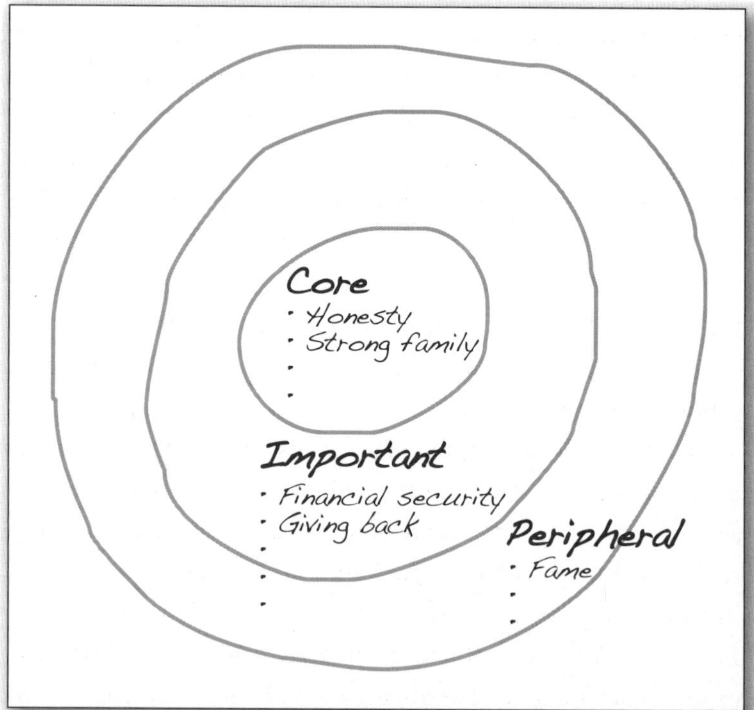

- **List #3: Nonnegotiable Habits and Routines** Based on your reflections about your story, write down the bare minimum routines and practices for staying sane and healthy and for keeping in touch with your core strengths and values. Try to keep it to a critical few, listing separately any that are helpful but not nonnegotiable. Decide whether you are ready to commit to your list of nonnegotiables or, alternatively, identify what it would take for you to be ready.

You can use your journeyline and these lists, along with Decision Point Tool #1: Activating Your Strengths, anytime you face unhealthy pressure. To help you stick to your core routines and practice your strengths and values, you can also use these lists proactively when you are setting goals or prioritizing your tasks. *Allow 10 to 15 minutes for this step.*

Optional variation Many people find it astonishingly helpful to have a private image or symbol of themselves at their full strength. To give this a try, ask yourself, *Who am I when I am at my most clear, courageous, and capable?* Notice what qualities or associations come to mind. Then think of someone you consider a role model of those qualities or associations—a historical figure, a mythical character, a comic book figure, even a superhero or movie character. Try to find an image or photo of that individual, or look through old magazines for iconic figures or images that capture that spirit.

Once you've found an image, consider giving it a title or finding a quote to capture the qualities or values you find yourself embodying when you are at your best. For example, in one recent workshop people adopted titles such as *the Voice of Reason, Advocate for Accountability, the Spirit of Courage,* and *Warrior for Innovation.* You can both have some fun with this and use it to experiment with how powerful images and phrases are for evoking the clarity, courage, and energy you feel when you are in touch with your strengths. Of course, the key is knowing that you don't have to show anyone if you don't want to!

ACTIVITY #2

Redefining-the-game Opportunity Map

Foundation: See the larger field

Purpose: To identify inherent tensions in your business and survey opportunities to redefine the game that would make a difference to your organization or your role

Timing: 1 to 2 hours

Number: Can be done individually, with a partner or coach, or in a group of seven to twelve participants

This activity helps you uncover the inherent tensions and opportunities to redefine the game in your business, role, or industry. You start by mapping what gets attention and what is important but tends to fade from view.

Step 1 Draw a map of what gets your attention As Saul Steinberg demonstrated in his famous *New Yorker* map, what is near and frequently visited looms large in your attention and what is farther away, in the future, or not as emotionally vivid gets lumped together and fades onto the horizon. With that in mind, start by drawing a rough horizon line on your map, then sketching in blocks, shapes, or figures in the foreground of what gets your attention day to day, where there is the most "heat and light." What data are most vivid and urgent—your performance metrics, the company stock price? On whom do you focus most—bosses, senior executives, employees? What events tend to get your focus—presentations, deadlines, crises? What places are most real to you? Don't worry about making the map elegant; just sketch some representation of the important demands on your attention. (See figure A-3 for a sample map.) *Spend 5 to 10 minutes working on your own.*

Step 2 Add what tends to fade in the distance We only have so much ability to focus. As your attention is drawn to these pressing issues, what tends to recede into the background? What is easy to neglect or postpone in your industry, business, or role because it is intangible, delayed, or remote? Who or what is important but rarely urgent—significant relationships, processes, assets, core knowledge? Who depends on you or your company to be trustworthy? Add the most important of these factors to your map, perhaps in the middle or background areas. *Work for another 5 to 6 minutes individually.*

Step 3 Highlight the tensions Now share your map with a partner. Looking at the whole landscape together, ask yourselves: *What are the inherent tensions here, especially between what is immediate, local, and tangible and what is delayed, remote, or intangible? Where are there trade-offs or either/or choices? Which of the areas that fade from view are important to future success? Where could discounting or ignoring an important factor come back to haunt the organization?* Using a different color, draw circles around the factors that might be underweighted in decision-making and arrows between each side of the either/or trade-offs. For example, you might draw arrows between the cost metrics in the foreground and customer quality in the background to show that these areas are often in tension. *Allow 10 to 15 minutes total for pair discussions.*

Figure A-3 Sample Redefining-the-game Opportunity Map

Step 4 Highlight the redefining-the-game opportunities Finally, working with your partner, take a step back and reflect on the tensions you highlighted and the opportunities they suggest. Think about them from the perspective of who you are as a person, parent, or citizen. What needs more attention in this situation? What needs more weight in decision-making? Where is innovation needed to reduce the pressure to make unhealthy trade-offs? Make a few notes about these redefining-the-game opportunities. *Allow 10 to 15 minutes total for pair discussions, and 15 to 20 minutes for small-group debriefing.*

You can use your Redefining-the-game Opportunity Map to identify areas where you can bring "more of reality" into decision-making processes or focus your efforts on innovation. See if it gives you any hint of what is important enough to be a professional quest for you. (You'll get to explore this further in Activity #3: Discovering Your Professional Quest.) Or, you might share it with others and invite them to help you upgrade your understanding.

Optional variation Here's a variation to make this activity even more useful. Try taking a field trip to check out the situation on the ground. Talk with those whose priorities tend to fade from view, who are important but rarely urgent to your organization. See if you can visit customers or suppliers; go to the neighborhoods or businesses where your products are made or used. Visit those people who seem to think your business is the enemy. Or try a virtual field trip via the Internet and search for magazine articles and/or blogs that show the state of the world on the ground in the places where your organization does business.

ACTIVITY #3

Discovering Your Professional Quest

Foundation: Define a worthy enough win

Purpose: To help you discover the unique professional quest that unlocks strength and guides you to what is really worth doing while developing and clarifying your professional guidelines

Timing: 1 to 2 hours

Number: Can be done individually, with a partner or coach, or in a group of seven to twelve participants

This activity helps you uncover a sense of a professional quest by looking for the links between your strengths and gifts and the particular situation and opportunities around you. It also helps you bring that into action by identifying professional guidelines you can use to make day-to-day decisions based on that sense of mission or purpose.

Step 1 Revisit your story, strengths, and values Take a moment to revisit what you discovered in Activity #1: Finding the Strengths in Your Story. Or reflect on these questions: *What does your story explain about who you are? What are the personal strengths you most enjoy using, the ones you bring in a unique way to whatever situation you are in? What are the most important values that define you and why are they important? Who are you when you are at your most clear, courageous, and capable?* If you came up with an image or title in Activity #1, take a look at it now and recall how it connects to your strengths. Jot down a few notes. *Allow 5 to 10 minutes for individual work here.*

Step 2 Reflect on what needs attention in the world Take a moment to revisit your Redefining-the-game Opportunity Map from Activity #2, or reflect on these questions: *What are the most challenging inherent tensions in your business or role? Who or what tends to fade to the background because they are important but not urgent? Where are there opportunities for improving decision-making by raising the visibility of important factors or innovating to reduce the need to make trade-offs?* Now step back and ask yourself, just as a person, citizen, parent, or human being: *What most needs attention these days? What opportunities seem most important, and what concerns are most troubling?* Don't limit yourself to your current setting or industry. Jot down a few notes. *Allow 5 to 10 minutes for individual work here.*

Step 3 Draw the connections Working with a partner, briefly describe your story, strengths, and values and what you see needs attention in the world—using your judgment about which details feel comfortable and appropriate to share. Then, reflecting together, ask yourself these self-discovery questions:

- What connections do you see between your gifts and strengths and what needs attention?
- Given your strengths, gifts, and values and what you see most needs attention in the world, where are you uniquely situated to contribute? What would you most like to offer or contribute?
- What opportunities or possibilities seem most necessary and inspiring? What are you most curious or energized to explore?

Invite your partner to work with you to craft a short statement or a few sentences that capture your sense of a professional quest or mission. You might even try framing it as a question. There is no "right" level of ambition or importance here—your passion might be creating a culture of mutual respect at work, making customers' lives easier, or designing transformative healthcare experiences. (It should be something beyond caring for your children because it will be most powerful if it is something that makes your children proud, something you can use to help model the life you hope they might lead.) To ensure that your professional quest thoroughly galvanizes your energy, you might check that it has these qualities:

- It is worthy of you; it taps your highest potential.
- It is singular and unique, such that only you can fulfill it.
- You really want it; you don't just think you *should* want it.
- It's intrinsically valuable to you, whether or not others approve.
- It is concrete and reflects what is needed in the world.

Allow 10 to 15 minutes per person, 20 to 30 minutes total for this pair activity.

Step 4 Clarify your professional guidelines Considering your professional quest, what professional guidelines would allow you to bring it to life in your day-to-day decisions? Given the inherent tensions in your industry, business, or role, what principles will you use to make practical decisions that incorporate both what is immediate and measurable and what is important but less visible or measurable? What commitments do you need to make to be trustworthy to those who must count on you? (For a reminder, see figure 7-1, Jim Lehrer's Personal Work Guidelines.) Start by making a list of just three or four guidelines so that you can try them out first. Share them briefly with a partner and refine them to ensure that they help you be "angular" to the pressures in your industry rather than automatically opposed or completely compliant. Then, if you are working in a small group, you might want to come back together to debrief. *Allow 10 minutes individually, then 5 minutes per person in pairs and 15 to 20 minutes for the group.*

ACTIVITY #4

Strengthening Your Connections with Allies

Foundation: Find your real team

Purpose: To take stock of your most critical relationships and develop a plan for deepening and forming new connections

Timing: 1 to 2 hours

Number: Can be done individually, with a partner or coach, or in a group of seven to twelve participants

With this activity you can survey your current relationships, identify where you would like to form stronger alliances, and craft the first steps toward doing so. It includes a list of Dinner-table Conversation Starters to help you deepen the conversation in informal settings with your family, friends, or allies.

Step 1 List your relationships Working on your own, draw lines to create four columns on a sheet of paper and label the columns *Family, Allies,* and *Network.* Leave the last column blank. In the first column, list the names of your immediate family members or people you consider family. Under Allies, list your closest friends and connections at home and work—the people who make sure you have a birthday party, who you can call on in a pinch. Finally, in the third column, list those who are in your broader network—friends, professional connections, extended family, members of your community, acquaintances, and so on. Notice how you feel as you write each name and whether you are drawn to connect more actively with that person. *Take 5 to 10 minutes for individual work.*

Step 2 Circle those you'd like to cultivate further Now circle the names of those people who are or could be most aligned and supportive of the person you want to be, regardless of whether they are currently close to you. Include people you admire, learn from, get the most satisfaction from spending time with, those who "get" you, and those who stretch you in positive ways. For your family, circle those with whom you suspect there are ways to deepen or further align the relationship. In the last column enter and circle any additional names that come to mind as you think about potential members of your real team. Now sit back and take a look: Where are your circles? Which potential allies most attract your curiosity and interest? Which current relationships would you like to deepen? Take a moment to share any aha's with a partner. *Allow 5 to 7 minutes for individual work and 5 minutes for partner sharing.*

Step 3 Identify two or three ways you can deepen or extend your relationships with allies Select two or three relationships from those you circled and think about how you might get to know the individuals better or connect on a deeper level. For those to whom you are already close, are there ways you could acknowledge them or ask for their help (or offer it)? For those who are farther out, how might you reach out to them? This can be quite informal. The Dinner-table Conversation Starters below can help you get started. Briefly share your plans with a partner. *Allow 5 minutes for individual work, 5 minutes for partner sharing, and 2 to 3 minutes per pair to debrief as a group.*

Dinner-table Conversation Starters

In the world of computers, cell phones, text messaging, and television, a good conversation is in danger of becoming a lost art. Yet when someone takes the initiative to ask a really good question, others often respond enthusiastically. Here are a few you might try with your spouse, partner, children, friends, and allies—or use these for inspiration in crafting a few of your own:

- How did you come to be in the field you're in? How does your work relate to your priorities, values, or strengths as a person?
- What do you like most about your work (or school)? What really engages you?
- What pressures do you face at work (or school)? What do you like least?
- Where have you had to compromise for work (or at school)? Why?
- How do you find yourself changing as you grow in your profession (or your skills at school)?
- What are your bottom lines? Have you ever had to stand up for something you believed in at work (or school)?

- What makes one thing work and another play? What work would you really *want* to do?
- Whom do you consider really successful? Why?
- What is "enough" for you? What do you consider extra, a luxury? What helps you avoid getting caught up in always needing more?

Further options At some point you may want to move beyond informal conversations to form an ongoing support group. To help you get started, I have crafted a guide for forming your own "professional quest group" or hosting larger-scale conversations as part of a retreat or leadership development program. For more information, please see "Online Resources."

ACTIVITY #5

Redefining-the-game Action Planning

Foundation: Make positive plays

Purpose: To recognize opportunities to make a positive play and think through which best fits your situation (over a longer time horizon than with Decision Point Tool #5: Which Positive Play?)

Timing: 2 to 4 hours

Number: Best done in a small group of two or three individuals, then vetted and upgraded with others who have similar inspiration to influence the situation

This series of questions helps you identify which action to take and when, especially in more prolonged and challenging efforts.

Step 1 What is needed here? If possible, before you do this step, make a Redefining-the-game Opportunity Map for the organization or role you are concerned with. Then, with your small group, explain your map and brainstorm: *What needs to happen here? What needs to be made more visible? Where would innovation help? What would it look like to redefine the game at a higher level? What is the worthy enough win?* Look for leverage, where the smallest effort can have the greatest positive impact. You will be most effective if you can think it through without blame, imagining how each person or group views the situation differently. *Allow 15 to 20 minutes per person in small groups of 2 or 3 individuals.*

Step 2 What is within my control? Now, working on your own, brainstorm: *Where might I start with myself in pursuing what is needed here? What experiments might I try? What new habits might I adopt? What information might I provide to others? How could I capture what I learn in a way that helps tell the story to others?* Jot down a few ideas. *Allow 5 to 15 minutes for individual work, then 15 to 30 minutes to compare notes in small groups.*

Step 3 Where do I need to connect with others? Returning to your small groups, expand your horizon to consider additional potential allies, sponsors, or even worthy opponents you might engage. Ask yourselves: *Who might improve our thinking? Who sees the risks and the opportunities most clearly? Who could act differently to help the right thing happen? Who might already be working on this issue?* Try to identify the important stakeholders from these different perspectives, how they view the world, and why you think it might be in their interest to consider the worthy enough win you are proposing. Consider how you might tell the story, what you'd like to understand better from each of them, and what you want to propose or request of them. Jot down a few notes for each key conversation. *Allow 15 to 30 minutes in small groups, then 5 to 10 minutes for individuals to summarize their final plans. If you are working in a multiple-group setting, do a quick general debriefing,* *then ask 2 or 3 individuals to share their plans; have the larger group work with them to identify how they would know they were successful and what they might expect to learn from the experience.*

Step 4 Identify your first steps Take a moment on your own to jot down a few first action steps you want to take in terms of testing your assumptions or assessments of the situation, trying your own experiments, or meeting with others. *Allow 5 to 10 minutes for individual work. If meeting in a group, close the session with a round of reflections on any aha's or responses to this thought process.*

Each time you go through this process, taking action yourself and connecting with others, you broaden the group involved as well as your impact, refining your story, clarifying what you can act on directly, and identifying new places to connect. This becomes part of a reinforcing loop as a greater number of people get involved in helping redefine the game and you each get clearer about what is needed and what is possible. To learn more, I encourage you to check out the further reading described under "Online Resources."

ACTIVITY #6

Personal Goal Review

Foundation: Keep your own score

Purpose: To bring your goals into greater alignment with your professional quest or mission, including developing independent ways to gauge your success and reinforce your efforts

Timing: 1.5 to 2 hours

Number: Can be done individually, with a partner or coach, or in a group of seven to twelve participants

This activity helps you reshape your goals to align more closely with your true priorities and what you consider "enough" by reviewing

your current goals and spending. It also invites you to craft a uniquely personal celebration to acknowledge the work you have put into achieving greater alignment.

Step 1 Reflect on your current goals Take a moment to jot down your current goals—implicit or explicit—then ask yourself the following questions to see how well they align with your sense of your quest or mission.

- Why do I want these goals? What feelings/experiences will they get me? Are these goals intrinsically valuable to me, or are they a means to an end?
- Are these mostly playing-along-with-the-game goals or redefining-the-game goals? Are there redefining-the-game goals lurking behind any of the playing-along ones? (See figure A-4.)
- Finally, which of these goals might I want to refine or let go of, knowing that it may no longer fit for me? Which might I want to watch carefully in case it costs too much?

Figure A-4 Playing-along-with-the-game and Redefining-the-game Goals

Playing-along-with-the-game Goals	Redefining-the-game Goals
■ I'll *be* somebody if I do this. ■ This will prove I'm not a loser. ■ Everyone will admire me when I get there. ■ If I make a ton of money, I won't have to deal with these clowns. ■ Once I show them, I can do what I really want.	■ I am fully engaged when I work on this. ■ I need to earn a living, but I don't need to "win" to keep doing this. ■ This is worth doing whether or not I get credit. ■ This is part of what my life is all about. ■ I may not work on this all the time, but I still value it.

Take a moment to briefly share your insights with a partner, using your judgment about which details feel comfortable or appropriate to share. Jot down a few notes about what adjustments you might make based on your reflections. *Allow 10 to 15 minutes for individual work and 5 to 10 minutes total for pairs.*

Step 2 Get clearer about what is enough Think for a moment about what "survival" really means to you, jotting down notes as you reflect on the following questions:

- How have you and your family defined survival and security, implicitly or explicitly? What have you personally viewed as a comfortable life, a luxurious life, and a life of hardship? How does your family feel about each of these?
- Which of your financial commitments, purchases, and activities are inherently, directly pleasurable to you? Which are more oriented toward social standing? Which are a result of your efforts to deal with stress? (You may want to revisit an old budget or spending records for this.)
- Where do you feel scarcity in your life? Where do you feel there is enough? Where is there too much? How do you think your family would answer?

Again, take a moment to share your insights with a partner; strategize together on how you might initiate these sorts of conversations with your family. Then identify some experiments you might try with different ways of using your time and resources to see whether they increase your sense of well-being and satisfaction. *Allow 30 minutes total for pair work, then 15 to 20 minutes for a small-group debriefing.*

Step 3 Design a celebration As an experiment in the use of appreciation, gratitude, and intrinsic satisfaction (and all the hard work of doing these activities), work with your partner to craft a celebration with your family, friends, or circle of allies. What's the right way to celebrate what's working in your life—for you? A toast over a meal, an awards ceremony, an outing, a roast? Whom would you invite? What would you say? *Allow 10 to 15 minutes total for brainstorming in pairs. If you are in a larger group, allow 15 minutes for sharing "best ideas," then close with a round of reflections from each person.*

Online Resources

To download these additional materials, please visit:
www.WorkLore.com/CompromiseTrap

Diagnostic Questionnaires

These two online questionnaires help you target your efforts to stay out of the compromise trap and expand your ability to redefine the game. The **Organizational Pressure Diagnostic** allows you to take stock of the type, source, and strength of healthy and unhealthy pressure in your organization. The **Self-diagnostic** helps you identify the constraints that may be limiting your ability to engage at a higher level and the personal foundations that are likely to be of most use.

Decision Point Tools

To help you tap your personal foundations in the moment, the Decision Point Tools that appear throughout the book are available in a single document that you can download and print or work with online.

Individual and Small-group Activities

The Individual and Small-group Activities at the back of the book are available electronically in several short documents designed to be used over a period of six to twelve weeks, for yourself or someone you are coaching. As I develop new activities, I post them to the Web site, so you may want to check back from time to time.

Professional Quest Groups

If you would like to connect with other professionals for mutual support and encouragement as you put these ideas into practice, check this link to learn about groups forming online or in your area. You can also check here for information about convening your own groups or hosting larger-scale conversations as part of a retreat or leadership development program.

More about the Interviews

For those interested in the inquiry that led to this book, this gives you more detail about the research method, interview questions, participant demographics, and findings (such as the data that are the basis of figure 2-1). In addition, I have compiled a selection of quotes that do not appear in the book but which give you a richer and deeper sense of the conversations.

Further Reading

As I mentioned in the Introduction, each of the personal foundations in this book represents a stepping-stone on a path to greater and greater capacity to redefine the game and engage at a higher level. To continue your progress, I highly recommend exploring this list of related books and articles. I continually update the list, so you may want to check back periodically.

Acknowledgments

Because this book is the culmination of several thousand conversations, I am struck by the immense debt of gratitude I owe to all those who shared their stories, insights, and philosophies as well as by the sheer impossibility of acknowledging everyone who had a significant influence. Yet certain conversational threads stand out particularly bright and strong in the weave that brings this together and need to be named.

I owe the deepest debt of gratitude to all the interview participants, formal and informal, who generously shared their experiences and reflections on organizational life. My hope is that at least some small portion of the wisdom, understanding, and humor in your tales comes through in the translation.

I would like to thank William Ury and the dedicated individuals who contribute to the Harvard Negotiation Project, the Abraham Path, and other efforts to demonstrate the creative power of constructive conflict. They have given me a living model of what it means to redefine the game without apology or fanfare, and Dr. Ury's ideas, especially on the power of a positive no, are visible here throughout. And to Art Kleiner, I am indebted for the provocative idea of core groups and, more personally, for his spontaneous emotional response to the stories I had gathered, the introduction to Berrett-Koehler, and his invaluable advice on "writing without strain."

Thanks also to the other thought leaders in this field who shared their time to improve these ideas, including Bill Torbert, Joe Badaracco, Max Bazerman, Earl Palmer, Maureen O'Hara, Bob Fuller, and Stanley Keleman. Beyond these personal interactions, several authors' works have proved foundational to the concepts here, including those of Marvin Brown, Lynn Sharp Paine, Ira Chaleff, Peter Block, Debra Meyerson, Ian Mitroff, Parker Palmer, David Whyte, and Václav Havel. Also, I would especially like to thank Jim Lehrer for sharing the guidelines that help him and the team at the *NewsHour* model such high-quality journalism.

There have been several "circles of allies" from whom and with whom I have been fortunate to learn. The tenaciously disorganized Bay Area fractal of the Society for Organizational Learning has been a wonderfully fruitful incubator, and I am very grateful for my colleagues there. More broadly, the members of the global Society for Organizational Learning offer practical models of how to be a positive force during a necessary revolution. Some of my most vivid learning experiences have centered around the Grace Group, including Mitch Saunders, Anne Dosher, Craig Fleck, and Glenna Gerard; more recent students of that work, Rod Bacon and Matthew Frazer; and those on a parallel path, John Ott, Jon Rubenstein, and Rose Pinard. And finally, thank you to all the business storytellers for proving the startling power of learning from our own experience, especially Terri Tate and Kat Koppett for their help in crafting the story-circle method.

For reasons known best to themselves, several brilliant and talented individuals stepped forward to help shepherd this work as it took shape. Thank you to Bob Horn, whose flexible and energetic intellect spurred my thinking and who helped introduce me to Berrett-Koehler as well as the writings of Reinhold Niebuhr and Robert Kegan. Thanks also to Hanley Brite, for lending the brilliant spotlight of his playful intelligence to this work and for all the provocative conversations over the past twenty years that, in the end, were about compromise traps and redefining the game; and to Alain Gauthier, for coming alongside my work as our inquiries converged and for the delightful survey of French meanings for the term *devil's bargain.* To Joe Durzo, thank you for sharing from your inexhaustible well of encouragement and for guidance in walking the line between realism and exposé; and to Mike Maginn, for tirelessly brainstorming titles, reading drafts, and helping bring the practice of self-reflection to the foreground. To Seetha Kammula-Coleman, Brian Coleman, and Julian, thanks for sharing their home, their family, their stories, and their new ventures in one of the biggest games of this century; and to Andrea Dyer, Kristin Cobble, Stacey Smith, Nancy Murphy, David Isaacs, Lisa Voss, Badal Chaudhari, and Anna Meyer, for making it a special priority to see this effort come to fruition and for reinforcing my commitment as it first began to emerge in its finished form. And thanks to Marijke Rijsberman, for her rigorous and principled reasoning, for our long IM chats about the processes of compromise, and for sharing the writing cabin with my dogs.

Many of the most important ideas and examples here came from infrequent but foundational conversations with people whose paths I crossed only occasionally, but with great value, including Alex Gilmete, Ana and Joao Santos, Bernice Moore, Bo Gyllenpalm, Cathy Rodgers, Charlene Grabowski, Clive Chafer, David and Linda Belle-Isle, David Drake, David Sonke, Debbie Arce, Dennis Reidlinger, Diana Verhalen, Eduardo Salaz, Gayle Wessel, Gerald Harris, Greg Veerman, Herb Wimmer, Jeff Dunn, Janet Aguilar, Jeff Venable, Jerry Curtin, Jerry Michalski, Joy

Strassel, Julie Van Hove, Kay Faubert, Keith McCandless, KoAnn Skrzniarz, Mahammed Mahbouba, Marcia Rayene, Mark Sommer, Michael Gordon, Nancy Southern, Natalie Zeituny, Norma Olmos, Pat Murphy, Robert Fisher, Roger Saillant, Sally Al-Daher, Sarita Chawla, Scott Mills, Shane Rogers, Stacy Ferratti, Tom Hurley, Tom McLaren, Tracie Lofgren, the Special Forces sniper from Peru, the cab driver from Kabul, and many, many others.

Thank you also to my clients and their organizations, especially my friends at Archstone-Smith, Intuit, and CDM, for the opportunity to partner in pursuit of their visions and for the flexibility they offered during the process of completing this manuscript. Thanks also to my HBS classmates, whom I leave unnamed out of respect for their anonymity in the stories herein, and for allowing themselves to be engaged, and occasionally disrupted, by my questions.

I am enormously grateful to Steve Piersanti at Berrett-Koehler Publishers for the honor of having my ideas passed through the crucible of his brilliant "denseness" and for yet another reminder of what it looks like to redefine the game without apology or fanfare. Thank you to Jeevan Sivasubramaniam for seeing the energy in a positive approach to the dark side, and to all the staff at BK for their willingness to help shape a book for an audience who might not always recognize that compromise could go too far. Thanks also to Gary Palmatier, copyeditor Elizabeth von Radics, and the production team at Ideas to Images for their artful ability to turn electronic ideas and images into something as enduring as a book. To the BK author community, I am grateful for the welcoming support every first-time author undoubtedly needs but only gets in the remarkable network that forms around a publisher with a mission like helping create a world that works for all.

To Ken Homer, Diane Fischler, Stephanie Tristan, Kim Criswell, and Naraya Stein, I owe deep thanks for helping me keep my sanity, giving "legs" to the book as it goes out into the world, and letting themselves occasionally get inspired.

Thank you to Jan Hetherington and Joe Davis for attending any and every experimental storytelling event I ever concocted (I'm sorry the book has a subtitle). Thank you to David Nelson for showing up on our second date with a book on integrity to help my research—and then going dancing every week for three years. And thanks to Jack, Lorraine, Dana, Kim, Mark, Cynthia, Simon, Melissa, Ralph, Ellen, and all the Zydeco dancers who asked me every Friday night, "How's the book coming?" and assured me as we danced the two-step that I really ought to finish it soon.

Finally, I would like to extend my deepest appreciation and gratitude to my family, who are also my friends. The conversations this inquiry prompted have helped me know you all the better, and I have been enriched by that connection.

Notes

Foreword

1. C. S. Lewis, *The Silver Chair* (New York: HarperTrophy, 2000), p. 166.

Introduction

1. *Enron: The Smartest Guys in the Room*. Los Angeles: Magnolia Home Entertainment, 2005.
2. See Marvin T. Brown, *Corporate Integrity: Rethinking Organizational Ethics and Leadership* (Cambridge: Cambridge University Press, 2005); and John Beebe, *Integrity in Depth* (Carolyn and Ernest Fay Series in Analytical Psychology) (Bryan, TX: Texas A&M University Press, 1992).
3. John Briggs and F. David Peat, *Seven Life Lessons of Chaos: Spiritual Wisdom from the Science of Change* (New York: HarperCollins, 1999), p. 43.

Chapter 1: The Compromise Trap

1. "Credit and Credibility," *Now* on PBS: online video. http://www.pbs.org/now/shows/446/index.html.
2. Michael Isikoff, "The Fed Who Blew the Whistle," *Newsweek*, December 22, 2008. http://www.newsweek.com/id/174601.
3. See James P. Carse, *Finite and Infinite Games* (New York: Ballantine Books, 1987) for an interesting discussion of games as a metaphor for how we engage in everyday life.
4. "Confessions of a Wal-Mart Hit Man," extended bonus scenes from *Wal-Mart: The High Cost of Low Price*. Documentary film. Robert Greenwald Films, 2005. http://www.youtube.com/watch?gl=GB&hl=en-GB&v=-mQH9DloKD8.

5. "Credit and Credibility," *Now* on PBS: online video.
6. David Whyte, *Crossing the Unknown Sea* (New York: Riverhead Books, 2001), p. 56.

Chapter 2: A Devil's Bargain by Degrees

1. For more on this pressure to conform, see Richard Sennett, *The Corrosion of Character: The Personal Consequences of Work in the New Capitalism* (New York: W. W. Norton, 2000).
2. Chris Argyris, "Skilled Incompetence," *Harvard Business Review* (September/October 1986): 74–79.
3. Linda K. Trevino and Katherine A. Nelson, *Managing Business Ethics: Straight Talk about How to Do It Right* (Hoboken, NJ: John Wiley & Sons, 2007), p. 195.
4. Ethics Resource Center, *2007 National Business Ethics Survey: An Inside View of Private Sector Ethics* (Arlington, VA: Ethics Resource Council, 2007), pp. 9, 39. http://www.ethics.org/research/NBESOffers.asp.
5. Johann Wolfgang von Goethe, *Faust: A Tragedy* (New York: Norton, 2001), p. 324.
6. Robert B. Cialdini, "Commitment and Consistency: Hobgoblins of the Minds," in *Readings in Managerial Psychology,* eds. Harold J. Leavitt, Louis R. Pondy, and David M. Boje (Chicago: University of Chicago Press, 1988), p. 145; and Elliot Aronson, "The Rationalizing Animal," in *Readings in Managerial Psychology,* 134.
7. Max H. Bazerman and Margaret A. Neale, *Negotiating Rationally* (New York: Free Press, 1994).
8. Arthur G. Miller, "What Can the Milgram Obedience Experiments Tell Us About the Holocaust? Generalizing from the Social Psychology Laboratory," in *The Social Psychology of Good and Evil,* ed. Arthur G. Miller (New York: Guilford Press, 2004), p. 210.
9. For example, see "Fixes That Fail" in *The Fifth Discipline Fieldbook* by Peter M. Senge, Art Kleiner, Charlotte Roberts, Rick Ross, and Bryan Smith (New York: Doubleday, 1994), p. 125.
10. Barry Adamson and Murray Axmith, "The CEO Disconnect: Finding Consistency between Personal Values and the Demands of Leadership," *Ivey Business Journal* (May/June 2003): 3.

Chapter 3: Ten Misconceptions about Compromise at Work

1. Martha Brannigan, "Auditor's Downfall Shows a Man Caught in Trap of His Own Making," *Wall Street Journal,* March 4, 1987.
2. Francesca Gino, Don A. Moore, and Max Bazerman, "See No Evil: When We Overlook Other People's Unethical Behavior," *HBS Working Knowledge,* January 11, 2008. http://hbswk.hbs.edu/item/5839.html.
3. Linda K. Trevino and Katherine A. Nelson, *Managing Business Ethics: Straight Talk about How to Do It Right* (Hoboken, NJ: John Wiley & Sons, 2007), pp. 121–47.
4. Guy B. Adams and Danny L. Balfour, *Unmasking Administrative Evil* (Armonk, NY: M. E. Sharpe, 2009), p. 94.
5. *Buell-Wilson v Ford Motor Co.* 16 (Cal. App. 4th. 2006) http://caselaw.lp.findlaw.com/data2/californiastatecases/d045154.pdf.
6. Chester I. Barnard, *The Functions of the Executive* (Cambridge, MA: Harvard University Press, 1968), p. xi; and Adams and Balfour, *Unmasking Administrative Evil,* p. 94.
7. William Shakespeare, *Hamlet,* act 1, scene 3 (New York: Simon and Schuster, 2003).
8. This would not work well for sociopaths, of course, though that is a less frequent cause of harm than is usually assumed. See Roy Baumeister and Kathleen D. Vohs, "Four Roots of Evil," in *The Social Psychology of Good and Evil,* ed. Arthur G. Miller (New York: Guilford Press, 2004), p. 91.
9. Gino, Moore, and Bazerman, "See No Evil," p. 26.
10. Carol Tavris and Elliot Aronson, *Mistakes Were Made (But Not by Me): Why We Justify Foolish Beliefs, Bad Decisions, and Hurtful Acts* (Boston: Houghton Mifflin Harcourt, 2007), p. 42.
11. Tavris and Aronson, *Mistakes Were Made,* p. 129.
12. Trevino and Nelson, *Managing Business Ethics,* p. 133.
13. Philip G. Zimbardo, *The Lucifer Effect: Understanding How Good People Turn Evil* (New York: Random House, 2007), p. 266.
14. Arthur G. Miller, "What Can the Milgram Obedience Experiments Tell Us About the Holocaust? Generalizing from the Social Psychology Laboratory," in *The Social Psychology of Good and Evil,* ed. Arthur G. Miller (New York: Guilford Press, 2004), p. 210.
15. Adams and Balfour, *Unmasking Administrative Evil,* p. 60.
16. Zimbardo, *Lucifer Effect,* p. 212.

17. Trevino and Nelson, *Managing Business Ethics*, p. 142.
18. Zimbardo, *Lucifer Effect*, p. 266; and http://en.wikipedia.org/wiki/Groupthink.
19. Robert B. Cialdini, "Commitment and Consistency: Hobgoblins of the Minds," in *Readings in Managerial Psychology*, eds. Harold J. Leavitt, Louis R. Pondy, and David M. Boje (Chicago: University of Chicago Press, 1988), p. 145.
20. Daniel Goleman, *Vital Lies, Simple Truths: The Psychology of Self-deception* (New York: Simon and Schuster, 1996).
21. Art Kleiner, *Who Really Matters: The Core Group Theory of Power, Privilege, and Success* (New York: Currency/Doubleday, 2003).
22. John Briggs and F. David Peat, *Seven Life Lessons of Chaos: Spiritual Wisdom from the Science of Change* (New York: HarperCollins, 1999).
23. See Barbara Kellerman, *Bad Leadership: What It Is, How It Happens, Why It Matters* (Boston: Harvard Business School Press, 2004); and Jean Lipman-Blumen, *The Allure of Toxic Leaders: Why We Follow Destructive Bosses and Corrupt Politicians—and How We Can Survive Them* (New York: Oxford University Press, 2006).
24. Zimbardo, *Lucifer Effect*, p. 272.
25. Zimbardo, *Lucifer Effect*, p. 271.
26. Howard Gardner, "The Ethical Mind," *Harvard Business Review* (March 2007): 5.
27. See Martin Seligman, *Authentic Happiness: Using the New Positive Psychology to Realize Your Potential for Lasting Fulfillment* (New York: Free Press, 2004); and Jonathan Haidt, *The Happiness Hypothesis: Finding Modern Truth in Ancient Wisdom* (New York: Basic Books, 2006).
28. Tim Kasser, *The High Price of Materialism* (Cambridge, MA: MIT Press, 2003).
29. Johann Wolfgang von Goethe, *Faust: A Tragedy* (New York: Norton, 2001), p. 329.
30. "The Giant Pool of Money," *This American Life*, Chicago Public Radio, May 9, 2008. http://www.thisamericanlife.org/radio_episode.aspx?sched=1242.
31. Daniel Reingold and Jennifer Reingold, *Confessions of a Wall Street Analyst: A True Story of Inside Information and Corruption in the Stock Market* (New York: Collins, 2006), p. 205.
32. House Committee on Energy and Commerce Subcommittee on Oversight and Investigations hearing, "The Salmonella Outbreak: The Continued Failure to

Protect the Food Supply" (February 11, 2009). See the February 10, 2009, letter from Michelle Pronto to Chairman Henry Waxman and Chairman Bart Stupak. http://energycommerce.house.gov/Press_111/20090211/prontoletterto waxmanandstupak.2.10.2009.pdf.

33. Barry Adamson and Murray Axmith, "The CEO Disconnect: Finding Consistency between Personal Values and the Demands of Leadership," *Ivey Business Journal* (May/June 2003): 3

34. Lynn Sharp Paine, *Value Shift: Why Companies Must Merge Social and Financial Imperatives to Achieve Superior Performance* (New York: McGraw-Hill, 2003), p. 172.

35. In Zimbardo, *Lucifer Effect,* p. 278, the author reports that cockpit analyses of thirty-seven serious plane accidents showed that in 81 percent the first officer did not properly monitor or challenge the captain when he had made errors. A second study of seventy-five accidents concluded that excessive obedience may cause as many as 25 percent of all airplane accidents. Robert M. Wachter and Kaveh Shojania's *Internal Bleeding: The Truth Behind America's Terrifying Epidemic of Medical Mistakes* (New York: Rugged Land, 2004) describes the huge number of deaths due to medical errors, mostly because of ineffective handoffs, faulty data, and other poor systems.

36. H. Thomas Johnson and Anders Broms, *Profit Beyond Measure: Extraordinary Results through Attention to Work and People* (New York: Free Press, 2000).

Chapter 4: How Do I Redefine the Game?

1. *Citizen Václav Havel Goes on Vacation.* Documentary film. Chicago: Facets Video, 2006.

2. Thank you to Carol Sanford of InterOctave Development (http://interoctave.com) for the concept of modes of behavior from fear, to ego, to purpose.

3. Peter M. Senge, Art Kleiner, Charlotte Roberts, Rick Ross, and Bryan Smith, *The Fifth Discipline* (New York: Doubleday, 1994), chapter 8.

4. Jim Collins, *Good to Great: Why Some Companies Make the Leap...and Others Don't* (New York: Collins Business, 2001).

5. Linda K. Trevino and Katherine A. Nelson, *Managing Business Ethics: Straight Talk about How to Do It Right* (Hoboken, NJ: John Wiley & Sons, 2007), p. 128.

6. J. Krishnamurti, *Commentaries on Living: Second Series* (Wheaton, IL: Quest Books, 1967).

7. Mimi Swartz with Sherron Watkins, *Power Failure: The Inside Story of the Collapse of Enron* (New York: Doubleday, 2003), p. xiii.
8. Etienne Wenger, Richard McDermott, and William M. Snyder, *Cultivating Communities of Practice* (Boston: Harvard Business School Press, 2002).
9. Václav Havel, *The Power of the Powerless: Citizens Against the State in Central Eastern Europe*, ed. John Keene (Armonk, NY: M. E. Sharpe, 1985).
10. David Halberstam, *The Children* (New York: Ballantine, 1998).
11. Václav Havel, *Disturbing the Peace: A Conversation with Karel Hvizdala* (New York: Knopf, 1990).

Chapter 5: Reconnect to Your Strengths

1. Joshua Weiss, Negotiation Tip: Time Pressure 8/3/05. http://www.negotiationtip.com/?p=18.
2. George M. Prince, "Anxiety and Becoming a Person." http://www.georgemprince.com/articles/Anxiety%20and%20Becoming.pdf.
3. Malcolm Gladwell, *The Tipping Point: How Little Things Can Make a Big Difference* (Boston: Back Bay Books, 2002), p. 164.
4. Ric Church, "Taming The Beast," in *Ethics Role Call, Center for Ethics in Law Enforcement* 10 no. 2 (Summer 2003): 4. http://www.theilea.org/ilea/publications/roll-call-summer03.pdf.
5. Earl Shorris, *Scenes from Corporate Life: The Politics of Middle Management* (New York: Penguin Books, 1984), p. 82. Shorris gives brilliant descriptions of the costs of inattention and excessive speed: "[A business executive may make] a tragedy of his life because he so desires to economize time that he believes he cannot afford to think" and "At great velocity, one may act in ways that would, if contemplated, be inimical to his beliefs, offenses to his own moral sense" (p. 66).
6. Malcolm Gladwell, *Blink: The Power of Thinking without Thinking* (Back Bay Books, 2007), p. 56.
7. Dan Ariely, "How Honest People Cheat," *Harvard Business Review* (February 2008): 9.
8. David Rock and Jeffrey Schwartz, "The Neuroscience of Leadership" in *Strategy + Business* 43 (Summer 2006): 79.
9. Abraham Maslow, "A Theory of Human Motivation," in *Readings in Managerial Psychology*, eds. Harold J. Leavitt, Louis R. Pondy, and David M. Boje (Chicago: University of Chicago Press, 1988). For an illustration of

Maslow's hierarchy of needs, see http://en.wikipedia.org/wiki/Maslow%27s_hierarchy_of_needs.

10. James Hillman, *The Soul's Code: In Search of Character and Calling* (New York: Random House, 1996).

11. "Choice," *RadioLab* program on WNYC, November 14, 2008. http://www.wnyc.org/shows/radiolab/episodes/2008/11/14; also Dan Ariely, *Predictably Irrational: The Hidden Forces That Shape Our Decisions* (New York: Harper, 2008).

12. Philip G. Zimbardo, *The Lucifer Effect: Understanding How Good People Turn Evil* (New York: Random House, 2007), p. 451.

Chapter 6: See the Larger Field

1. Alfred Korzybski: "The map is not the territory." See more at http://en.wikipedia.org/wiki/Map–territory_relation.

2. John Beebe, *Integrity in Depth* (Carolyn and Ernest Fay Series in Analytical Psychology) (Bryan, TX: Texas A&M University Press, 1992), pp. 30–32.

3. Linda K. Trevino and Katherine A. Nelson, *Managing Business Ethics: Straight Talk about How to Do It Right* (Hoboken, NJ: John Wiley & Sons, 2007), chapter 4; or Cynthia A. Brincat and Victoria S. Wike, *Morality and the Professional Life: Values at Work* (Englewood Cliffs, NJ: Prentice-Hall, 1999), chapters 2–5.

4. Robert S. Kaplan and David P. Norton, "The Balanced Scorecard: Measures That Drive Performance," *Harvard Business Review* (July/August 2005): 172–80; see also Andrew W. Savitz with Karl Weber, *The Triple Bottom Line: How Today's Best-run Companies Are Achieving Economic, Social, and Environmental Success—and How You Can Too* (San Francisco: Jossey-Bass, 2006).

5. Barry Johnson, *Polarity Management: Identifying and Managing Unsolvable Problems* (Amherst, MA: HRD Press, 1992).

6. Dwight D. Eisenhower: "If a problem cannot be solved, enlarge it." http://www.brainyquote.com/quotes/authors/d/dwight_d_eisenhower.html.

Chapter 7: Define a Worthy Enough Win

1. Frances Moore Lappe and Jeffrey Perkins, *You Have the Power: Choosing Courage in a Culture of Fear* (New York: Jeremy P. Tarcher, 2005), p. 206.

2. William Ury, *The Power of a Positive No: Save the Deal, Save the Relationship, and Still Say No* (New York: Bantam, 2007).

3. Definition of *quest.* Dictionary.com. *Dictionary.com Unabridged (v 1.1).* Random House, Inc. http://dictionary.reference.com/browse/quest (accessed: June 11, 2009).
4. Steve R. Covey, *The Seven Habits of Highly Effective People* (New York: Free Press, 2004).
5. Mihaly Csikszentmihalyi, *Flow: The Psychology of Optimal Experience* (New York: Harper Perennial, 1991).
6. Peter Block, *The Answer to How Is Yes: Acting on What Matters* (Berrett-Koehler, 2003), p. 18.
7. Bill George with Peter Sims, *True North: Discover Your Authentic Leadership* (San Francisco: Jossey-Bass, 2007).
8. Definition of *quest.* Dictionary.com.
9. Reinhold Niebuhr: "Nothing that is worth doing can be achieved in a lifetime." http://www.brainyquote.com/quotes/authors/r/reinhold_niebuhr.html.
10. Viktor E. Frankl, *Man's Search for Meaning: An Introduction to Logotherapy* (New York: Beacon Press, 1963), pp. 164, 175.
11. Robert W. Fuller, *Somebodies and Nobodies: Overcoming the Abuse of Rank* (Philadelphia: New Society Publishers, 2004).

Chapter 8: Find Your Real Team

1. Personal conversation with Jahn Ballard, son of Jack Ballard, member of the Laymen's Movement Executive Committee (August 3, 2006). See also obituaries for Jack Ballard: http://express-press-release.net/23/An%20American%20Success%20Story%20-%20%20Jack%20Ballard%20Remembered.php; and Weyman Huckabee, founder: http://www.nytimes.com/1981/03/28/obituaries/weyman-huckabee-77-headed-religion-center.html.
2. Carol Tavris and Elliot Aronson, *Mistakes Were Made (But Not by Me): Why We Justify Foolish Beliefs, Bad Decisions, and Hurtful Acts* (Boston: Houghton Mifflin Harcourt, 2007), p. 66.
3. Joseph L. Badaracco Jr., "We Don't Need Another Hero," *Harvard Business Review* (September 2001): 12.

Chapter 9: Make Positive Plays

1. Albert O. Hirschman, *Exit, Voice, and Loyalty: Responses to Decline in Firms, Organizations, and States* (Cambridge, MA: Harvard University Press, 1970).

2. *Pirates of the Caribbean: The Curse of the Black Pearl.* Feature film. Los Angeles: Walt Disney Studios Home Entertainment, 2003.
3. Thucydides: "The secret to happiness is freedom and the secret to freedom is courage." http://www.brainyquote.com/quotes/quotes/t/thucydides384481.html.
4. William Ury, *The Power of a Positive No: Save the Deal, Save the Relationship, and Still Say No* (New York: Bantam, 2007).
5. Ira Chaleff, *The Courageous Follower: Standing Up to and for Our Leaders* (San Francisco: Berrett-Koehler, 2003), p. 13.
6. Art Kleiner, *Who Really Matters: The Core Group Theory of Power, Privilege, and Success* (New York: Currency/Doubleday, 2003).
7. Malcolm Gladwell, *The Tipping Point: How Little Things Can Make a Big Difference* (Boston: Back Bay Books, 2002).
8. Debra E. Meyerson, *Tempered Radicals: How Everyday Leaders Inspire Change at Work* (Cambridge, MA: Harvard Business School Press, 2003).
9. Barbara Waugh, *The Soul in the Computer: The Story of a Corporate Revolutionary* (Makawao, HI: Inner Ocean Publishing, 2001); and Peter Block, *The Empowered Manager: Positive Political Skills at Work* (San Francisco: Jossey-Bass, 1991).
10. Philip G. Zimbardo, *The Lucifer Effect: Understanding How Good People Turn Evil* (New York: Random House, 2007), p. 456.
11. Meyerson, *Tempered Radicals.*
12. Ethics Resources Center, "Inside the Whistleblower Experience." http://www.ethics.org/ethics-today/1108/whistleblower.asp; and Linda K. Trevino and Katherine A. Nelson, *Managing Business Ethics: Straight Talk about How to Do It Right* (Hoboken, NJ: John Wiley & Sons, 2007), p. 87.
13. Joseph L. Badaracco Jr., "Personal Values and Professional Responsibilities," Harvard Business Publishing (January 2004). http://harvardbusinessonline.hbsp.harvard.edu/b01/en/common/item_detail.jhtml?id=304070.

Chapter 10: Keep Your Own Score

1. Merissa Marr, "Star Bucks: George Foreman: How the Former Heavyweight Champ Learned to Be More Aggressive with His Money," *Wall Street Journal,* January 16, 2006.
2. E-mail correspondence with the author, March 20, 2009. To learn more, please see http://www.georgeforeman.com.

3. Thomas Friedman, *Hot, Flat and Crowded: Why We Need a Green Revolution—and How It Can Renew America* (New York: Farrar, Straus, and Giroux, 2008).
4. Robert W. Fuller, *Somebodies and Nobodies: Overcoming the Abuse of Rank* (Philadelphia: New Society Publishers, 2004).
5. Eleanor Roosevelt: "No one can make you feel inferior without your consent." http://www.quotationspage.com/quote/137.html.
6. Robert W. Fuller and Pamela A. Gerloff, *Dignity for All: How to Create a World Without Rankism* (San Francisco: Berrett-Koehler, 2008).
7. Marina Krakovsky, "The Effort Effect," *Stanford Magazine*, March/April 2007. http://www.stanfordalumni.org/news/magazine/2007/marapr/features/dweck.html.
8. H. Thomas Johnson and Anders Broms, *Profit Beyond Measure: Extraordinary Results through Attention to Work and People* (New York: Free Press, 2000), chapter 2.
9. Frances Moore Lappe and Jeffrey Perkins, *You Have the Power: Choosing Courage in a Culture of Fear* (New York: Jeremy P. Tarcher, 2005), p. 168.
10. Bill Torbert, *Action Inquiry: The Secret of Timely and Transforming Leadership* (San Francisco: Berrett-Koehler, 2004).
11. Oliver James, *Affluenza* (London: Vermillion, 2008); and Tim Kasser, *The High Price of Materialism* (Cambridge, MA: MIT Press, 2003).
12. Vicki Robin, Joe Dominguez, and Monique Tilford, *Your Money or Your Life: 9 Steps to Transforming Your Relationship with Money and Achieving Financial Independence* (New York: Penguin, 2008).
13. Edward M. Hallowell, "Overloaded Circuits: Why Smart People Underperform," *Harvard Business Review* (January 2005): 55–62.
14. Cynthia A. Brincat and Victoria S. Wike, *Morality and the Professional Life: Values at Work* (Englewood Cliffs, NJ: Prentice-Hall, 1999).
15. John Welwood, *Perfect Love, Imperfect Relationships: Healing the Wound of the Heart* (Boston: Trumpeter, 2007), p. 158.
16. Lappe and Perkins, *You Have the Power*, p. 151.

Chapter 11: Thriving at Work

1. C. K. Prahalad, *The Fortune at the Bottom of the Pyramid: Eradicating Poverty through Profits* (Pennsylvania: Wharton School Publishing, 2006).

2. Wendell Berry, "Manifesto: The Mad Farmer Liberation Front," in *Mad Farmer Poems* (Berkeley, CA: Counterpoint Press, 2008).

3. Martin Seligman, *Authentic Happiness: Using the New Positive Psychology to Realize Your Potential for Lasting Fulfillment* (New York: Free Press, 2004).

4. Jonathan Haidt, *The Happiness Hypothesis: Finding Modern Truth in Ancient Wisdom* (New York: Basic Books, 2006), p. 85.

5. Mihaly Csikszentmihalyi. *Flow: The Psychology of Optimal Experience* (New York: Harper Perennial, 1991).

6. Haidt, *Happiness Hypothesis,* p. 174.

7. Haidt, *Happiness Hypothesis,* p. 224.

8. David Sirota, Louis A. Mischkind, and Michael Irwin Meltzer, *The Enthusiastic Employee: How Companies Profit by Giving Employees What They Want* (New Jersey: Wharton School Publishing, 2005).

9. Viktor E. Frankl, *Man's Search for Meaning: An Introduction to Logotherapy* (New York: Beacon Press, 1963), p. 77.

10. Carl Jung: "The greatest and most important problems of life are all fundamentally insoluble. They can never be solved but only outgrown." http://www.quotationspage.com/quote/29985.html.

11. Haidt, *Happiness Hypothesis,* pp. 196–99.

12. Barbara Waugh, *The Soul in the Computer: The Story of a Corporate Revolutionary* (Makawao, HI: Inner Ocean Publishing, 2001), p. 105, citing Dave Packard, *The HP Way: How Bill Hewlett and I Built Our Company* (New York: Collins, 1995).

13. Rev. Earl Palmer, "The People of Encouragement," from a series of talks (First Presbyterian Church, Berkeley, California, May 1985); private recordings.

14. "Credit and Credibility," *Now* on PBS: online video. http://www.pbs.org/now/shows/446/index.html.

15. "Confessions of a Wal-Mart Hit Man," extended bonus scenes from *Wal-Mart: The High Cost of Low Price*. Documentary film. Robert Greenwald Films, 2005. http://www.youtube.com/watch?gl=GB&hl=en-GB&v=-mQH9DloKD8.

16. Johann Wolfgang von Goethe, *Faust: A Tragedy* (New York: Norton, 2001), p. 329.

Chapter 12: It's Bigger Than a Game

1. Edmund L. Andrews, "Greenspan Concedes Error on Regulation," *New York Times,* October 24, 2008. http://www.nytimes.com/2008/10/24/business/

economy/24panel.html?_r=1&sq=alan%20greenspan%20testimony&st=cse&scp=1&pagewanted=print.

2. Chad Holliday, Stephan Schmidheiny, and Phillip Watts, *Walking the Talk: The Business Case for Sustainable Development* (San Francisco: Berrett-Koehler, 2002).
3. See http://www.mbaoath.com and Anne VanderMey, "Harvard's MBA Oath Goes Viral," *Business Week*, June 11, 2009. http://www.businessweek.com/bschools/content/jun2009/bs20090611_522427.htm.
4. Lynn Sharp Paine, *Value Shift: Why Companies Must Merge Social and Financial Imperatives to Achieve Superior Performance* (New York: McGraw-Hill, 2003), p. 172.
5. Simon Zadek, "The Path to Corporate Responsibility," *Harvard Business Review* (December 2004): 128–30.
6. Marvin T. Brown, *Corporate Integrity: Rethinking Organizational Ethics and Leadership* (Cambridge: Cambridge University Press, 2005).
7. M. Scott Peck, MD, *The Road Less Traveled and Beyond: Spiritual Growth in an Age of Anxiety* (New York: Touchstone, 1998), p. 50.
8. Václav Havel, *Temptation* (New York: Grove Press, 1986/1989).
9. Timothy Garton Ash, *The Magic Lantern: The Revolution of '89 Witnessed in Warsaw, Budapest, Berlin, and Prague* (New York: Vintage Books, 1993), p. 137.
10. Jung Chang, *Wild Swans: Three Daughters of China* (New York: Anchor Books, 1991), p. 224–25.
11. See Paul Buchheit's blog at http://paulbuchheit.blogspot.com/2007/06/quick-dbe.html.
12. Fred Reichheld, *The Ultimate Question: Driving Good Profits and True Growth* (Boston: Harvard Business School Press, 2006).
13. Garton Ash, *Magic Lantern*, pp. 102, 121, 138.
14. Mihaly Csikszentmihalyi, *Good Business: Leadership, Flow, and the Making of Meaning* (New York: Penguin, 2003), p. 19.

Individual and Small-group Activities

1. Tony Schwartz and Catherine McCarthy, "Manage Your Energy, Not Your Time," *Harvard Business Review* (October 2007).

Index

About the Author

Photo by Kristen Policy

Elizabeth Doty has spent thirty years working in and around large organizations, in three different careers. She began in the hospitality industry, where she served as a manager for more than eleven years, mostly in four-star hotels. After earning her MBA from Harvard in 1991, she joined one of the top ten U.S. reengineering firms, working in the trenches with client teams in a variety of industries to achieve radical improvements in quality, delivery time, and profitability. Finally, in 1994 she launched her own consulting firm, focused on diagnosing breakdowns and dysfunctions in large, complex organizations and helping such clients as Intuit, Hewlett-Packard, and Archstone-Smith capitalize on hidden opportunities to improve performance.

Based on these varied experiences, Elizabeth is intimately familiar with the inspirations, dilemmas, and absurdities of organizational life. Fundamentally concerned with the interlocking challenges of individual and organizational integrity in their broadest sense, Elizabeth brings a background in systems think-